Exp

Science
Communication

Sara Miller McCune founded SAGE Publishing in 1965 to support the dissemination of usable knowledge and educate a global community. SAGE publishes more than 1000 journals and over 800 new books each year, spanning a wide range of subject areas. Our growing selection of library products includes archives, data, case studies and video. SAGE remains majority owned by our founder and after her lifetime will become owned by a charitable trust that secures the company's continued independence.

Los Angeles | London | New Delhi | Singapore | Washington DC | Melbourne

Exploring

Science
Communication

A Science and Technology Studies Approach

Ulrike Felt and Sarah R. Davies

Los Angeles | London | New Delhi
Singapore | Washington DC | Melbourne

Los Angeles | London | New Delhi
Singapore | Washington DC | Melbourne

SAGE Publications Ltd
1 Oliver's Yard
55 City Road
London EC1Y 1SP

SAGE Publications Inc.
2455 Teller Road
Thousand Oaks, California 91320

SAGE Publications India Pvt Ltd
B 1/I 1 Mohan Cooperative Industrial Area
Mathura Road
New Delhi 110 044

SAGE Publications Asia-Pacific Pte Ltd
3 Church Street
#10-04 Samsung Hub
Singapore 049483

Editor: Michael Ainsley
Editorial assistant: Amber Turner-Flanders
Production editor: Imogen Roome
Copyeditor: Sarah Bury
Proofreader: Leigh C. Smithson
Indexer: Adam Pozner
Marketing manager: Lucia Sweet
Cover design: Lisa Harper-Wells
Typeset by: C&M Digitals (P) Ltd, Chennai, India
Printed in the UK

Library of Congress Control Number: 2019944246

British Library Cataloguing in Publication data

A catalogue record for this book is available from
the British Library

ISBN 978-1-5264-6439-2
ISBN 978-1-5264-6440-8 (pbk)

At SAGE we take sustainability seriously. Most of our products are printed in the UK using responsibly sourced
papers and boards. When we print overseas we ensure sustainable papers are used as measured by the PREPS
grading system. We undertake an annual audit to monitor our sustainability.

CONTENTS

ABOUT THE EDITORS AND CONTRIBUTORS

Nina Amelung is a post-doctoral research fellow at the University of Minho, Portugal. Nina's research focuses on the democratic challenges of cross-border biometric data-exchange and explores the making of publics in European crime, migration and border control regimes. She applies perspectives offered at the intersection of science and technology studies, political sociology and the sociology of science.

Dorothea Born holds a Master's degree in ecology, for which she researched climate change in the Arctic. In her PhD in Science and Technology Studies at the University of Vienna she investigates how climate change is constructed and shaped as a problem in popular science magazines. Her focus lies on the visual aspects of climate change communication.

Nadav Davidovitch, MD, MPH, PhD, is an epidemiologist and public health physician. He is a full professor and director of the School of Public Health at the Faculty of Health Sciences, Ben-Gurion University of the Negev in Israel. His research focuses on health policy, public health, one health/ecohealth, health promotion, the Israeli healthcare system, public health history and ethics, and global health.

Sarah R. Davies is a researcher at the Norwegian University of Science and Technology, having previously been associate professor at the University of Copenhagen, Denmark. Her work focuses on relations between science and society. Recent publications include the books *Hackerspaces* (2017, Polity) and *Science Communication: Culture, Identity, and Citizenship* (2016, with Maja Horst, Palgrave Macmillan).

Ulrike Felt is Professor of Science and Technology Studies (STS) and Head of the research platform 'Responsible research and innovation in academic practice'. Her research focuses on governance, democracy and public engagement as well as on changing academic research cultures. She has been editor of the journal *Science, Technology and Human Values* (2002–2007) and of the most recent *Handbook of Science and Technology Studies* (2017, MIT Press). Since 2017 she has been president of the European Association for the Study of Science and Technology (EASST).

Rafaela Granja is a post-doctoral research fellow and guest assistant lecturer at the University of Minho, Portugal, where she teaches Qualitative Methods and Social Studies of Crime at both Master's and BA levels. Rafaela's current research explores the interconnections between family, genetics, technology and crime, with a particular focus on emerging DNA technologies and its associated controversies. She has published in several journals, including *Science, Technology, & Human Values*, *Science as Culture*, *Probation Journal* and *Journal of Family Issues*.

Helena Machado is Full Professor of Sociology at the University of Minho, Portugal. She has been engaged in research on the intersection between science, technology and society studies, and criminology. In 2015, Helena was awarded a Consolidator Grant from the European Research Council (ERC) to conduct research into the societal, legal, ethical, and political challenges posed by criminal DNA databases, and the transnational exchange of DNA data in the context of policing and judicial cooperation in the EU.

Oliver Marsh is an Honorary Research Associate with the Science and Technology Studies Department at University College London. His research brings together sociology of knowledge and emotion, particularly in relation to social media. He has previously published on Carl Sagan and 'sci-lebrity', taught qualitative research methods, and worked on digital communication with the think tank Demos and the UK Civil Service. Twitter @olivermmarsh, blog sidewayslooks.wordpress.com.

Marcus Owens is an architect and lecturer in the College of Environmental Design at the University of California, Berkeley, where he recently completed a PhD in affiliation with the Berkeley Center for Science, Technology, Medicine, and Society.

Erika Szymanski is a research fellow at the University of Edinburgh, where she studies yeast and human-microbe working relations in contemporary biotechnology through STS, rhetoric of science and environmental humanities perspectives. She holds an MS in microbiology, an MA in rhetoric and writing studies, and a PhD in science communication, along with long-standing interests in fermentation, microbial relationships, and writing about science in a social context.

Erela Teharlev Ben-Shachar is a lecturer in the programme of Biological Thought at the Open University in Israel. She did her PhD at the Science and Technology Studies department at Bar-Ilan University. Her dissertation explores the transformations of body regimes in the history of Israel and the way these were co-produced with changes in society, dominant ideologies, and financial notions. In addition, she is a science journalist, writing about health and culture in Israeli magazines.

Karin Tybjerg is an associate professor at Medical Museion, University of Copenhagen. She has a background as PhD and research fellow in the Department of History and Philosophy of Science at the University of Cambridge and Head of Modern History and Ethnographic Collections at the National Museum of Denmark. She curated the award-winning *The Body Collected* exhibition on medical collections of body parts and has written on practical knowledge, on medical collections and on exhibiting objects of knowledge.

Louise Whiteley is an associate professor and curator at Medical Museion and the Novo Nordisk Foundation Center for Basic Metabolic Research, University of Copenhagen. Louise's research interests include how biomedical science affects how we understand mental wellbeing, and interdisciplinarity in science communication and exhibition-making. She is currently completing a research project on co-curation with artists and scientists, based on the exhibition *Mind the Gut*, which she led with Adam Bencard, and which was awarded the Bikuben Foundation Vision Prize in 2015 and UMAC (ICOM International Committee for University Museums and Collections) award in 2019.

1

INTRODUCTION

'We Should Reward Scientists for Communicating to the Public', wrote the popular science magazine *Scientific American* in 2018, in a piece that argued that researchers should be promoted according not just to their research and teaching but also to their participation in public engagement activities (Ngumbi 2018). In the same year the European Commission launched a funding programme that called for work that 'took stock and re-examined the role of science communication'. According to the Commission, there was an urgent need to 'improve the quality and effectiveness of interactions between scientists, general media and the public' (European Commission 2018: nn.), a need they perceived as relating to contemporary challenges such as the circulation of pseudoscience on social media and a 'crisis' in traditional science journalism due to funding reductions (Lunau 2016).

Such calls are not unusual. It is widely accepted that science communication plays a central role in society, and that it is something to be promoted (Davies & Horst 2016). As the involvement of the European Commission – an important actor in European research and in European politics generally – suggests, the promotion of science communication, alongside citizen engagement on science-related issues, has been seen as essential to the advancement of contemporary societies. Guides to science communication[1] published in connection with European funding programmes offer numerous explanations of why this is the case: more and better science communication is needed because it is important to sell one's science, because it is a possibility to restrain moral concerns

---

[1] See, for instance: www.youtube.com/playlist?list=PLvpwIjZTs-Lhe0wu6uy8gr7JFfm-v8EZuH

from gaining traction, because scientists have an obligation to the taxpayers who fund their research, because people need to be informed about science. This is not only a European phenomenon. Similar narratives, though perhaps with different foci, might be told about other regions in the world.

Science communication is thus tied to a specific vision of the relation between science and society (e.g. Bauer & Bucchi 2008). Academic and policy literature includes frequent references to public knowledge about science as being in need of improvement (Durant et al. 1989), or argues that 'a public' with too little knowledge of science and connection to science might constitute a potential threat to innovation-driven societies (Felt, Wynne et al. 2007; Marris 2015). This is often connected to the call for improving 'scientific literacy' (Miller 1998) among the wider population, under the assumption that this will lead citizens to follow the advice given to them in the name of science.

Just as public audiences are asked to become scientifically literate, politicians are frequently called to be guided by 'sound science' in their policies and choices (Stirling 2007). Evidence-informed policy making has been high on the agenda, and scientists have been urged to more proactively engage with policy; particularly, for instance, in the areas of energy or climate-related policies (Geden 2015). Ultimately, scientific knowledge is framed as being central to the functioning of modern democratic societies (Brown 2009; Jasanoff 2017).

Science communication is therefore something that deserves close reflection and attention, not just because of taken-for-granted assumptions about its importance, but exactly because of the ways that it is tied to political projects, and in particular to contemporary understandings of how democracy should function (Lövbrand et al. 2011). Such attention has been revealing. For instance, studies have shown that scientific literacy by no means clearly correlates with the positions citizens take when it comes to technoscientific controversies (Brossard & Nisbet 2007; Wynne 1992). Rather, 'value dispositions such as ideology, partisanship, and religious identity' as well as 'political context, and necessary trade-offs between costs, benefits, and risks' seem to matter (Nisbet & Scheufele 2009: 1768). Already by the early 1990s research sought to move discussion about science communication away from a 'deficit model' approach (in which publics are framed as not knowing enough about science and therefore are a problem) and from measuring the success of a communication activity against a set of scientific facts people are able to refer to. The focus increasingly shifted to exploring the ways that science is encountered in diverse science communication settings (Irwin & Wynne 1996; Wynne 1992) and to questioning the often complex ways citizens relate to science.

It has similarly become clear that science communication is something that not only affects public audiences and politicians, but that has considerable impact on both science and scientists' identities. Public communication – and particularly its emphasis on the success stories of science – can shape junior scientists' expectations of their work, leading to frustration when research turns out to be quite different from the ideals communicated and when success does not, in fact, immediately emerge (Felt & Fochler 2012, 2013). Science communication might also create the effect that not fully stabilised or still controversial knowledge can appear as robust, and thus travels and starts to be taken for granted in neighbouring fields; after all, scientists also read popular science magazines or watch science videos online, and are affected by the content of such communication (Jurdant 1993; Mellor 2003). Science communication therefore not only enables the negotiation of science in public contexts, but shapes science itself.

1.1 STUDYING SCIENCE COMMUNICATION

The role and effects of science communication in contemporary societies are therefore not straightforward. While – in our view – science communication is indeed essential to democracy, it is not a way to avoid the messiness of public debates or the voicing of concerns. And it is by no ways unidirectional, acting only on society: it acts upon science as much as upon its lay audiences. In interrogating these dynamics, science communication has in recent years become a lively field of scholarship (outlined in, for instance, Brossard & Lewenstein 2009; Bucchi & Trench 2014; Jamieson et al. 2017). It has professional associations and regular conferences that bring 'together practitioners, educators and researchers in the diverse and growing field of science communication'.[2]

This book aims to explore how approaches from the field of Science and Technology Studies (STS) can contribute to this field and to the study of science communication. Our starting point is that there is scope to further develop interactions between STS, science communication research and researchers, and science communication practice. We will suggest that the theoretical and conceptual developments of STS offer new perspectives for looking into science communication. Science communication is a key way that science–society relations are organised and managed. Accordingly, we also think that STS needs to engage more with diverse forms of science communication and with the changing spaces, processes and practices through which science communication takes place. The aim is to begin more of a conversation between STS and science communication research and practice.

We understand science communication in broad terms: it comprises communicative processes, within public settings, through which scientific knowledge is presented, transformed, negotiated or contested (Horst et al. 2017).

---

[2]https://pcst.co/conferences

These settings can include science TV, popular science writing, mass media accounts of science, and science museums, but also Facebook pages, podcasts, comedy events, activism or public consultations and policy advice that draw on or are oriented to scientific knowledge or cultures. Indeed, we consider any public setting where science is present(ed) to be of relevance to science communication scholarship. This includes spaces that are not explicitly aiming to communicate science, and that are oriented around other purposes but where science is present.

For instance, this volume features case studies such as courtrooms and parks, using these as examples of spaces where the reliability of particular scientific 'facts' are negotiated almost incidentally (courtrooms: see Chapter 11) or where ecological knowledge is embodied and communicated through landscape design (parks: see Chapter 5). Other examples might be the use of science by activist or protest groups, the ways that science is used in fiction (whether written or on film), or how particular technical knowledges implicitly shape the architecture of digital spaces. We therefore think it is productive to examine science communication beyond those contexts that have traditionally and explicitly been seen as 'science communication'. In our view, science communication permeates many aspects of contemporary societies, and science is present in much of mundane life.

Indeed, in most societies most of the time, knowledge is now central to politics, public debate, and decision making. The notion of the 'knowledge society' has sprung up (Felt, Wynne et al. 2007; Stehr 2012), in Europe in particular but also around the world. (National) economies are no longer structured around manufacturing products, but are making and utilising knowledge through innovation (the central buzzword of recent years); similarly, reliable knowledge is viewed as essential to guiding the choices that governments, institutions or individuals must make in complex and technologically oriented worlds. Science communication is an integral part of this. Science is essential to imaginations of democracy, both in terms of providing politicians with expert advice and in allowing an electorate to have access to robust knowledge that can inform public debate and voting decisions (Davies & Horst 2016; Ezrahi 2012).

At the same time that science, and science communication, have become integral to contemporary understandings of a well-functioning society, the fragility of these democratic imaginaries has also become clear (Jasanoff 2017; Stehr 2012). Ulrich Beck (1992) has argued that we live in 'risk societies', in which the unequal distribution of risk has to some extent replaced traditional social hierarchies, and where science and technology are widely acknowledged to have resulted in unwanted and dangerous effects, from climate change to agricultural pollution. High-profile public controversies about scientific issues have emerged across the globe: around genetic modification of agricultural crops in Europe (Horlick-Jones et al. 2007); around nuclear energy after technological disasters in Russia and Japan (Bauer 2015); around access to healthcare in Africa and the USA (Epstein 1996; Leach et al. 2005). As noted above, polities have tended to promote science communication in order to ensure a citizenry who are scientifically literate and supportive of science. While part of this promotion is tied to the belief that science and innovation are essential to a nation's economic wellbeing (de Saille 2015), it has also been related to efforts to smooth over public concerns about science's methods, values, and effects (Felt, Wynne et al. 2007; Gregory & Lock 2008).

Most recently – and as we write this text in 2019 – these dynamics have crystallised around concerns about 'post truth' public-sphere debate, acceptance of 'alternative facts', and the rising prevalence of 'fake news', as enabled by social and digital media (Jasanoff & Simmet 2017; Roche & Davis 2017; Temmerman et al. 2018). There is widespread concern that knowledge is being devalued. If climate change is publicly contestable even though it is backed by scientific consensus, if politicians can, seemingly, deliberately lie without consequences, if public debate is founded on an idea that 'people … have had enough of experts' (as was claimed by UK politician Michael Gove in the run-up to the 2016 Brexit referendum[3]) – what does this mean for the role and place of science in society? Anxiety about these developments has led, among other things, to increased activism in supporting and promoting science (Penders 2017; Roche & Davis 2017). Activities such as the 2017 March for Science – a global march that 'champions robustly funded and publicly communicated science' (March for Science 2019) – seek to use public communication to ensure that science maintains its uniquely authoritative role in the public sphere (Penders 2017).

An interest in science communication thus takes us very quickly to questions about the kind of societies we live in, and how they are and should be run. (Questions like: Whose knowledge counts? How should that knowledge be used?) The role of science communication and communicators in these debates has varied. Some have seen their role as being to defend or promote science, or to recruit young people into it; others frame their activities as empowering laypeople to access and make use of science on their own terms. The last two decades, in particular, have seen an emphasis on opening up science to wider public scrutiny, and on ensuring its public value (Jasanoff 2003; Stirling 2008; Wilsdon et al. 2005). Science communicators have developed and used dialogic and interactive methods, and sought to feed public views back to science and science policy (Trench 2008). Even previously promotional forms of science communication, such as the work of press offices, may now frame their activities as taking a wider role in supporting scientific accountability and democratic public debate (Shipman 2015).

---

[3] www.ft.com/content/3be49734-29cb-11e6-83e4-abc22d5d108c

1.2 A PROFESSION IN THE MAKING?

The preceding discussion should have helped the reader understand why we think it is important to study science communication, in all its forms. Science communication is clearly important to contemporary societies, and the ways in which it is carried out and discussed point to wider questions about the place of knowledge in those societies. Even the mundane and seemingly insignificant ways that science is presented in public – through soap adverts, science fiction TV shows, or dietary information on the back of cereal boxes, say – are suggestive of how the relation between science and society is understood. It is therefore important to examine science communication if we wish to better understand life in today's scientific and technologically saturated environments.

It is also important to research science communication because it is a growing area of professional practice (Trench 2017). Science communication is not a homogeneous field. Communicators understand the purposes of their activities in different ways, and it is certainly a very different kind of practice to build an exhibition than to organise a public engagement event or a protest, for instance. Despite the very real and continuing diversity of the field, however, science communication in all of its forms is increasingly populated by trained professionals. There are now many educational programmes that focus on the skills and knowledge necessary to work in science communication, both integrated into natural science education and as stand-alone Master's programmes or professional diplomas (Besley et al. 2015; Mulder et al. 2008; Trench 2012). Public communication of science is thus a field that is capitalising on its links to research, codifying particular ideas about good practice, and, importantly, critically reflecting on its activities, practices, and priorities.

It is these developments that in large part lie behind this book. Science communication students are often asked to carry out research projects, while science communicators may be required to evaluate their activities, or simply want to engage in personal reflections on them. Our view is that the academic field of Science and Technology Studies (STS) offers useful resources for such research and reflection. A key aim of this volume is thus to introduce students, scholars, and practitioners of science communication to STS, in order to show how its methodological tools and concepts might assist with critical reflection and analysis of public communication. At the same time, the book speaks to students in STS about the importance of exploring science communication in its diverse dimensions, of looking into the specific ways in which science, science–society relations, and scientific citizenship take shape, and of understanding why this matters in contemporary societies.

What is STS? While Chapters 2 and 3 can be taken as an extended answer to this question, STS is, in brief, 'an interdisciplinary field that investigates the institutions, practices, meanings, and outcomes of science and technology and their multiple entanglements with the worlds people inhabit, their lives, and their values' (Felt et al. 2017: 1). It is therefore a field that is centrally concerned with how knowledge is made and negotiated through interactions between people – whether scientists or others – and the material world. It is, as noted, highly interdisciplinary, drawing in scholarship and scholars from sociology, anthropology, history, philosophy, and organisation studies. At the same time, it is possible to identify a broadly shared set of key concepts and sensitivities. It is these that we suggest can be mobilised as a resource for the study of science communication, and that we build upon in our discussion in Chapters 2 and 3.

In particular, STS research offers an approach to science communication that views it not as primarily representational – a process in which extant scientific facts or aspects of science are straightforwardly represented or depicted – but as productive, involved in making the knowledge it presents. In this book, we therefore explore science communication as a space in which knowledge and social worlds are co-produced (Jasanoff 2004). This means that we are concerned with the work that science communication does upon (and with) the world around it. How does science communication matter? What effects does it have on the public audiences involved in it, perceptions of science, ideas about democracy, or scientific facts, for instance? It is these kinds of questions that we consider, through case studies of science communication that range from museums to Facebook pages to parks.

1.3 WHERE THE BOOK IS GOING

Chapters 2 and 3 outline in some detail the intellectual tools that STS offers the science communication practitioner, evaluator, or researcher. Chapter 2 introduces the main concepts an STS approach will involve. Here we follow John Law's (2017) argument that STS does not use methods, but *is* a method – a particular way of understanding and looking at the world. STS is thus a lens as much as a concrete set of methods or approaches. In Chapter 2 we discuss the notion of co-production, talk about knowledge production as occurring in 'knowing spaces', suggest that science communication is fundamentally relational, explore the centrality of practices in making realities and, finally, draw attention to how science communication can incorporate particular values.

Chapter 3 then explores in more detail what these concepts mean in practice for science communication, and digs down into how to mobilise them within research. We discuss seven sensitivities that can guide how researchers might examine science communication, starting with how publics are imagined and performed within science communication. We then explore the making of public facts, the creation and negotiation of expertise, and the materialities, spaces, temporalities, and atmospheres of science communication. Taken together these two chapters offer a grounding in key STS ideas, how these ideas have been mobilised in existing research on science in public, and how they can be put to work in investigations of and reflections on science communication.

The rest of the book further demonstrates how these concepts and sensitivities can be used within research. Chapters 4 to 11 comprise examples of how an STS-oriented approach allows us to address particular aspects of science communication. Each of these chapters, written by a different author or author group, offers an empirical analysis of science communication that is grounded in STS and which therefore puts the concepts and approaches outlined in Chapters 2 and 3 to work (albeit in very different ways). To help make explicit how each chapter is mobilising specific concepts, we, the editors, give a short introduction — 'reflections and connections' – that pulls out how the empirical analysis relates to our discussion in Chapters 2 and 3.

It is therefore possible to use this volume in a number of different ways. Those interested in specific aspects of science communication – the use of images, museums, the mass media – may wish to start with a chapter that covers that topic. Students of science communication who want to get to grips with the nature of STS should begin with Chapters 2 and 3, and can follow up on how particular STS ideas are realised in practice by going to one or more of the empirical chapters (Chapters 2 and 3 include pointers, presented in boxes within the body of the text, as to where these ideas are visible in the empirical studies). Those beginning research in science communication and wanting inspiration for this can engage with the book as a whole, which both offers a set of practical tools for research and raises questions and problematics that can inspire the framing of research projects.

The book closes with a short conclusion – Connections, Assemblages, and Open Ends. This pulls the key themes of the book together, reflecting on what we have learned from seeing the STS concepts described in Chapters 2 and 3 used in practice in Chapters 4 to 11. It also looks beyond the confines of this volume to consider what is missing from it and to point forward to future research needs. In this way, our aim is for the book to be the start of something, not the end. We look forward to seeing the work it might trigger or inspire.

REFERENCES

Bauer, Martin W. 2015. *Atoms, Bytes and Genes: Public Resistance and Techno-Scientific Responses*. Abingdon: Routledge.

Bauer, Martin W., and Massimiano Bucchi. 2008. *Journalism, Science and Society: Science Communication between News and Public Relations*. Abingdon: Routledge.

Beck, Ulrich. 1992. *Risk Society: Towards a New Modernity*. London: Sage.

Besley, John C., Anthony Dudo, and Martin Storksdieck. 2015. 'Scientists' Views about Communication Training'. *Journal of Research in Science Teaching* 52 (2): 199–220.

Brossard, Dominique, and Bruce V. Lewenstein. 2009. 'A Critical Appraisal of Models of Public Understanding of Science'. In Lee Ann Kahlor and Patricia A. Stout (eds.),

Communicating Science: New Agendas in Communication, pp. 11–39. New York: Taylor & Francis.

Brossard, Dominique, and Matthew C. Nisbet. 2007. 'Deference to Scientific Authority among a Low Information Public: Understanding U.S. Opinion on Agricultural Biotechnology'. *International Journal of Public Opinion Research* 19 (1): 24–52.

Brown, Mark B. 2009. *Science in Democracy: Expertise, Institutions, and Representation*. Cambridge, MA: The MIT Press.

Bucchi, Massimiano, and Brian Trench. 2014. *Handbook of Public Communication of Science and Technology* (2nd edition). Abingdon: Routledge.

Davies, Sarah, and Maja Horst. 2016. *Science Communication: Culture, Identity and Citizenship*. New York: Palgrave Macmillan.

de Saille, Stevienna. 2015. 'Innovating Innovation Policy: The Emergence of "Responsible Research and Innovation"'. *Journal of Responsible Innovation* 2 (2): 152–168.

Durant, John, Geoffrey Evans, and Geoffrey P. Thomas. 1989. 'The Public Understanding of Science'. *Nature* 340: 11–14.

Epstein, Steven. 1996. *Impure Science: AIDS, Activism and the Politics of Knowledge*. Berkeley, CA, and London: University of California Press.

European Commission. 2018. 'Taking Stock and Re-Examining the Role of Science Communication (SwafS-19-2018-2019)'. https://ec.europa.eu/info/funding-tenders/opportunities/portal/screen/opportunities/topic-details/swafs-19-2018-2019.

Ezrahi, Yaron. 2012. *Imagined Democracies: Necessary Political Fictions*. Cambridge: Cambridge University Press.

Felt, Ulrike, and Maximilian Fochler. 2012. 'Re-Ordering Epistemic Living Spaces: On the Tacit Governance Effects of the Public Communication of Science.' In Simone Rödder, Martina Franzen and Peter Weingart (eds.), *The Sciences' Media Connection – Communication to the Public and its Repercussions. Yearbook of the Sociology of the Sciences*, pp. 133–154. Dordrecht: Springer.

Felt, Ulrike, and Maximilian Fochler. 2013. 'What Science Stories Do: Rethinking the Multiple Consequences of Intensified Science Communication'. In Patrick Baranger and Bernard Schiele (eds.), *Science Communication Today: International Perspectives, Issues and Strategies*, pp. 75–90. Paris: CNRS Editions.

Felt, Ulrike, Rayvon Fouché, Clark A. Miller, and Laurel Smith-Doerr (eds.). 2017. *The Handbook of Science and Technology Studies* (4th edition). Cambridge, MA: The MIT Press.

Felt, Ulrike, Brian Wynne, Michel Callon, Maria Eduarda Gonçalves, Sheila Jasanoff, Maria Jepsen, Pierre-Benoît Joly, Zdenek Konopasek, Stefan May, Claudia Neubauer, Arie Rip, Karen Siune, Andy Stirling, and Mariachiara Tallacchini. 2007. *Taking European Knowledge Society Seriously*. Luxembourg: Office for Official Publications of the European Communities.

Geden, Oliver. 2015. 'Policy: Climate Advisers Must Maintain Integrity'. *Nature* 521 (7550): 27–28.

Gregory, Jane, and Simon Jay Lock. 2008. 'The Evolution of "Public Understanding of Science": Public Engagement as a Tool of Science Policy in the UK'. *Sociology Compass* 2 (4): 1252–1265.

Horlick-Jones, Tom, John Walls, Gene Rowe, Nick Pidgeon, Wouter Poortinga, Graham Murdock, and Tim O'Riordan. 2007. *The GM Debate: Risk, Politics and Public Engagement*. New York: Routledge.

Horst, Maja, Sarah R. Davies, and Alan Irwin. 2017. 'Reframing Science Communication'. In Ulrike Felt, Rayvon Fouché, Clark A. Miller, and Laurel Smith-Doerr (eds.), *The Handbook of Science and Technology Studies*, p. 4. Cambridge, MA: The MIT Press.

Irwin, Alan, and Brian Wynne. 1996. *Misunderstanding Science? The Public Reconstruction of Science and Technology*. Cambridge: Cambridge University Press.

Jamieson, Kathleen Hall, Dan M. Kahan, and Dietram Scheufele (eds.). 2017. *The Oxford Handbook of the Science of Science Communication*. New York: Oxford University Press.

Jasanoff, Sheila. 2003. 'Technologies of Humility: Citizen Participation in Governing Science'. *Minerva* 41: 223–244.

Jasanoff, Sheila. 2004. *States of Knowledge: The Co-Production of Science and the Social Order*. Abingdon: Routledge.

Jasanoff, Sheila. 2017. 'Science and Democracy.' In Ulrike Felt, Rayvon Fouché, Clark Miller, and Laurel Smith-Doerr (eds.), *The Handbook of Science and Technology Studies*, pp. 259–287. Cambridge MA: The MIT Press.

Jasanoff, Sheila, and Hilton R. Simmet. 2017. 'No Funeral Bells: Public Reason in a "Post-Truth" Age'. *Social Studies of Science* 47 (5): 751–770.

Jurdant, Baudouin. 1993. 'Popularization of Science as the Autobiography of Science'. *Public Understanding of Science* 2 (4): 365–373.

Law, John. 2017. 'STS as Method'. In Ulrike Felt, Rayvon Fouché, Clark Miller, and Laurel Smith-Doerr (eds.), *The Handbook of Science and Technology Studies*, pp. 31–57. Cambridge, MA: The MIT Press.

Leach, Melissa, Ian Scoones, and Brian Wynne. 2005. *Science and Citizens: Globalization and the Challenge of Engagement*. London: Zed Books.

Lunau, Kate. 2016. 'Science Journalism's Identity Crisis'. *Motherboard*. 2016. http://motherboard.vice.com/en_ca/read/science-journalisms-identity-crisis-CSWA-NASW.

Lövbrand, Eva, Roger Pielke, and Silke Beck. 2011. 'A Democracy Paradox in Studies of Science and Technology'. *Science, Technology & Human Values* 36 (4): 474–496.

March for Science. 2019. March for Science Website, 'About Us'. www.marchforscience.com/our-mission

Marris, Claire. 2015. 'The Construction of Imaginaries of the Public as a Threat to Synthetic Biology'. *Science as Culture* 24 (1): 83–98. https://doi.org/10.1080/09505431.2014.986320

Mellor, Felicity. 2003. 'Between Fact and Fiction: Demarcating Science from Non-Science in Popular Physics Books'. *Social Studies of Science* 33 (4): 509–538.

Miller, Jon D. 1998. 'The Measurement of Civic Scientific Literacy'. *Public Understanding of Science* 7 (3): 203–223.

Mulder, Henk A. J., Nancy Longnecker, and Lloyd S. Davis. 2008. 'The State of Science Communication Programs at Universities around the World'. *Science Communication* 30 (2): 277–287.

Ngumbi, Esther. 2018. 'We Should Reward Scientists for Communicating to the Public'. *Scientific American*, 8 July 2018. https://blogs.scientificamerican.com/observations/we-should-reward-scientists-for-communicating-to-the-public/.

Nisbet, Matthew C., and Dietram A. Scheufele. 2009. 'What's Next for Science Communication? Promising Directions and Lingering Distractions'. *American Journal of Botany* 96: 1767–1778. doi: 10.3732/ajb.0900041

Penders, Bart. 2017. 'Marching for the Myth of Science: A Self-Destructive Celebration of Scientific Exceptionalism'. *EMBO Reports* 18 (9): 1486–1489.

Roche, Joseph, and Nicola Davis. 2017. 'Should the Science Communication Community Play a Role in Political Activism?' *Journal of Science Communication* 16 (1): L01–1.

Shipman, W. Matthew. 2015. *Handbook for Science Public Information Officers: Chicago Guides to Writing, Editing, and Publishing*. Chicago, IL: University of Chicago Press.

Stehr, Nico. 2012. 'Knowledge Societies'. In George Ritzer (ed.), *The Wiley-Blackwell Encyclopedia of Globalization*. Chichester: John Wiley & Sons.

Stirling, Andrew. 2007. 'Risk, Precaution and Science: Towards a More Constructive Policy Debate. Talking Point on the Precautionary Principle'. *EMBO Reports* 8 (4): 309–315.

Stirling, Andy. 2008. '"Opening Up" and "Closing Down": Power, Participation, and Pluralism in the Social Appraisal of Technology'. *Science, Technology & Human Values* 33 (2): 262–294.

Temmerman, Martina, Renée Moernaut, Roel Coesemans, and Jelle Mast. 2018. 'Post-Truth and the Political: Constructions and Distortions in Representing Political Facts'. *Discourse, Context & Media*, October.

Trench, Brian 2008. 'Towards an Analytical Framework of Science Communication Models'. In Donghong Cheng, Michel Claessens, Toss Gascoigne, Jenni Metcalfe, Bernard Schiele, and Shunke Shi (eds.), *Communicating Science in Social Contexts*, pp. 119–135. Dordrecht: Springer.

Trench, Brian. 2012. 'Vital and Vulnerable: Science Communication as a University Subject'. In Bernard Schiele, Michel Claessens, and Shunke Shi (eds.), *Science Communication in the World: Practices, Theories and Trends*, pp. 241–58. Dordrecht: Springer.

Trench, Brian. 2017. 'Universities, Science Communication and Professionalism'. *Journal of Science Communication* 16 (05). https://doi.org/10.22323/2.16050302.

Wilsdon, James, Brian Wynne, and Jack Stilgoe. 2005. *The Public Value of Science: Or How to Ensure that Science Really Matters*. London: Demos.

Wynne, Brian. 1992. 'Misunderstood Misunderstandings: Social Identities and the Public Uptake of Science'. *Public Understanding of Science* 1: 281–304.

PART I
STS CONCEPTS AND SENSITIVITIES

2

CONCEPTUAL FRAMINGS: STS RESEARCH FOR SCIENCE COMMUNICATION

2.1 INTRODUCTION

This chapter introduces the STS-related conceptual frames we identify as key to studying and doing science communication. It discusses basic assumptions about the nature of knowledge, communication, and research, as well as how these are related to societal challenges. In Chapter 3 we will explore in more detail core sensitivities of STS and what they mean in practice, digging down into the details of how to mobilise them within research practice when analysing science communication. In this chapter we prepare for this by critically reflecting on the nature of communication and of knowledge through, in particular, the notions of co-production and knowing spaces. We also frame science communication as heterogeneous, as processual, and as requiring specific attention to practice. We close by thinking about values in science communication in research and practice.

2.2 CO-PRODUCTION: WHERE WAYS OF LIVING IN AND KNOWING ABOUT THE WORLD MEET

Perhaps the most fundamental idea that we make use of in this volume is that of co-production. We understand the entities we study, and particularly 'science' and 'society', not as independent or pre-existing entities but as co-produced. To use the idiom of co-production means, to quote Sheila Jasanoff (2004: 2), acknowledging that 'the ways in which we know and represent the world (both nature and society) are inseparable from the ways in which we choose to live in it' and therefore to view knowledge or technological and social orders as being produced together. Co-productionist accounts emphasise symmetry: they call 'attention to the social dimensions of cognitive commitments and understandings, while at the same time underscoring the epistemic and material correlates of social formations' (ibid.: 3).

Our central framework is thus that knowledge production, and ways of knowing more generally, are always connected to particular forms of life – with science communication playing a central role in materialising this mutual shaping of science and society. Jasanoff (2004) suggests that co-production often runs along particular pathways, clustering within specific moments and places in which particular natural and social orders relate to each other. Specifically, she identifies four 'ordering instruments' which work 'at the nexus of natural and social order' (ibid.: 39–42). As will be visible in many of the chapters in this volume, these are key when studying and doing science communication, as they 'stabilize both what we know and how we know it' (ibid.: 39).

The first ordering instrument is the making, negotiation, and reshaping of *identities*, scientific or otherwise, in our case through the process of science communication. Attributing expert positions or describing human bodies and selves in specific ways – for instance, when scientists are represented as heroic or intellectually brilliant in popular media, or when human bodies and behaviours are represented in health-related narratives – are examples of such identity-related moments of co-production.

Second, *institutions* matter, particularly in the ways in which they become central players in defining what is to be regarded as valid and valuable knowledge. In science communication, looking at this institutional angle can be of particular interest: mass media, for instance, are powerful institutions that participate in defining what is to be seen as a given fact and what needs to be questioned. Media are also arenas for constructing institutional actors and attributing or denying credibility to institutions that make public knowledge claims. Science communication is thus shaped by, and (re)produces, institutions such as universities or media organisations.

The third ordering instrument involves the making of *discourses*. Discourses – languages that 'give accounts of experiments, persuade sceptical audiences, link knowledges to practice or action, provide reassurances to various publics, and so forth' (Jasanoff 2004: 40–41) – are central to linking knowledge, practice and action, and always address specific publics. As many of the chapters in this volume illustrate, science communication often embraces existing discourses (such as scientific framings), thus tacitly subscribing to specific ways of understanding nature and society. But science communication also has the potential to create ruptures and shape new ways of seeing and speaking, visualising and writing the world through the languages it mobilises.

Finally, *representations* comprise the fourth ordering instrument of co-production. They are the means by which the world around us is made intelligible; they also connect, however, to questions of political and social representation. Looking at the ways in which visualisations of science-related phenomena – such as climate change – are produced and deployed is one example of the centrality of critically investigating representations.

To view science communication through the idiom of co-production is thus to make a fundamental shift away from the understanding that it is about straightforwardly representing science and scientists in public. The latter understanding takes for granted that museum exhibitions, online videos, science cafés, or other forms of science communication involve the presentation of already existing scientific facts, theories, people, or practices. In this view, people or ideas are depicted in different media or through different techniques, more or less successfully. This commonsense view of science communication has led to a number of concerns within science communication research and practice. Scientists, for instance, are often worried about the accuracy of the science that is portrayed. Are public representations of science potentially 'dumbing down' science or leading to harmful misunderstandings (Hansen 2016)? Others have been more preoccupied with how the culture and practice of science are represented. Studies of gender and ethnicity in science coverage, for example, have shown not only that female scientists are in the minority in such coverage, but that they are described in rather different ways from their male colleagues, for example with more attention given to their appearance and clothing (Chimba & Kitzinger 2010). Science communication may thus represent science as populated by particular kinds of identities.

In Chapter 7 Ulrike Felt looks at the role of anecdotes in media accounts of obesity. Such anecdotes are spaces in which knowledge, social worlds, and value systems are co-produced. They simultaneously enact a specific understanding of obesity and normative beliefs about how 'good' citizens should relate to their bodies.

These dynamics of representation are important – particularly, we would suggest, those related to the way in which science is depicted as a particular kind of practice for particular kinds of people. It matters if science is largely presented as being something for those of a particular race, class, gender, personality-style or sexuality (a point relating to the question of values and responsibilities in science communication that we discuss in section 2.5). But from a co-productionist position these exclusions are important, because science communication is not representational but generative. Science communication does not simply show the world as it already is, but participates in enacting or performing it in specific ways. It is involved in co-producing realities, whether those are concerned with particular scientific facts (which may be stabilised by their dissemination within public communication) or with the culture of science. In this book we will therefore look at, and investigate, science communication not as turning on (good or bad) representations, but as a set of processes through which all actors involved in it are mutually shaping and being shaped. In this view, science communication doesn't just show things, it makes them.

This co-productionist approach is closely intertwined with STS scholarship that has emphasised that there is no straightforward 'reading off' of scientific facts from descriptive or experimental science, and that scientific knowledge is itself co-produced with particular social orders. What are understood as 'facts' or 'reality' are produced through interactions between the material world, scientific instruments, social processes, and narratives (Latour and Woolgar 1986). Indeed, these cannot readily be distinguished – they are produced together, and cannot be described outside their relations. A commonsense understanding of the scientific process might be that a scientist, standing at a lab bench and performing experiments, is engaging with and reporting on a static external reality (the nature of certain biochemical reactions, the composition of the earth's crust, or whatever it might be). A co-productionist approach instead emphasises that that scientist relies on layers and layers of intervention and understanding to make sense of her experiments and report on that external world. As Law writes, '[r]eality ... is not independent of the apparatuses that produce reports of reality' (2004: 31). Scientific knowledge only makes sense in the context of the (inscription) devices and techniques that are used to produce it; similarly, as that knowledge is produced, it reinforces the nature and value of those devices and techniques.

As Jasanoff (2004) argues, then, knowledge orders and social orders are produced together. These dynamics have been captured through a number of further conceptual developments. The first addresses the question of how states and their citizens manage to collectively arrive at knowledge-related decision making. Here the notion of *civic epistemologies* is helpful, as it aims to draw our attention to how knowledge and political orders are intertwined. It points to the ways in which political systems always involve specific styles of reasoning, dominant argumentative strategies, standards of evidence generation, and ways to attribute expertise. Furthermore, civic epistemology captures what publics expect the state to know and how it reasons in specific ways as part of its decision making (Jasanoff 2005; Miller 2008).

Future orientations are also essential to how social orders are made, and science communication is deeply involved in projecting and anticipating sociotechnical developments. The notion of *sociotechnical imaginaries* points to the role of such future visions and the anticipatory work done around science and technology in public. Imaginaries not only point to the visions present in a society, but draw our attention to the 'collectively held, institutionally stabilized, and publicly performed visions of desirable futures, animated by shared understandings of forms of social life and social order attainable through, and supportive of, advances in science and technology'

(Jasanoff & Kim 2015: 4). As multiple, potentially competing, imaginaries can co-exist within any given society, science communication (potentially) contributes to staging some imagined futures as more desirable than others. This may happen through embracing specific science and technology-related visions and performing them publicly (Felt 2015). Finally, *technopolitical cultures* encapsulate how particular 'technologies are interwoven into a specific society' and how knowledge and its material realisations get embedded in and perform a specific kind of political culture (Felt et al. 2010: 528). These terms all carry their own histories and nuances, and we will draw on them at different points throughout the book. Here we introduce them as a way of conveying what co-production means: that scientific and technical knowledge and ways of living in particular places are always made together.

A co-productive approach which emphasises the interdependence of scientific knowledge with human practices does not mean that we think that there is no reality, or that we can never produce reliable knowledge. As Bloor and Edge write, society, and particularly the norms of the scientific community, is actually 'enabling. We know reality through it, not in spite of it' (2000: 159). But taking this approach does mean that we view both science and science communication as *productive* – making the things they purport to describe. There are no 'neutral' representations, either in scientific practice or science communication. Taking a co-productionist approach means looking at moments and instances of science communication and exploring how apparently pre-existing categories or entities, such as 'science', 'the public', or 'dialogue', are mutually constituted within those communication practices. It also means understanding science communication as a space in which co-productive work – the articulation of social orders and knowledge orders – happens.

The starting point for this book is thus that science communication involves and is the locus of co-production: it performs the different entities involved in it. An STS approach to science communication looks at it through the lens of co-production, exploring how identities, institutions, discourses and representations are made through public communication, and how these ordering devices themselves shape the kinds of communication that are possible.

2.3 SCIENCE IS ONE KNOWING SPACE OF MANY

In the previous section we outlined our overall approach, one that focuses on co-production. Here we use these ideas in order to think more explicitly about what the 'science' in science communication is, as a process or culture. What kind of activity do we mean, in this volume, when we refer to science? The process of knowledge production, we have already suggested, is carried out through the interactions of people, experimental set-ups, objects, theories, and communities. Here we explore this further, using John Law's notion

(2017) of 'knowing spaces' to discuss how we understand knowledge-making. Our view is that science communication is a process and practice that is not solely about reporting the outcomes of scientific work, but a knowing space in its own right.

Our starting point is that scientific knowledge and facts are not direct and straightforward expressions of an objective reality, but are contingent on the conditions of their production. STS has repeatedly shown that any kind of knowledge is produced through complex interactions between objects, instruments, people, texts, organisations and cultures (see, for example, Knorr-Cetina 1981; Latour & Woolgar 1986). One way of framing this is by saying that knowledge production occurs within communities with specific practices and norms, and that the outputs of science – knowledge, theories, facts – are dependent on the nature of those communities. Writing in the 1930s, the Polish microbiologist Ludwik Fleck argued that scientific (and other) ways of knowing emerge out of 'thought collectives' with distinctive 'thought styles' (Fleck 1979 [1935]). A thought style is an epistemology, or a way of asking questions and seeking answers; for Fleck, scientific communities operate according to particular thought styles that encapsulate a shared knowledge base, assumptions about what is possible or impossible, and methods and approaches. A thought style has an invisible but powerful grip upon one's thinking: an 'individual within the collective is never, or hardly ever, conscious of the prevailing thought style, which almost always exerts an absolutely compulsive force upon his [sic] thinking and with which it is not possible to be at variance' (Fleck 1979 [1935]: 41). Cognition is thus never individual. Scientists rely on a shared well of knowledge, and knowledge about knowledge. Stepping outside the thought style of your community, while you are within it, is virtually impossible.

In Chapter 11 Nina Amelung and her co-authors take us to the legal system, and more specifically to the knowing space of the courtroom. Focusing on forensic genetics as a thought collective, they discuss how the norms at work in this knowing space shape scientific practice, as well as affecting how public communication is perceived by forensic geneticists.

However, an individual never belongs to a single thought collective. Think of a scientist who works in more than one discipline, or one who is simultaneously committed to a specific scientific field, to a religious faith, and to a political party. Each of these can be understood as different thought collectives with specific thought styles. Thought collectives fundamentally shape the kind of knowledge that is produced. Building on this insight, later authors have emphasised the role of objects, spaces, and embodiment within knowledge production. It is not only one's thought collective that shapes how science is done, but the spaces one works in, the equipment used, and the materials that are studied. Latour (1983), for instance, argues that the laboratory is a key infrastructure that allows science to interact with and operate on the wider world. The laboratory is a carefully controlled space where knowledge can be generated, but it is also the means by which that knowledge can be taken up in other contexts through the extension of 'laboratory conditions'. 'Scientific facts are like trains', writes Latour (1983: 155); 'they do not work off their rails' – where the 'rails' are the conditions under which facts can be produced and reproduced. Scientific knowledge thus brings with it specific sets of practices and assumptions, many of which do not travel well to other domains.

If we are to talk of 'science', 'facts', or 'scientific knowledge', then, we should not imagine eternal laws of nature (as Fleck (1979 [1935]) notes, scientific thinking is continually 'mutating') or direct representations of reality. Knowledge production is, as Law (2004: 29) argues, an 'activity that involves the simultaneous orchestration of a wide range of appropriate literary and material arrangements'. He underlines that:

> knowing and its methods are materially complex and performative webs of practice that imply particular arrays of subjects, objects, expressions or representations, imaginaries, metaphysical assumptions, normativities, and institutions. (Law 2017: 47)

These heterogeneous arrays together form the background, or a 'hinterland', behind every fact or piece of knowledge: they are the conditions that make knowledge possible and allow it to last. 'The orchestration of suitable and sustainable hinterlands' (Law 2004: 29) is thus key to stabilising how and what we know. Law has written about these orchestration processes as occurring within specific 'knowing spaces', which 'set more or less permeable boundaries to the possible and the accessible' (Law 2017: 47).

To exist within a particular knowing space is thus to be able to call, often implicitly, upon a specific array of 'subjects, objects, expressions or representations, imaginaries, metaphysical assumptions, normativities, and institutions' (ibid.: 47), and to make sense of statements or claims that occur within that knowing space, as well as to make such claims oneself. Within academic research, for instance, there are established ways of producing knowledge. As scientists progress in their careers, they become adept at using the right genre of language in writing and speaking, handling their research materials in an agreed-upon manner, publishing in the right kinds of places, developing more effective experimental set-ups, collaborating with the right kind of institutions and people, and so forth. They develop expertise in how one knows in their particular field and discipline. Such knowing spaces are specific, not universal: what 'counts' as reliable knowledge may differ between disciplines, or even from lab to lab (Collins 2001). As Law writes, in 'any given location it is easier to know in some ways than in others' (2017: 48). To exist within a particular knowing space means following familiar and well-worn grooves of practice and claim-making.

This is a central challenge for science communication. Communication within science – through articles or conference presentations – tends to focus on explaining the conditions under which new knowledge has been produced, making it possible for others in the thought collective to scrutinise, question, and critique that knowledge. Scientific knowledge is thus always more than what often gets called a 'scientific fact' – the results that get referred to in scientific publications and beyond – but always includes the hinterland, that is, 'the pre-existing social and material realities of its production' (Law 2004: 13). Science communication in more public settings does not generally include these details. Scientific findings, often called 'facts', are (often quite radically) decontextualised, i.e. stripped of the situatedness of their production and validation and then recontextualised in new spaces: in diverse societal thought collectives, in situated sociopolitical environments, in spaces where other events and experiences are present. 'Scientific facts' and related innovations must then be articulated in a manner recognisable to public modes of thought. If we understand knowledge as situated and defined through these respective hinterlands, then science communication should be understood as a transformation process, *creating distinct ways of knowing the world* (for a schematic representation of this process see Figure 2.1).

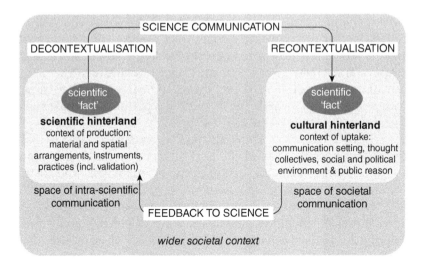

Figure 2.1 Schematic presentation of communicative processes

We have already noted that individuals exist within more than one knowing space. Among other things, this means that knowledge production is not exclusive to science. There are numerous instances of knowing spaces that do not involve the traditional scientific apparatus we have become accustomed to (laboratories, experiments, peer review, university researchers), and of these different kinds of knowing spaces coming into contact with each other. For example, Helen Verran has written about the 'ontological non-coherence' faced by bilingual students who exist within both Indigenous and Western cultures (Ayre & Verran 2010; Verran 2007). Nigerian students who speak both Yoruba and English encounter different methods of quantifying matter. In their day-to-day lives, they must negotiate two entirely different ways of knowing and being in the world (Verran 2007). Another example is of consultation processes and other spaces that seek to bring different groups together to debate a particular scientific issue. To engage with a particular medical condition, for example, is to bring together multiple knowing spaces: the knowledge-producing systems of different kinds of researchers, of doctors, of patients, and of care-givers, among others (Callon et al. 2009). These (doubtless overlapping) knowing spaces each enact particular ways of knowing. More generally, any of us exist within diverse knowing spaces if we engage with the media, live in and with particular communities (such as faith- or hobby-based groups), or make use of different aspects of institutionalised knowledge production: all of these can be considered thought collectives in that they involve sets of assumptions about what it is to know and what reliable knowledge looks like. This further suggests that communication is never a one-way enterprise, even in cases – such as classical news settings or a public lecture – where there seems to be a clear directionality of information flow (Davies & Horst 2016). Audiences are always engaged in interpretation: they judge whether or not information is interesting, noteworthy or relevant to them (Michael 1992), and have to integrate new information with pre-existing knowledge and experience (Wynne 1992).

In the context of this book, we consider (different settings of) science communication as opening up knowing spaces, as well as being knowing spaces in their own right. Public communication of science develops its own situated logics of what knowledge is and what is suitable for public consumption. For instance, journalistic media operate according to ideas about balance, and the need to show two different sides of a story; this can have dramatic effects on how science is depicted in public (Hansen 2016). Again, this leads us to a view of communication not only as a space in which knowledge is represented and narrated, but where it takes shape and is reconfigured in specific ways. Public knowing spaces can help solidify scientific knowledge in particular forms, or promote specific theories or ideas. For Baudouin Jurdant (1993), for instance, popular science books act as the 'autobiography' of science, making concrete a narrative concerning truth claims in a particular field. The knowing space (and literary conventions) of a genre of writing acts to secure the nature of scientific knowledge. Steven Epstein, in his analysis of the history of AIDS research and treatment, shows the impact of engagements between medical researchers, activists, policy makers, and publics at large on the complex processes and 'credibility struggles' in the making of knowledge about AIDS (Epstein 1996). Here, then, the knowing spaces of AIDS activists and traditional scientific research come into contact. To give another example, focus group research in the area of nanotechnologies shows how participants struggle to make sense of these novel materials by assembling different elements (including information) in context-specific ways. This reveals the non-fixed character of the discursive process and the ways in which a knowing space may be constructed within the specific, time-limited setting of a focus group (Felt et al. 2015).

The core argument of Dorothea Born's chapter (Chapter 6) is that popular science magazines can be understood as knowing spaces. In a longitudinal study of climate change communication in *National Geographic*, she unpacks the specific ways in which climate change was established as a human-made phenomenon, allowing engagement with its real-world consequences.

Ultimately, those engaged in science communication are always part of multiple thought collectives. One challenge for science communication research is to engage with the specificities of the knowing spaces being communicated about, as well as interrogating the knowing spaces of science communication itself. The key point here is that, in studying or performing science communication, we cannot take scientific knowledge for granted. It is not something immutable, but is produced by specific sets of methods and relies on specific assumptions. Scientific knowing spaces are also not impermeable: they both affect science communication and are affected by public knowing spaces.

2.4 SCIENCE COMMUNICATION IS RELATIONAL

The previous sections have discussed co-production and knowing spaces. Building on this, we now consider the nature of a science communication process. How can we think about what happens as someone reads a popular science magazine, attends a science festival, or visits an exhibition? Our key suggestion is that these are relational processes. They are defined by the components – human and non-human – from which they are assembled, as well as by the relations between these components.

Our starting point is that science communication is a flexible category rather than a fixed set of activities or formats. Indeed, one of the things we might study is how certain labels – 'popularisation' or 'public communication', for instance – become applied to particular activities, and what the effects of those labels are. In practice, it is impossible to make a clear distinction between intra-scientific communication, understood as being between scientists and involving knowledge production, and 'popular' or public communication, understood as directed at laypeople and involving knowledge dissemination. Stephen Hilgartner has shown this particularly clearly. In a 1990 paper, he followed the way in which the findings of a review article were taken up in the media, policy, and other public forums, showing not only that there was no clear moment at which these findings were definitively transferred into the public domain, but also that they continued to be queried and transformed even when they were. 'Scientific facts' remained unstable and subject to new interpretations within public communication as much as in scientific discussion. Hilgartner writes:

> The point ... is not that there are no differences between a report on DNA repair in *Cell* and an article on the same topic in *The Baltimore Sun*; obviously, there are. The point is simply that 'popularization' is a matter of degree. The boundary between real science and popularized science can be drawn at various points depending on what criteria one adopts, and these ambiguities leave some flexibility about what to label 'popularization'. (Hilgartner 1990: 528)

It is fruitless to try to draw a sharp line between 'real science' and 'popularized science'. Hilgartner follows up on this thought by exploring the work that the label 'popularisation' itself can do. Rather than being a statement of fact, he argues, it is a political tool. Labelling something a popularisation can serve to discredit it by removing the authority attached to 'real science'. It also serves other purposes: even well-meaning efforts to 'improve public understanding of science' or to 'bridge the gap' between science and the public will serve to reify the distinction between these entities even as they seek to bring them closer together, or will solidify science's status as uniquely authoritative (Felt 1999). The labels applied to a piece of science communication, and how it is understood, are therefore contextual, dependent on the situation and the sets of relations in which that communication sits.

This returns us to an earlier point: that science communication acts in the co-production of the entities involved in it. In Hilgartner's example, different statements of what was ostensibly the same piece of scientific knowledge are framed and reframed as differently authoritative and even different in content. As researchers, we should thus be aware of the work that the labels applied to science communication – whether that is 'popularisation', 'translation', 'mediation', or anything else – do. But we should also be attentive to what the science communication processes that we study are composed of. One key idea that we take from STS is heterogeneity, or diversity. We have already started to touch on this concept obliquely; Law, for example, talks about knowing spaces as heterogeneous arrays of 'subjects, objects, expressions or representations, imaginaries, metaphysical assumptions,

In Chapter 4, Tybjerg and co-authors describe the biography of a particular object, a 'gene gun' (a tool for changing the biological make-up of cells) produced by a hacker. As it moved through different communication spaces, it sparked into being different stories, social relations, ideas about the public, and forms of science communication.

normativities, and institutions' (2017: 47). Knowing spaces are complex entanglements of many different things, from the elusive or discursive ('imaginaries' or 'normativities') to the concrete and mundane ('objects'). An STS approach not only trains us to look out for this diversity within the construction of knowledge, but suggests that science communication should itself be understood as heterogeneous.

Heterogeneity implies – as the name suggests – that any instance of science communication will involve many different things. A news article is likely to involve several voices or positions; a live event brings together different kinds of people; a museum exhibition may have many similar objects but is likely to catalogue their differences. The idea of heterogeneity highlights multiplicities and differences within our research material that we need to attend to. But looking at Law's list (quoted above) of the kind of things that come together in knowing spaces also helps us to see that science communication will involve many different *kinds* of things. Subjects, objects, representations, imaginaries, and metaphysical assumptions are not all the same type of stuff. The idea of heterogeneity therefore encourages us not only to look out for difference and diversity – for instance, in views, voices, or actors – but also to investigate how different kinds of entities relate to each other and are assembled and hang together – a notion we might capture through the idea of choreography. This notion reminds us to be attentive to 'how different entities are connected, how they overlap and intertwine, and how they collectively shape' science communication (Felt 2016: 192). We should expect that any particular moment of science communication will be enacted through the interactions of multiple kinds of stuff, from people to narratives to national cultures. Those interactions, or relations, will also be diverse and heterogeneous.

Another way of thinking about heterogeneity is through the concept of ethno-epistemic assemblages (Irwin & Michael 2003). Irwin and Michael are concerned with conceptualising the relation between science and society in a way that moves away from simplistic distinctions between categories such as 'science' and 'the public'; the reality of science communication, they say, is much more 'blurred' or 'mixed up'. With ethno-epistemic assemblages (hybrid entities that mix together the natural and the social) as a heuristic – a tool for research and thinking – they examine the way that many interactions between science and wider society involve diverse coalitions or assemblages. Again, they want to emphasise that a range of 'entities, actors, processes and relations' (ibid.: 114) come together in different science communication spaces (their examples include public consultations and websites for patients), and that the alliances that form are rarely about being 'for' or 'against' science. Rather, actors gather around different kinds of issues, from the fashioning of a particular kind of identity to a concern for a certain local neighbourhood, and bring together diverse resources from both scientific and public domains (a patient group might mobilise scientific knowledge, an environmental action campaign might include both environmental scientists and local residents).

Importantly, they view these assemblages not as fixed but fluid, their constituents and relations shifting as circumstances change. *Processuality* is therefore also an important aspect of how science communication is assembled and composed.

All of this means that an STS approach to science communication will be attentive to the heterogeneity of an instance of science communication and to the relations that comprise it. It will not – or will at least try to not – filter out some kinds of actants, or presences, as unimportant. For instance, Davies (2009, 2013) was interested in studying science dialogue events – public events where visitors heard short presentations from scientists before the floor was opened up for discussion. She looked at the content of what was said, identifying themes in how scientific knowledge was presented and negotiated and thus how science was performed. But she also studied some perhaps quite surprising aspects of these events, such as the shape of the room they were held in, the colour scheme, how long it took for microphones to be passed around, and the ways in which the events mirrored interactional genres like talkshows or news interviews. These aspects also contributed to making the dialogue events what they were; the events were, by nature, heterogeneous assemblages that came together for a period before being disassembled, and the physical space and colour scheme and food served at the bar were as much part of that assemblage as the explicit discussion of science.

This processual or 'in flux' nature of science communication means that it can be thought of as a continual, dynamic process of 'becoming'. Horst and Michael (2011) offer a framework for thinking about science communication in these terms by arguing for its 'eventfulness'. As in the accounts above, they view science communication as mobile (changeable and in flux) and productive (implicated in the co-production of science and society). Their notion of science communication as 'event' loses the colloquial meaning of an event: they view all public communication in these terms, not just public events or meetings. They use the notion of the event to signal the coming together of the kinds of heterogeneous assemblages we have already discussed and the entanglement of 'entities that are social and material, human and non-human, macro and micro, cognitive and affective, available and unavailable to consciousness' (ibid.: 286). They also emphasise that an event is something that emerges. The coming together of diverse entities leaves those entities changed: 'the interactions of [an event's] constitutive elements change those elements' (ibid.).

In this view, science communication is about becomings. Assemblages are not static, comprised of fixed actants and relations. Both the components of any science communication 'event' and the relations between them are constantly in flux. A further important point for how we understand and analyse science communication is that we can view this process as operating on multiple different scales. The size of an assemblage is always a matter of analytical choice (Michael 2016). To return to the example mentioned earlier, the science dialogue events Davies (2009, 2013) studied were heterogeneous – composed of diverse actants, from scientist-speakers to brightly coloured furniture – and eventful: they emerged in a particular form, before being disassembled. But we could extend the notions of assemblage and processuality to look at this particular instance of science communication on a number of different scales. What wider networks did these dialogue events fit into? (They were hosted in a science museum, but we could also look at the professional networks their organisers were part of, or their regional and national context.) How does their use as a format relate to wider dynamics in the development of science communication in that particular location? What connections did they have to other instances of science communication, science policy, or scientific issues? Asking such questions leads us to other entities, assembled in other ways. Understanding science communication as an eventful, heterogeneous assemblage therefore does not limit us to looking at the small scale, or at single instances of communication. Instead, it can also help us examine what Chilvers and Kearnes (2016: 273) have called 'ecologies of participation': 'diverse socio-material collectives of participation and public involvement' that are co-present around a particular topic or a controversy. In other words, it can help trace the connections and interactions between different forms of science communication, and to understand the landscape of science and society as a whole.

Our view of science communication is thus that it is relational. As we have seen, it is flexible (in that it is impossible to sharply define the distinction between communication that is internal to science, and that which 'popularises' it), heterogeneous (composed of many diverse elements), and processual (continually in flux). A useful question for science communication researchers to consider is how any particular instance of science communication is *assembled*. That might mean looking at the assembly of a single science communication 'event', investigating the elements present in the assemblage as well as their connections, or at how a participation or communication 'ecology' as a whole comes together and collectively shapes a particular issue.

2.5 PRACTICES MAKE REALITIES

So far, we have made a number of conceptual claims relating to how we should think about science, knowledge more generally, and the nature of science communication. Our previous point was that science communication is not stable but in flux; we should therefore be attentive to the temporalities and flows of how it is assembled (an idea we will return to in Chapter 3). In this section, we suggest that this processuality can be further understood through the study of practices. Practices are 'arrays of activity' (Schatzki et al. 2001: 11): they are the routinised things we do as we go about living in the world.

At its very simplest, taking a practice approach means exploring what people *do* rather than focusing on what they say they do or the products that they make (Soler et al. 2014). Studying practices therefore helps us to explore how science communication is done. It draws attention not just to the finished product (a science communication 'event'), but to how this product is achieved and to the flows and becomings that comprise it.

The argument for studying practices comes not just from STS but from a wider move in social research. This approach, sometimes known as a 'practice turn', argues that the traditional topics for social and cultural research – language, culture, or institutions, for instance – are best studied by exploring not their final articulations, but how they are 'done' via practices. Studies of practices, writes Theodore Schatzki, are:

> joined in the belief that such phenomena as knowledge, meaning, human activity, science, power, language, social institutions, and historical transformation occur within and are aspects or components of the *field of practices*. The field of practices is the total nexus of interconnected human practices. (Schatzki et al. 2001: 11)

In STS, practice theory has often emphasised that practices are actually not only 'interconnected human practices'. Other kinds of agents are also involved in the scripts, routines and behaviours that make up a 'field of practice'. As with the concept of heterogeneous assemblages, then, a practice approach draws attention to the diverse entities that are involved in science communication, and the work that they do. In this view, practices are both embodied and entangled with diverse actants, human and non-human. To use John Law's language, a practice approach involves looking at 'how theories, methods, and materials are used in practice in specific social, organizational, cultural, and national contexts' and at 'the effects of those practices' (Law 2017: 31). In the context of science communication, this takes our focus from the thing itself – an isolated instance of science communication – to its making, negotiation, and effects. How is science enacted in different public contexts, and what work is this doing?

There are many fields of practice that are relevant to science communication. We have already mentioned mass media, and the fact that they operate according to particular norms and values. These assumptions, which lie behind how the reporting of science is framed and carried out, can certainly be understood in terms of practices, from the way in which journalists operate (Hansen 2016; Rosen et al. 2016) to the historical power of the press to shape shared understandings of social order (Anderson 2006). The central point is that these practices establish science in the public arena in a specific way – one that is not natural or inevitable, but a result of practices that could be otherwise. Felicity Mellor (2015), for instance, has written not only about news values – factors that help decide what kind of stories are 'newsworthy', including proximity, the presence of elites, and conflict – but about what she calls 'non-news values', 'features of science that are systematically deemed un-newsworthy and are excluded from news reports' (ibid.: 93). Decisions about the aspects of science that should be reported – decisions that are made implicitly because they are part of newsroom culture – ultimately mean that science journalism tends to 'draw on, and reproduce, an image of science as unassailable and devoid of vested interests' (ibid.: 110). Similarly, Penkler et al. (2015) explore media narratives of obesity to show that the conventions of reportage in this area are not innocent, but stage the condition in deeply moralistic terms; ultimately, obese individuals become a threat to society and are called to act in the name of the collective good. In the context of museums, taken-for-granted practices of display and interpretation also perform knowledge in specific, culturally loaded ways (Bennett 2004; Macdonald 1998).

The key point is that *practices do things*. In particular, from an STS view, they make realities. Law (2011), as we have seen, has talked about the way in which science and other knowledge-producing systems bring particular realities into being. We have already argued that science communication is (co-)productive. Focusing on practices encourages us to consider exactly what entities are being performed within science communication, and how they exist differently in different spaces or moments.

Erika Szymanski, in Chapter 8, is interested in media texts as practices. In her view, meaning is constructed through practices of writing texts. In her case study – of media accounts of synthetic yeast – she therefore explores how yeast is 'made' in public texts.

A practice-based approach therefore also brings us to the idea of *ontological multiplicity* – the view that reality is multiple. When we look at what different practices do, and the diverse realities they conjure into being, it is not that these 'realities' are different facets of, or perspectives on, a single reality that is 'out there'. Reality is itself multiple. Annemarie Mol has argued for ontological multiplicity based on an ethnography at a Dutch hospital, where she followed the condition of atherosclerosis from out-patient consultations to surgeries or the pathology lab in order to explore how it was enacted at different moments. What she found was that atherosclerosis was something that was 'done', rather than something existing 'out there' in a stable, singular manner – even though it seemed to exist as a single disease that was clearly described in medical textbooks. The reality of atherosclerosis was performed differently in different places. Its study therefore required 'keep[ing] track as persistently as possible of what it is that alters when matters, terms, and aims travel from one place to another' (Mol 2002: viii). Yet these realities were not independent or uncoordinated; indeed, atherosclerosis was, in the hospital, gathered together and turned into a single entity, so that it could be treated as a singular disease. In this process, some realities were able to 'win' over others – they obtain priority. At other times, realities are played off against each other, with a 'negotiation' between the practices (clinical notes, findings from the pathology lab, pressure measurements) that produced them.

The key point here is that it is important how science communication is done. Practices matter because they perform realities; by studying practices, we can explore what is being produced by science communication activities but also which practices science communication is choosing to report about. We should also be attentive to multiplicity. If different practices perform different realities, how are these coordinated in public communication of science?

2.6 VALUES, VALUATION, AND CARE

Implicit in our discussion thus far – of heterogeneous assemblages, fluid relations, and productive practices – is that an STS approach will frequently involve fine-grained analysis and close attention to the details of any instance of science communication. It will tend to look at specifics, rather than generalities. In part this is because attending to heterogeneity means attending to contingency and locality. If a science communication 'event' is understood as multifarious, complex, and fluid, it can always be otherwise; we should be hesitant, then, about grand theorising or a priori assumptions about the dynamics that are at play (Michael 2016). Similarly, an interest in practices implies a focus on the local and situated (Mol 2002). As a method, a practice approach involves unpacking the details of what is happening – what is being done – in specific moments and sites, and exploring the complexities of this. It is only through attending to the specifics that we get closer to understanding the situated meanings of the larger-scale collective imaginaries such as democracy or citizenship (Ezrahi 2012; Nowotny 2014) that shape the ways in which we investigate and perform science communication.

One important thing to say about an STS approach to science communication is thus that it is attentive to the situatedness of instances of public communication, while simultaneously understanding such communication as allowing insight into larger developments. It will explore contingencies and the specificity of particular case studies. This means looking at, for instance, how science is done differently in communication about different disciplinary traditions, the constituents of different science communication assemblages, or the practices and values associated with a particular form of science communication. Indeed, we might take this as something of an ethical imperative in that we want to *do justice* to our research material (Wray 2018). This idea brings us to the final aspect of STS that we want to discuss in this chapter: its attention, particularly in recent years, to questions of *values*, *valuation*, and *care*.

This attention has several aspects. It can be articulated through a concern with implicit values present within the empirical cases we study; it calls for explicit reflection on the kinds of issues we find worth engaging with or which we decide to ignore; it denotes a concern for social practices through

In Chapter 10, Erela Teharlev Ben-Shachar and Nadav Davidovitch engage with the complex question of how nutritional communication becomes a space in which 'national values' and knowledge about food are co-produced. They show how specific versions of the state and citizenship are performed, rendering other options invisible. Dietary prescriptions thus become expressions of basic values to be shared.

which value(s) are assessed, negotiated, established, or contested; and it means being attentive to the ways in which we carry out our research, and the values and sensitivities expressed through it. In other words, it involves both a concern *with* values in our research (exploring how diverse values are articulated and contested within science communication), and a concern *for* the values of that research (interrogating our own values, and the ways these are expressed in how we carry out research). Both of these concerns build on STS interest in how particular versions of science and society are assembled and staged, and the implications of this.

Concretely, STS offers at least five ways forward for thinking about how we can engage with values and valuation within our research.

First, it is worth highlighting that recent STS work has drawn particular attention to values such as responsibility, democracy, and justice in scientific research and innovation. One aspect of this has been a concern with 'responsible research and innovation' (Owen et al. 2012). The aim has been to 'democratically open up and realise new areas of public value for science and innovation' (ibid.: 754) – to encourage reflection on scientific values and the implications of research trajectories, and to render these both open and publicly accountable (Stirling 2008; Wynne 2006). Similarly, research that uses notions of co-production is explicit that, if science and society are not predefined, stable entities but are co-produced, then values and valuation practices come to matter on many different levels. Co-production is 'not only about how people organize or express themselves, but also about what they value and how they assume responsibility for their inventions' (Jasanoff 2004: 6). Civic epistemologies and sociotechnical imaginaries similarly express values in relation to knowledge and technological developments and the futures they bring about.

Second, value judgements are at work in what is excluded, or put into the background, through public communication. We should thus also be interested not only in the performativity of science communication, but in what is *not* being performed, and which is thereby rendered invisible. John Law has written about these dynamics in terms of what he calls 'collateral realities', versions of the world that are brought into being by scientific, social scientific, or other knowledge practices but which thereby push other realities into the background (2004, 2011). The point is that the realities that are performed by science or science communication shouldn't be taken for granted, but viewed as a choice involving specific values. Law summarises this as follows:

> If, performatively, representations do realities in practice, then those realities might have been done differently. We find ourselves in the realm of politics. (Law 2011: 161)

An integral aspect of an STS approach to science communication is therefore an interest in *how things could be otherwise*. What realities are produced, what wider implications do they have, and what realities are being shut down or sequestered? This approach is concerned with the co-productive processes that take place within science communication, but focuses on the values and moral judgements that are being promoted through these. Here, as an example, we might again return to the way in which science is performed through media practices. If media mainly frame obesity as a moral problem tied to individuals' undisciplined ways of living that poses a threat to the nation (Penkler et al. 2015), what other versions and lived experiences of obesity, and what bodily identities, are suppressed by this discourse and thus rendered illegitimate? 'By choosing rhetorical devices and selecting evidence, [media] construct specific accounts of health issues, unfold moral narratives, and distribute responsibilities' (ibid.: 317).

Third, these concerns with values of responsibility and justice, and the politics of what is (not) represented within public communication, have led to more applied efforts to open up scientific governance and enhance democracy (Stilgoe et al. 2014). Here an interest in values becomes a normative call to action: if scientific accounts of the world are not straightforward readings of a stable external reality, but interventions that produce specific realities, it is important to allow for the voicing of other, related realities. This is especially the case where there might be existing realities, pressing in their own ways, that are routinely silenced by scientific, policy, or bureaucratic narratives. Callon et al. (2009: 136) argue for 'hybrid forums', spaces that bring together different actors 'in search of a common world'. They particularly focus on cases where 'secluded research' – research under laboratory conditions, cloistered from the wider world – comes into contact with real-world experiences, knowledges, and practices, such as medical research or the siting of nuclear waste storage facilities. In such cases, hybrid forums may arise naturally when patients, activists, scientists, policy makers, and others interact, but there is also an argument for the careful creation of spaces where deliberation between such actants can occur:

> Instead of resorting to established experts and the maintenance of the monopoly of secluded research in the investigation of possible worlds, and instead of resorting to institutional spokespersons who keep emergent concerned groups at arm's length, the setting up and organization of hybrid forums is favoured. Now the distinction between facts and values is not only blurred in these forums, it is quite simply suppressed. It is through the exploration of possible worlds that identities are reconfigured, these identities in turn leading to new questions. (Callon et al. 2009: 232)

The creation of different kinds of hybrid forums is therefore one concrete way in which STS scholarship has sought to promote values of justice, to enhance democratic engagement with science, and to interrogate the moral judgements that scientific knowledge may implicitly incorporate.

Fourth, and closely connected to the call to allow the voicing of diverse sets of actors and values, feminist studies of technoscience (Mol et al. 2010) have called attention to care as a value to be both explored in our analyses and practised within our research. Care has been conceptualised as a practice that brings attention to under-represented voices and experiences – 'engaging neglected things', to use the language of Maria Puig de la Bellacasa (2011) – but which also requires inhabiting, and acknowledging, affective states. As an approach, this involves attention not just to abstract values of democracy or justice, or to instances of under-represented carework, but to the specificities of research situations, and our own emotional entanglement in them. It involves a commitment to living out particular values by caring for those situations, and the actants implicated in them, and thus asking what is needed from us at that moment. 'Caring is more about a transformative ethos than an ethical application', writes Puig de la Bellacasa (ibid.: 100). 'We need to ask "how to care" in each situation.' Caring about science communication will thus look different in different contexts; what is more general, however, is that we should expect to feel something – even something awkward or uncomfortable – about our research. Indeed, science communication can be seen as an act of care for specific matters of (public) concern: it is an intervention that opens up particular topics to wider debate, allowing us to question what has seemed unquestionnable. Ultimately, if we are interested in interrogating the realities that instances of science communication open up and shut down, we should be prepared to acknowledge our own entanglement in these realities.

Fifth, recent STS work has turned explicitly to the study of processes of valuation, that is, to explore how values are enacted within the sciences (Dussauge et al. 2015). While STS has always taken for granted that facts and values are co-produced, such valuation studies focus more specifically on what is valued, in what ways, within scientific knowledge-making. One strand of work, for instance, interrogates what is valued within contemporary scientific careers: How is credit given, promotion gained, and work assessed? Often, metrics – such as the number of articles published and how many times these have been cited – are key to such evaluations, becoming a proxy for scientific value (Fochler & de Rijcke 2017; Müller & de Rijcke 2017). More generally, valuation studies help us to think about processes and cultures of assessment and evaluation, which are increasingly important in science communication as well as science itself (Boltanski & Thévenot 2006). This line of work might therefore encourage us to ask: what is *valued* in science communication, how is such value attributed, and in what ways are value attributions reproduced but also questioned in science communication settings?

Ultimately, being attentive to values can be understood as a concern for the choices we make in carrying out our research, and their effects, as well as the choices made in producing science communication, and the effects of these. This can lead us to ask questions such as: What are the values furthered through specific kinds of communication practices? What is being furthered by this research, or this way of describing the world, and what is my position on this? Are there other values we want our work to promote?

2.7 CONCLUSION

This chapter has outlined some of the core ideas of STS, and reflected on what these mean for science communication research. We have explored the notion of co-production, argued that knowledge is made within specific 'knowing-spaces', suggested that science communication is relational, and shown how practices are a central means to examine what science communication is and what it does. In the preceding section, we suggested that we should be attentive to the fact that seemingly 'neutral' science communication encodes values, and that one task for us, as researchers and practitioners, is to interrogate these values. What does our communication assume about the actors and worlds it speaks of and to? What responsibilities, judgements, or valuations are written into these descriptions?

We have worked through these ideas almost through a set of keywords: co-production; knowing spaces; heterogeneity; becoming; practices; values; care. These are not approaches that should form a rigid framework; rather, they should be mobilised and worked with as and when our research material, and the cases that we are engaged with, demands it. But taken together, we think that they provoke particular reflections, or lead us to a particular set of sensitivities, as we carry out science communication research or do science communication. They encourage us to view science communication events, moments, and activities as fluid, complex processes that act to co-produce science and society, and that are responsible for bringing particular realities into being. Given this understanding of science communication, the chapter that follows discusses the implications for our research. If we view science communication in these STS-oriented terms, what specific sensitivities and questions will we bring to our research practices and material?

REFERENCES

Anderson, Benedict. 2006. *Imagined Communities: Reflections on the Origin and Spread of Nationalism*. London: Verso.

Ayre, Margaret, and Helen Verran. 2010. 'Managing Ontological Tensions in Learning to Be an Aboriginal Ranger: Inductions into a Strategic Cross-cultural Knowledge

Community'. *Learning Communities: International Journal of Learning in Social Contexts* 1: 2–18.

Bennett, Tony. 2004. *Pasts beyond Memory: Evolution, Museums, Colonianism.* Abingdon: Routledge.

Bloor, David, and David Edge. 2000. 'For the Record (Knowing Reality through Society)'. *Social Studies of Science* 30 (1): 158–160.

Boltanski, Luc, and Laurent Thévenot. 2006. *On Justification: Economies of Worth. Princeton Studies in Cultural Sociology.* Princeton, NJ: Princeton University Press.

Callon, Michel, Pierre Lascoumes, and Yannick Barthe. 2009. *Acting in an Uncertain World: An Essay on Technical Democracy.* Translated by Graham Burchell. Cambridge, MA: The MIT Press.

Chilvers, Jason, and Matthew Kearnes. 2016. *Remaking Participation: Science, Environment and Emergent Publics.* Abingdon: Routledge.

Chimba, Mwenya, and Jenny Kitzinger. 2010. 'Bimbo or Boffin? Women in Science: An Analysis of Media Representations and How Female Scientists Negotiate Cultural Contradictions'. *Public Understanding of Science* 19 (5): 609–624.

Collins, Harry M. 2001. 'Tacit Knowledge, Trust and the Q of Sapphire'. *Social Studies of Science* 31 (1): 71–85.

Davies, Sarah R. 2009. 'Doing Dialogue: Genre and Flexibility in Public Engagement with Science'. *Science as Culture* 18 (4): 397–416.

Davies, Sarah R. 2013. 'The Rules of Engagement: Power and Interaction in Dialogue Events'. *Public Understanding of Science* 22 (1): 65–79.

Davies, Sarah R., and Maja Horst. 2016. *Science Communication: Culture, Identity and Citizenship.* London: Palgrave Macmillan.

Dussauge, Isabelle, Claes-Fredrik Helgesson, and Francis Lee (eds.). 2015. *Value Practices in the Life Sciences and Medicine.* Oxford: Oxford University Press.

Epstein, Steven. 1996. *Impure Science: AIDS, Activism and the Politics of Knowledge.* Berkeley, CA, and London: University of California Press.

Ezrahi, Yaron. 2012. *Imagined Democracies: Necessary Political Fictions.* Cambridge: Cambridge University Press.

Felt, Ulrike. 1999. 'Why Should the Public "Understand" Science? A Historical Perspective on Aspects of the Public Understanding of Science'. In Meinolf Dierkes and Claudia Von Grote (eds.), *Between Understanding and Trust: The Public, Science and Technology,* pp. 7–38. Amsterdam: Harwood Academic Publishers.

Felt, Ulrike. 2015. 'Keeping Technologies Out: Sociotechnical Imaginaries and the Formation of Austria's Technopolitical Identity'. In Sheila Jasanoff and Sang-Hyun Kim (eds.), *Dreamscapes of Modernity: Sociotechnical Imaginaries and the Fabrication of Power,* pp. 103–125. Chicago, IL: Chicago University Press.

Felt, Ulrike. 2016. 'The Temporal Choreographies of Participation: Thinking Innovation and Society from a Time-Sensitive Perspective'. In Jason Chilvers and Matthew Kearnes (eds.), *Remaking Participation: Science, Environment and Emergent Publics,* pp. 178–198. Abingdon: Routledge.

Felt, Ulrike, Maximilian Fochler, and Peter Winkler. 2010. 'Coming to Terms with Biomedical Technologies in Different Technopolitical Cultures: A Comparative Analysis of Focus Groups on Organ Transplantation and Genetic Testing in Austria, France, and the Netherlands'. *Science, Technology & Human Values* 35 (4): 525–53.

Felt, Ulrike, Simone Schumann, and Claudia Schwarz. 2015. '(Re)assembling Natures, Cultures, and (Nano)technologies in Public Engagement'. *Science as Culture* 24 (4): 458–483. doi: 10.1080/09505431.2015.1055720.

Fleck, Ludwik. 1979 [1935]. *Genesis and Development of a Scientific Fact*. Chicago, IL: University of Chicago Press.

Fochler, Maximilian, and Sarah De Rijcke. 2017. 'Implicated in the Indicator Game? An Experimental Debate'. *Engaging Science, Technology, and Society* 3 (February): 21.

Hansen, Anders. 2016. 'The Changing Uses of Accuracy in Science Communication'. *Public Understanding of Science* 25 (7): 760–774.

Hilgartner, Stephen. 1990. 'The Dominant View of Popularization: Conceptual Problems, Political Uses'. *Social Studies of Science* 20 (3): 519–539.

Horst, Maja, and Mike Michael. 2011. 'On the Shoulders of Idiots: Re-Thinking Science Communication as "Event"'. *Science as Culture* 20 (3): 283–306.

Irwin, Alan, and Mike Michael. 2003. *Science, Social Theory and Public Knowledge*. Maidenhead: Open University Press.

Jasanoff, Sheila. 2004. 'The Idiom of Co-Production'. In Sheila Jasanoff (ed.), *States of Knowledge: The Co-Production of Science and Social Order*, pp. 1–12. Abingdon and New York: Routledge.

Jasanoff, Sheila. 2005. *Designs on Nature: Science and Democracy in Europe and the United States*. Princeton, NJ, and Oxford: Princeton University Press.

Jasanoff, Sheila, and Sang-Hyun Kim (eds.). 2015. *Dreamscapes of Modernity: Sociotechnical Imaginaries and the Fabrication of Power*. Chicago, IL: University of Chicago Press.

Jurdant, Baudouin. 1993. 'Popularization of Science as the Autobiography of Science'. *Public Understanding of Science* 2 (4): 365–373. https://doi.org/10.1088/0963-6625/2/4/006

Knorr-Cetina, Karin D. 1981. *The Manufacture of Knowledge: An Essay on the Constructivist and Contextual Nature of Science*. Oxford: Pergamon Press.

Latour, Bruno. 1983. 'Give Me a Laboratory and I Will Raise the World'. In Karin D. Knorr-Cetina and Michael Mulkay (eds.), *Science Observed: Perspectives on the Social Study of Science*, pp. 141–70. Thousand Oaks, CA: Sage.

Latour, Bruno, and Steve Woolgar. 1986. *Laboratory Life: The Construction of Scientific Facts*. Princeton, NJ: Princeton University Press.

Law, John. 2004. *After Method: Mess in Social Science Research*. Abingdon: Routledge.

Law, John. 2011. 'The Explanatory Burden: An Essay on Hugh Raffles's Insectopedia by Hugh Raffles'. *Cultural Anthropology* 26 (3): 485–510. https://doi.org/10.1111/j.1548-1360.2011.01108.x.

Law, John. 2017. 'STS as Method'. In Ulrike Felt, Rayvon Fouché, Clark Miller, and Laurel Smith-Doerr (eds.), *The Handbook of Science and Technology Studies*, pp. 31–57. Cambridge, MA: The MIT Press.

Macdonald, Sharon (ed.). 1998. *The Politics of Display: Museums, Science, Culture*. Abingdon and New York: Routledge.

Mellor, Felicity. 2015. 'Non-News Values in Science Journalism'. In Brian Rappert and Brian Balmer (eds.), *Absence in Science, Security and Policy: From Research Agendas to Global Strategy*, pp. 93–113. Global Issues Series. London: Palgrave Macmillan. https://doi.org/10.1057/9781137493736_5.

Michael, Mike. 1992. 'Lay Discourses of Science: Science-in-General, Science-in-Particular, and Self'. *Science, Technology & Human Values* 17 (3): 313–333.

Michael, Mike. 2016. *Actor Network Theory: Trials, Trails and Translations*. London: Sage.

Miller, Clark. 2008. 'Civic Epistemologies: Constituting Knowledge and Order in Political Communities'. *Sociology Compass* 2 (6): 1896–1919. doi: 10.1111/j.1751-9020.2008.00175.x.

Mol, Annemarie. 2002. *The Body Multiple: Ontology in Medical Practice*. Durham, NC: Duke University Press.

Mol, Annemarie, Ingunn Moser, and Jeannette Pols. 2010. *Care in Practice: On Tinkering in Clinics, Homes and Farms*. Bielefeld: Transcript Verlag.

Müller, Ruth, and Sarah de Rijcke. 2017. 'Thinking with Indicators: Exploring the Epistemic Impacts of Academic Performance Indicators in the Life Sciences'. *Research Evaluation* 26 (3): 157–168.

Nowotny, Helga. 2014. 'Engaging with the Political Imaginaries of Science: Near Misses and Future Targets'. *Public Understanding of Science* 23 (1): 16–20. doi: 10.1177/0963662513476220.

Owen, Richard, Phil Macnaghten, and Jack Stilgoe. 2012. 'Responsible Research and Innovation: From Science in Society to Science for Society, with Society'. *Science and Public Policy* 39 (6): 751–760. doi: 10.1093/scipol/scs093.

Penkler, Michael, Kay Felder, and Ulrike Felt. 2015. 'Diagnostic Narratives: Creating Visions of Austrian Society in Print Media Accounts of Obesity'. *Science Communication* 37 (3): 314–339.

Puig de la Bellacasa, Maria. 2011. 'Matters of Care in Technoscience: Assembling Neglected Things'. *Social Studies of Science* 41 (1): 85–106.

Rosen, Cecilia, Lars Guenther, and Klara Froehlich. 2016. 'The Question of Newsworthiness: A Cross-Comparison among Science Journalists' Selection Criteria in Argentina, France, and Germany'. *Science Communication* 38 (3): 328–355.

Schatzki, Theodore R., Karin D. Knorr-Cetina, and Eike von Savigny. 2001. *The Practice Turn in Contemporary Theory*. Abingdon and New York: Routledge.

Soler, Léna, Sjoerd Zwart, Michael Lynch, and Vincent Israel-Jost. 2014. *Science after the Practice Turn in the Philosophy, History, and Social Studies of Science*. Abingdon: Routledge.

Stilgoe, Jack, Simon J. Lock, and James Wilsdon. 2014. 'Why Should We Promote Public Engagement with Science?' *Public Understanding of Science* 23 (1): 4–15.

Stirling, Andy. 2008. '"Opening Up" and "Closing Down": Power, Participation, and Pluralism in the Social Appraisal of Technology'. *Science, Technology & Human Values* 33 (2): 262–294. https://doi.org/10.1177/0162243907311265.

Verran, Helen. 2007. 'The Educational Value of Explicit Noncoherence'. In David W. Kritt and Lucien T. Winegar (eds.), *Education and Technology: Critical Perspectives, Possible Futures*, pp. 101–124. New York: Lexington Books.

Wray, Brittany D. D. 2018. *'Listen, Why Should I Care?': Emotion, Affect, and Expert Participation in Public Engagement about Synthetic Biology*. Københavns Universitet, Det Humanistiske Fakultet.

Wynne, Brian. 1992. 'Misunderstood Misunderstandings: Social Identities and Public Uptake of Science'. *Public Understanding of Science* 1 (3): 281–304.

Wynne, Brian. 2006. 'Public Engagement as Means of Restoring Trust in Science? Hitting the Notes, but Missing the Music'. *Community Genetics* 9 (3): 211–220.

3

WHAT DOES AN STS APPROACH TO SCIENCE COMMUNICATION LOOK LIKE?

3.1 INTRODUCTION

The previous chapter was centrally concerned with unfolding how STS could contribute to the analysis of science communication, as well as how it is carried out. It highlighted the importance of thinking of science communication in co-productive terms, that is, looking at how knowledge, people, and society are made in one and the same move. This approach invites a move away from a purely representational perspective to being attentive to the performative character of any science communication effort. We have stressed the importance of considering the multiplicity of knowing spaces (Law 2017), which leads to heightened attention not only to the places where knowledge is produced, but also to the ways in which science communication itself is a space where knowledge gets (re)shaped. And we underlined the fluid character of science communication, a fluidity that means that we see science communication as a practice of creating situated heterogeneous assemblages of human and non-human actors, creating and distributing a broad range of narratives. These narratives in turn feed imaginaries about science, technology, and how societal pasts, presents, and futures co-evolve. In this view, science communication constantly allows new ways of knowing the world in which we live as well as of imagining the future worlds we want to live in.

This in turn has led us to stress three major sensibilities. First, practices of communication should be at the core of attention when analysing science communication; second, it is important to look out for complex, often hidden, *choreographies* of what gets assembled and connected in specific ways in any moment of science communication; and finally, we put notions such as *justice*, *democracy* and *care* at the centre, asking how science communication relates not only to scientific knowledge but also to the realisation of specific values. We position science communication as being at the core of contemporary knowledge societies, but, embracing a co-productionist gaze, we also understand this practice as formative for the science system itself (Felt & Fochler 2013; Irwin & Michael 2003). In science communication, both science and society mutually shape each other. This perspective frames science communication as central to any effort towards research and innovation being responsible towards society (as with efforts to promote 'responsible research and innovation', RRI), but also to understanding the role that science plays in contemporary societies.

Based on this central framework, this chapter offers a set of insights into what such an STS approach (or, better, such STS sensitivities) can offer to the analysis and practice of science communication. We will discuss seven overlapping perspectives, each focusing on a specific aspect of what a wider STS approach would add to more classical science communication approaches. They all allow us to rethink and reconceptualise making and doing science communication; as we discuss each perspective, we outline the key ideas on which they are based before pulling out some practical implications for studying science communication with them.

3.2 PUBLICS ARE NEVER SIMPLY OUT THERE

First, an STS approach to science communication must engage with how science communication always produces a specific imagination of those who are being addressed. Publics are never simply 'out there', but are made through science communication practices.

STS scholarship has studied in detail how any form of interaction around technoscientific issues always performs a vision of the relevant actors to be engaged with or 'invited to the table' (Irwin 2001; Lezaun & Soneryd 2007). Public actors are represented in multiple ways, and are assumed to have a variety of roles with regard to science. These figures are named differently according to the communicative setting – they might be, for instance, members of the public, citizens, stakeholders, patients, audiences, a readership, consumers, visitors, or clients. While in some settings addressees are expected to learn about science in order to be able to make the 'right' decision, in others they should simply enjoy science, and through this emotional attachment create closeness and support, while in yet others audiences are meant to develop trust in both the knowledge and the recommendations attached to it (Weingart & Guenther 2016). These visions of addressees shape the ways in which relevant actors are addressed, engaged with, and given voice: they produce the publics they describe. Even more important, such visions perform acts of boundary-drawing around scientific knowledge and other forms of knowing the world (Felt 1999; Gieryn 1999), and define who is given agency when it comes to issues of science and technology.

Taking a Facebook page as his case study, Oliver Marsh (Chapter 9) shows how particular kinds of public emerge in this setting. This virtual space invites specific forms of engagement with science, and, at the same time, specific audiences to perform this engagement. He also shows that expression of emotions towards science is used to include or exclude particular publics.

All this should be understood in the context of a political moment in which policy actors are increasingly concerned with challenges of environmental sustainability, climate change, energy alternatives, health and ageing, food safety or other issues of comparable importance. In this context, there is a growing concern 'that publics should be able to respond to compelling scientific insights' and embrace 'urgent associated policy prescriptions' (Felt et al. 2007: 11). Indeed, there is a high degree of awareness that any intervention in areas that carry the label of 'grand challenges' of our time can never solely be based on centralised state policies or new technological solutions, but will always demand a range of different and multi-sited interventions – science communication being a central example. At a time when public participation and engagement are held in high regard (in theory if not always in practice), and there are calls for communicating science in a responsible manner, we encounter a latent contradiction: the communicators construct the very publics to whom they are supposed to be listening as they imagine their audiences, design participation processes according to these imaginations, and define the agency of participants (see Felt et al. 2007; Jasanoff 2005; Wynne 2006). These publics are made not only through 'discursive, linguistic or procedural terms', but through material practices and devices (Marres & Lezaun 2011: 490). Techniques for participation are not only imaginative or linguistic, but are embodied in particular objects and spaces (see section 3.4).

In sum, publics are never simply out there, waiting to be drawn into an act of communication, but are deliberately (if tacitly) formed through those same acts. At the same time, people engaging with science and technology also have their own visions and beliefs about the role they should have. Those visions and beliefs construct a version of society and its relation to science and technology; in this way, audiences can resist the roles

Publics are made in different ways through science communication. Chapter 5, by Marcus Owens, describes how park design embodied particular 'ecological publics'. Both the physical design and interpretative material framed park users as active, engaged citizens with wider commitments to ecological diversity.

that communicators impose upon them, and construct alternative visions – of their role in communication or of the place of science in society – for themselves (Felt et al. 2008, Felt & Fochler 2010).

What does this mean for the kinds of questions that should be considered when analysing and carrying out science communication?

- What kinds of publics are *imagined and brought to life in a particular act of communication*, and, relatedly, *who is tacitly excluded from it?* becomes a central question. This means investigating 'whether there are implicated actors [...] who, while they do not participate actively (for whatever reasons), are the targets of or will likely be affected by actions taken within the social world or arena' (Clarke 1998: 16). Such 'implicated actors' are imagined within an instance of science communication: we might identify them by studying the discursive work that is done to cast the addressees in specific ways, by exploring the ways in which material, non-human elements take an active role in shaping an act of science communication and its participants, or by being attentive to the spatio-temporal configurations communication is part of.

- We can further ask: what kinds of *issues* are the publics of science communication concerned with, and *how do particular actors frame those issues?* For instance, STS studies on disputes around technoscientific issues – such as controversy around genetically modified crops – have shown that while scientists and policy makers are mainly concerned with probabilistic statements concerning the risk of harm, members of the public showed more concern about the character of the institutional actors speaking in the name of science, and whether or not they could be trusted (Felt et al. 2007; Irwin & Wynne 1996; Nelkin 1995). Unpacking diverse issue framings, and differing views on what is at stake, can thus help identify the co-productive work taking place in science communication.

- Questions of the *wider context and technopolitical cultures* (Felt et al. 2010) in which an act of communication is embedded need to be posed. Taking such a perspective speaks to the dynamics of responsibility, agency, and democracy. It helps us to unpick, in a particular situation, what (if any) traditions exist to give citizens a voice on complex technoscientific issues, and how such engagements are practised.

- This attention to the formation of publics invites analysts and practitioners to engage with questions of justice and power, of inclusion and exclusion, and of authority and hierarchies of knowing by looking into the *distribution of agency* across different settings of communication, that is, *who can gain a voice and take action in which setting.*

3.3 MAKING FACTS PUBLIC – MAKING PUBLIC FACTS

The second sensitivity puts the notion of 'scientific facts' at the centre, inviting reflection upon what gets labelled, staged, addressed as science and as stable knowledge within science communication.

When discussing issues of public participation and science communication, much recent debate in STS has gravitated around the many ways in which the making of publics and making of issues are entangled. Most prominently, Noortje Marres (2005: 62) has formulated this as a rule of 'no issue, no politics, no public'. Inspired by the pragmatist thinker John Dewey (1927), she argues that 'the public may then be understood as *an effect* of particular political processes of issue formation' (Marres 2005: 62, emphasis ours). In the context of science communication, this means that publics are not simply addressed by media reports, exhibitions, or other communicative settings, but are made through the very act of transforming something into a 'public issue'. In reading this rule through a co-productionist lens (Jasanoff 2004), however, we need to extend this perspective and shift our attention to how publics, issues, specific kinds of political interventions, and scientific knowledge are always produced in one and the same move (Felt & Fochler 2010). It is not clear what comes first; rather, all these elements are closely intertwined.

We can start by looking at what making a scientific fact means – something we started to explore in the previous chapter. STS has a long tradition of investigating the complex socio-epistemic struggles of fact making in the laboratory and beyond. These studies have opened up processes of fact making and have scrutinised the substantial effort that goes into making knowledge claims, how such claims can gain stability, and how they become part of the widely accepted corpus of knowledge (Knorr-Cetina 1981; Latour & Woolgar 1986). These writings make us aware of the contingent and negotiated character of the scientific knowledge, which is – in the context of science communication – often taken as a given. Sismondo (2010: 107) has summarised the negotiated nature of knowledge making: 'Conversations decide what it is at which the scientists are looking. Negotiations decide what can be written into manuscripts. Rhetorical manoeuvres help shape what other scientists will accept.' From diverse studies of knowledge production STS has come to the basic assumption that knowledge claims (and technological developments) are always situated in specific contexts (Haraway 1988) and thus necessarily reflect a particular moment in time, cultural context, and array of heterogeneous networks used to produce such claims and developments (Felt et al. 2017).

If facts are contingent on the circumstances of their production, how do they become 'public facts'? Or, to express it in a more co-productionist manner, how do scientific and public fact making relate to each other? When scientific knowledge has to move out of the space in which it was produced (see Figure 2.1 in Chapter 2), it needs to develop new types of contextualisations and forms of proofs in order to make sense and become or remain robust.

Indeed, as Jasanoff (1995) and others have argued, scientific claims do not generally deliver easily applicable knowledge about real-life situations. As we discussed in Chapter 2, the laboratory is a location where simplification happens in the name of robust outcomes. In the real world, however, many of these simplifications show limitations and become inadequate. Work needs to be done in ensuring that as scientific facts circulate, they remain trustworthy, sufficiently robust, and relate to societal concerns in meaningful ways. Studying science communication can therefore involve attention to the diverse processes through which 'scientific facts' are captured and reconfigured in acts of communication, how these facts manage or not to become shared and tied into what can be regarded as public knowledge, and how this in turn relates to wider societal issues and concerns. From such a perspective, it makes little sense to judge science communication's quality solely in terms of its accuracy (Hansen 2016); rather, we should explore how facts are made and stabilised within such communication.

Relatedly, it is essential to remember that 'matters of fact' do not come first and only later relate to 'matters of concern' – to use Bruno Latour's (2004) distinction. On the contrary, we can observe how the issues societies talk about, the values they cherish, and ways they connect to and frame science (Callon et al. 2009; Latour 2004) shape some of the ways that research can call for support. For example, in the European context, we can see discussion of 'grand challenges' and mission-oriented research as one way of thinking about how matters of concern frame research. Societal concerns – such as climate change, sustainability, or health – are used to instigate and focus scientific research, to create a whole language of scientific relevance for society, and thus support some forms of knowledge generation more than others.

Facts are made alongside matters of concern in public spaces. Felt, in Chapter 7, explores how obesity is assembled in the media as a matter of public concern. She analyses how anecdotes of 'life with obesity' are a specific means of public fact making, while simultaneously delivering moral judgements.

What do these points mean for the kinds of questions that should be considered when analysing and carrying out science communication?

- When looking at science communication we can no longer take scientific facts as the stable starting point for investigation. Instead of fixating on accuracy, an STS approach encourages us to look at *what gets opened up to questioning* - thus making visible processes of knowledge production and the values involved - and what is closed down in order to achieve a specific predefined outcome (Stirling 2008). How is knowledge brought into the public domain?

- Second, we can ask: how do facts *emerge out of public matters of concern*, and at the same time how do matters of fact *reinforce specific matters of concern*? This means investigating how the sciences that are supposed to produce public facts are brought into different public arenas, and how it is managed that facts and concerns can speak to each other.

- But it also means looking into *the processes* through which scientific facts are transformed into and positioned as public facts, becoming widely shared and taken for granted by large groups within society. We know from research on climate change, for instance, that the relation between matters of societal concern and scientific knowledge are less than straightforward. An STS approach can help us explore *how* public knowledge is presented, negotiated, and – perhaps – rendered stable and trustworthy.

3.4 EXPERTISE AND EVIDENCE

A third perspective, or sensitivity, closely relates to the two we have just described. Given an interest in how publics are made, and how scientific knowledge finds its way into society, a number of questions arise. In particular: what roles do evidence and expertise play in the stabilisation of 'public facts', and who can lay claim to such expertise? This also means thinking about questions of authority, as well as how issues of uncertainty and ignorance or non-knowledge are addressed.

Indeed, the question of what counts as relevant expertise and credible evidence to support a specific agenda or to trigger corresponding action is key when investigating or performing science communication, in particular when it comes to sensitive issues such as health- or environment-related problems. STS has a long-standing tradition in addressing these issues. A basic tenet concerning expertise is that it is not simply related to the specific kind of scientific knowledge or technical skills a person possesses, nor can the persons claiming the status of experts straightforwardly claim the moral virtues of disinterestedness and impartiality. Instead, it is contextual and relational: the question of who holds relevant expertise and is accepted as an expert is the outcome of a complex interaction between participants in an issue (Gieryn 1999; Grundmann 2017; Limoges 1993). In this view, expertise is not seen as a property of a person, but as something that needs to be re-established in every new situation (Kerr et al. 2007). The way in which expertise is exercised or performed therefore matters, calling for thorough examination (Hilgartner 2000).

The unstable and negotiated character of expertise becomes particularly clear in the context of public debates over controversial issues or communication following disasters, when it is often far from clear what relevant evidence or information is and therefore who has applicable expertise. Shobita Parthasarathy (2010: 355) speaks in this context of an 'expert barrier, which often blocks those lacking specialized knowledge from full participation'. However, her work also shows how activists have developed strategies to overcome this barrier by claiming specific kinds of expertise (e.g., in the case of medical conditions), by introducing new facts, or by proposing a different argumentative logic. Ideas about relevance – what is useful knowledge and who has it – develop exactly as issues take shape, and as such these kinds of controversies are a moment when co-production can be observed. Even outside such moments of crisis, what is regarded as relevant information or data very often depends on the assumptions people hold; when assumptions differ, relevance (or relative importance) cannot be easily decided upon. We can often observe that the same data are referred to but that there is disagreement about how to interpret these data and draw conclusions. As with scientific facts more generally, 'data' and 'evidence' therefore cannot be understood in straightforward terms. It is essential to look closely into the processes by which expertise and evidence are established, not just in the lab but also in acts of communication.

Who knows what is best for a nation in the making to eat? This is the question at the core of Chapter 10 (by Teharlev Ben-Shachar and Davidovitch). By longitudinally investigating different forms of nutritional communication in Israel through the 20th century, the authors explore how expertise is constructed within such communication, and its intended (and unintended) governance effects.

In particular, at a moment in time when talk of the importance of big data is high on the public and policy agenda, it is essential to be aware of how deeply values and judgements become embedded into the ways that data are collected, modelled, and finally read in automated forms through algorithms. Speaking of evidence in the 21st century very often means talking about big data and the insights they seem to provide into the complexities of the world around us. This means that a specific kind of reasoning is necessary. It is essential to be aware that objects and subjects are not simply described through the processes of collecting, analysing, and presenting data – they are brought into being through these data and related methods (Ruppert et al. 2017). All this needs to be considered against the backdrop of 'data' and the 'evidence' they produce often being a trump card in science communication: trust is higher when numbers can be presented (Porter 1995). The value-laden and contingent character of such data is thus often made invisible through public communication, where it is brandished as unquestionable and objective.

This has the danger of making science communication through big data and corresponding algorithms unresponsive to societal questioning, a danger that is particularly urgent when the authority to interpret data is unevenly distributed.

It is therefore important to ask who is able to present themselves as having authority. In the past, expertise could be demonstrated through an established repertoire of performances – institutional affiliations, prestigious careers, and excellent media connections were often a guarantee for a stable position of authority. However, as public matters of concern that touch upon scientific and technological developments have become more complex, and the settings in which communication and debates about them have multiplied, authority has become a much more fluid and unstable concept. It now needs continuous work in order to become and remain robust (Hajer 2009; Hilgartner 2000). A world that offers many different locations in which technoscientific issues are communicated, discussed, assessed, and integrated into other forms of knowledge offers more possibilities to present other kinds of evidence. It therefore allows for the creation of thought collectives looking at issues from diverse perspectives, and has made the question of how authority is constructed, distributed, or challenged an important aspect for studies of science communication.

The final issue to be addressed in the context of expertise is uncertainty and non-knowledge. There is a long tradition in STS of reflecting on 'the other' of knowledge, that is, addressing the limits of how and what we can know through science (Böschen et al. 2010; Gross & McGoey 2015). Such work has, for example, explored how uncertainty and unknowns are understood and framed by scientists, the ways in which ignorance may have strategic uses, or how scientific uncertainty may be politicised. Similarly, research on public negotiations of science has shown that 'not knowing' may have social purposes and uses (Irwin & Wynne 1996; Michael 1996). What is of interest here is to better grasp how, in particular communication settings, non-knowledge is more or less recognised and addressed, how it is understood and described by the actors involved (e.g., as temporary, as science will soon be able to know or technologies might solve a problem at stake), and, as a consequence, how it is dealt with in a specific communicative context. We also find examples where the non-knowledge or uncertainty that is embedded in what is presented as 'facts' is consciously *not* addressed, in order to sustain an authoritative stance or to push a solution to a specific problem. This means that it is essential to be attentive to what is represented as, in principle, knowable, and where the limits of our scientific understanding of complex real-world phenomena are situated. In sum, it is as essential to investigate the production and distribution of non-knowledge as it is to explore the presentation of robust knowledge. This is of particular importance when studying areas where controversies matter and where the knowledge–action nexus plays an essential role.

What do these points mean for the kinds of questions that should be considered when analysing and carrying out science communication?

- These reflections should invite the analyst or practitioner to ask: how is expertise *represented and contested* in any instance of science communication, and *who is allowed to lay claim to it*? In particular we should be prepared to explore how scientific expertise is produced through public communication, and how scientific authority is maintained (Hilgartner 1990). Science communication has a long history of reinforcing the boundaries around science, and of ensuring that it is viewed as more authoritative than other forms of knowledge (Gieryn 1999). Does this happen in the instances of science communication that we study, or are other forms of expertise on display (Kerr et al. 2007)?
- We can extend this by posing the question: in what ways are *different voices and claims to knowledge* weighed against each other within a particular cultural context (see Jasanoff's civic epistemologies; Jasanoff 2005)? As we have outlined, expertise in a particular situation is something that has to be established. The mechanisms through which this can be done will be shaped by the norms of particular local cultures, and by national imaginations of science's place in society. Studying how expertise is produced and managed within science communication can thus provide insight into civic epistemologies and imaginaries.
- And, to give another indication of how this angle might help us better understand science communication, we need to extend the focus on knowledge, and aim to gain a better understanding of how non-knowledge and uncertainties are *addressed or silenced*. What kinds of actions are therefore presented as quasi-unavoidable and rational to take? Whose expertise is foregrounded and whose is silenced?

3.5 MATERIALITY IN SCIENCE COMMUNICATION

As we saw in Chapter 2.2, STS work on science and technology has argued convincingly for the centrality of the material means through which knowledge is developed, encountered, and made tangible. Although science communication has often focused on the transmission or acquiring of disembodied ideas, concepts, or knowledges (Michael 2002), attention to materiality is fundamental to understanding science communication practice. Spatial issues related to communication will be treated in more depth in section 3.6. Here we aim to draw attention to materiality from a range of other perspectives.

First, it is essential to reflect upon the changing media landscape in which science communication takes place and the ways this is articulated through particular objects and material arrangements. These materialities include the multiplication of technological devices that connect people to the internet (phones, watches, tablets...), the search engines that guide exactly what information we can find (Mager 2009), or the new ways we can sense our environment and thus engage with knowing the world in thus far unprecedented ways (Gabrys et al. 2016). These developments offer opportunities and affordances to those engaged in communication – be it those who aim to provide information or those looking for it – but also calls for careful reflection. These new technological infrastructures, whether we call them Web 2.0, the internet of things, or ubiquitous computing, allows the targeting of previously unreachable audiences, involvement in communication activities by a broad set of actors, and for actors to take many different roles. Citizens can become science communicators by using social media, new thought collectives can emerge and gain stability, science stories can take shape in many different forms, and can multiply and diffuse in new ways targeting diverse audiences with specific interests. These new infrastructures offer new possibilities of presenting knowledge through the combination of textual and audiovisual formats, as well as hypertextuality and virtual reality, and have thus changed and continue to change ways of accessing knowledge. This, however, forces us to ask new questions concerning how people choose, combine, and process this multiplicity of information, or how power is exercised in new ways (through algorithms and search engines, for instance).

Relatedly, we should also take note of how opportunities for public participation and engagement with science and technology are being shaped by these new technological infrastructures. This relates to the materially sensitive account of public engagement that Marres and Lezaun (2011) propose. They invite us to move beyond solely focusing on human agents to broaden 'the range of entities that ought to be considered relevant to the fabric of political communities' (ibid.: 493) and the ways that these engage with the sociotechnical worlds around them. This view of participation and citizenship takes into account human actors' relationships with a range of sensing devices and other kinds of objects, and how that brings about different forms of engaging with and knowing about sociotechnical issues. Communication about the world around us is being profoundly shaped by the technological possibilities of sensors (see, e.g., Gabrys et al. 2016) and the information collected and distributed to them. The range of entities engaged in communication is exploding in number (an explosion addressed in the idea of an *internet of things*), and these new possibilities need to be encompassed in understandings of science communication. New devices for sensing and sharing environmental readings, from air quality to the temperature of one's fridge, produce sets of data that become key in how we understand and act in the world. An interest in the materiality in science communication may therefore involve attention to the ways in which engagement with questions of science, society, and citizenship takes place not only through traditional political action – such as participating in a debate or town hall meeting – but through interactions with sensing devices and other mundane data-producing technologies.

The third way in which materiality matters concerns the objects at the centre of communication activities. These are present in at least two ways: communication about or around objects, and communication through objects. In both cases such objects can act as 'boundary objects' (Star & Griesemer 1989), which sit at the intersection of different knowing spaces and allow their connection. Communication about objects often starts from the assumption that such objects already have a clear status that we can communicate and discuss. However, drawing on John Law, Sergio Sismondo (2010: 86) reminds us that 'objects are defined by their places in networks, and their properties appear in the context of tests, not in isolation'. Objects, just like facts, cannot be taken for granted as stable entities: as we discussed in Chapter 2, science communication is productive rather than representational, and therefore produces the objects it purports to describe. It is therefore essential to reflect on how an object is brought into being in particular communicative settings, how the wider assemblage it is part of gives shape to the object, and how the object's own agency is reflected. Objects in this sense are not immutable. We should think of them as fluid, taking ever new (temporary) forms.

Objects can be used as a focal point for research into science communication. In Chapter 4 Tybjerg and co-authors follow one particular object – a homemade 'gene gun' – and use this to explore how the materiality of an object structures public communication around it.

However, objects do not only emerge and take shape through communication, but are also prominent agents of communication. This raises a slightly different set of concerns. We could point here to museums or exhibitions, which often stage specific objects as nodes of communication, using them to illustrate or address wider questions (Bennett 2004; Dudley 2009). In the next section, when speaking about the courtroom as a space of science communication, we will allude to visual evidence – such as of DNA matches – produced for use in the courtroom. Here knowledge is communicated by being able to point to a specific material object – a photograph, for instance – that is meant to represent this evidence. Objects are thus often understood as demonstrating or embodying particular pieces of information. One task for science communication research is to examine what meanings are imputed to such objects by different actors, as well as how their material properties function to shape a communication event.

Images and graphics are central to science communication. In Chapter 6, Dorothea Born examines the work that visuals do in the magazine *National Geographic*, showing that, while they always involve interpretative flexibility, they also enact particular visions of science, society, and politics.

Finally, materiality also matters as we closely engage with representational technologies. Living in a visual culture (Mitchell 1994), visual representations have become a central part of any effort to communicate. But representations go beyond images or visuals: the body language through which we convey our message; the different literary technologies we deploy, from anecdotes to analogies or simple highlighting practices; the symbols or visual metaphors we introduce – all of these should be understood as interventions rather than as neutral ways of transmitting information (e.g., see Nerlich 2018). They actively shape and give form and meaning to the issues we want to convey, and are often key to what Latour (1983) has called a 'public proof' – a seeming closure of or agreement on a technoscientific matter of concern. But representational technologies allow a high degree of interpretative flexibility, and are open to becoming part of different explanatory environments and wider imaginaries of the world around us. 'Images and imaginations … are rhetorical tools in the construction of a public meaning' (Van Dijck 1998: 197). An attention to images and other forms of non-discursive representation will therefore again give insight into science communication's role in the co-production of knowledge and social orders.

A sensibility towards the material aspects of science communication opens up a number of entry points into analysis:

- It calls for careful reflection upon how science communication is *mediated through particular technological arrangements* (How is it different to encounter science on a phone or in a newspaper? Or on Facebook or Twitter?), or how public participation may happen as much through material engagement as through explicit discursive addressing of issues.
- Our attention is drawn to objects as important actors in science communication. They offer interesting starting points for investigating science communication. In doing so, however, we need to conceptualise them not as stable entities about which or through which communication happens, but rather follow *how they take form and become imbued with meaning*, as well as what kinds of *active roles they take* in shaping science communication.
- It is important to ask how different material elements or infrastructures create the possibility of – to refer back to Fleck's concept of thought collectives (Fleck 1979 [1935]) – seeing things together, of creating ways of relating matters of fact and matters of concern. This means looking into how *specific issues at stake can be materially framed* in ways that create spaces of thinking together.
- Representational objects are often central to science communication. This leads us to further explore the work that *images, graphics*, and *visualisations* may do: how are they used, and what effects do they have?

3.6 SPACE OF/IN SCIENCE AND TECHNOLOGY COMMUNICATION

The fifth sensitivity concerns the spaces of science communication. Where is science performed, how does space matter when we engage with issues relating to science and technology, and how does science communication become a space in which to experiment with the relations of science and society?

One straightforward aspect of this is to investigate the spaces in which science communication takes place – museums, science centres, or scientific institutions that open their doors to wider societal actors, for instance. In being attentive to the spatial aspects of science communication, we understand space as a relational arrangement of human and non-human entities in a specific place (Löw 2016). Löw suggests that spaces are created by practices of deploying, placing, and (re)arranging human and non-human entities in specific ways, that is, 'creating the distribution of materiality in a potential scene' (ibid.: v). These operations are deeply entangled with perception, imagination, and memory practices. They thus draw our attention to the cultural environments in which science and technology are communicated.

Being attentive to space in the context of communicating science also means being aware that different kinds of spaces can take form in one and the same place. It also means acknowledging the different meaning of space, ranging from physical to social or more conceptual, symbolic, or imagined forms. Here we briefly outline some of the key dimensions that matter when investigating or performing science communication.

In Chapter 5 Owens introduces the park as a space for public engagement with science. Although parks may not be explicitly framed as spaces of science communication, he shows how particular parks – in San Francisco and Berlin – embody specific pedagogies and relations to nature.

First, science is communicated and negotiated in specific kinds of spaces, many of which have received relatively little attention in research on science communication. This means considering how specific spaces structure interactions with science (Gieryn 2000, 2002; Stimson 1986). One example of a space where science is important, but which is rarely framed as 'science communication', would be the courtroom (Dumit 1999; Lynch & Cole 2005). In her investigation of science and the law, Jasanoff (1995) points to the fact that in this situation key questions are asked concerning what kind of scientific facts can be used in the legal context, to what degree science is capable of supporting ideas of causality, reason, and justice in the law, and finally, how scientific experts supplement the work of jurists, advocates, and other actors engaged in securing social stability and order. She shows how the courtroom becomes a theatre in which things are not only referred to but also demonstrated in order to compel belief. The law generally, as well as the physical environment of the courtroom specifically, is thus a key space in which the relation between science and society is negotiated. When scientific evidence is brought into the courtroom, it needs to be persuasive, it has to come with the authority of standards, and it also has to appeal to the commonsense of judges and juries. This means that legal practitioners become science communicators and fact makers through their efforts to weave objects, images, and a specific legal-scientific rhetoric into a coherent narrative that only allows one interpretation by the audience. The challenge in all this is that all the different actors in this communicative setting do not necessarily belong to a single thought collective (Fleck 1979 [1935]). Considerable work therefore needs to be done to be able to develop a shared understanding.

We can also think of science communication as a space where technosciences and their relations to society can be experimented with and tested. STS has a long tradition of thinking about testing as a key moment in developing knowledge and technologies. Our view is that we can understand communication settings as a test space in which specific articulations of science or technology with society are examined for 'workability'. For instance, Nelly Oudshoorn's 2003 book *The Male Pill* pointed to the important role media play in shaping the cultural feasibility and acceptability of a new technology, in this case the male contraceptive pill. She shows that while in different labs and in a number of clinical trials this new medical product was being tested, 'journalists put the trial results to another test. This time it was not the artifact that was on trial, but the potential user' (2003: 200). This public testing out of the technology enrolled new kinds of experts and expertise – members of the public – with scientists figuring 'merely as commentators on public opinion' (ibid.). Science communication, in this case in the mass media, is thus actively engaged not only in imagining potential audiences, but also in developing and rehearsing specific ideas about affected citizens or prospective users of scientific knowledge or technological innovations.

STS can also look back to a long-standing interest in the kinds of public space in which science and diverse publics encounter each other, and where publics can potentially 'speak back' to science. Nowotny and her co-authors stress the importance of spaces in which 'recontextualization' takes place (2001; see also Figure 2.1), where such recontextualisation involves putting technoscientific developments into wider societal contexts. This, in their view, leads to knowledge being 'continually subjected to testing while in the process it is becoming more robust' (ibid.: 247). They are particularly interested in the notion of the *agora* as a space in which science and technology are tested. The agora is '[n]either state nor market, neither exclusively private nor exclusively public'. They suggest that it 'is the space in which societal and scientific problems are framed and defined, and where what will be accepted as a "solution" is being negotiated' (ibid.: 247). While it remains open exactly what this agora is, we would like to argue that we have many different forms of agora in which such negotiations take place, ranging from hybrid spaces where citizens, patients and professionals meet (Callon et al. 2009) to new media, museums, or private environments.

Taken together, the preceding points mean that we can see science communication as opening up a space quite similar to the laboratory, but involving a very different genre of testing of science and technology. While in the lab the successful replication of experiments is seen as what leads to robust results, in spaces of communication it is 'literary replication' (Secord 1989) – the taking up and repetition of a specific assemblage of an issue in different venues – that is viewed as a sign of success.

Finally, thinking about space in science communication also calls for consideration of the wider cultural spaces within which these activities take place. These spaces may overlap with national spaces – for instance with regard to traditions of public debate on issues related to science and technology (Horst & Irwin 2010) – or they may co-construct the role science and technology are understood to take in a specific society or community. This could be more specifically framed as 'technopolitical cultures' (Felt et al. 2010): the practices, structures, and mechanisms through which science, technologies, and a specific society are entangled (see Chapter 2). For instance, empirical work with focus groups has shown how important public debate is for people's capacity to express a position towards technoscientific issues. Individual ways of 'coming to terms with [a] technology are framed by the broader context of a technopolitical culture and by its ways of understanding, narrating, and governing technologies' (Felt et al. 2010: 549). This invites us to look for analogies and visions that are broadly shared in particular cultures, but also for what Jasanoff calls 'civic epistemologies: culturally specific, historically and politically grounded, public knowledge-ways' (Jasanoff 2005: 249; see Chapter 2). However, when we speak of national and cultural spaces and their relation to science, there are three things to consider. First, different issues will relate to and be embedded into a cultural environment in quite different ways. This means that communication about health-related topics might happen very differently from that concerning the environment, driverless cars, or robotics, for instance. Second, while national or cultural environments do matter, in these times of the internet and search engines, it is safe to say that we are witnessing ideas about technology cut across national borders. This international space of communication, connection, and exchange also needs close consideration. Third, we should bear in mind that physical and cultural spaces will interact with each other. For instance, a courtroom's physical construction may structure what kind of communication happens there – they are often built to convey a sense of authority and seriousness, and to partition speakers and non-speakers from each other – but the wider technopolitical space in which it is embedded will also shape what occurs.

What do these points mean for the kinds of questions that should be considered when analysing and carrying out science communication?

- Straightforwardly being sensitive to the spatial dimension means asking: how do specific spaces *impact upon and shape* any particular instance of science communication? This means paying attention to the kinds of spaces that impinge upon how science communication is articulated, whether those are physical, cultural, or imaginative.
- In what ways do spaces include or exclude specific forms of engagement and participation? *How is expertise*, and *what counts as evidence or proof*, related to space? And what kinds of recontextualisations does a specific space allow for/demand?
- We can also ask: *what is being tested in this space and how?* If science communication is a form of public trial, what is being put to the test? Perhaps the public robustness of particular 'facts', but potentially also the imaginations of publics, users, or versions of society.

3.7 TIME AND THE ANTICIPATORY WORK OF COMMUNICATION

Sensitivities to space also invite reflection on 'the invisible other' (Adam 1998: 9) of space – time. The sixth perspective we wish to consider is thus that of time and temporality, specifically in the way science is framed in the context of communication, as well as the temporal orders in/for science and society that are produced through communicating science.

We start by using our co-productive lens to perceive time as being produced through science communication. We should also explore how specific cultural understandings of time bring about particular forms of communicating and engaging with science and technology-related questions. Being sensitive to temporal aspects is particularly important as 'time works outside and beyond the reach of our senses' (Adam 1998: 9), while simultaneously being a force structuring how we can grasp and communicate about the world around us. Time matters on a variety of levels in communication, and studying it in more depth often helps to identify otherwise invisible phenomena. Studying focus group discussions of citizens and newspaper reports on obesity, for example, Felt et al. (2014) showed how temporal narratives shaped people's perceptions of obesity as a medical phenomenon alongside their views of their bodies and lives in contemporary societies.

What are the different forms that time takes when thinking about engagements of science and society, and how is this projective and anticipatory work performed through public communication of science and technology? First,

Amelung and her co-authors (Chapter 11) look at expectation management in the context of forensic genetics, where 'enthusiastic publics' in the criminal justice system are understood as expecting too much from forensic science. According to forensic geneticists, the prominence of forensic science in popular culture raises expectations to a degree that might actually have negative consequences for criminal investigations and the judicial system.

much has been written in STS on how futures have become a central element in thinking about action in the present – what Sloterdijk (1989) has described as an unquenchable hunger for the future. All too often these future narratives produced in the context of science communication are tacitly (and sometimes even explicitly) tied to the idea of progress through science (in the form of advanced knowledge) and technological development (Borup et al. 2006; Brown & Michael 2003; Selin 2008). 'Standing still means falling behind' (Adam & Groves 2007: 1) is then an underlying assumption, supporting an imagination of a continuous flow of innovations. We peer into the future and tell of the opportunities it would offer to be the first to colonise this. Such narratives of anticipation, progress, and continuous acceleration (Rose 2003) result in feelings of urgency. Science communication plays a major role in performing this projective work, given that it often features narratives about where innovations might lead us. This is linked to the emergence of an 'economics of technoscientific promises' (Felt et al. 2007: 24), a kind of symbolic economy that 'trades' promises for a better future in the context of scientific and technological developments. But it is not that the future is always bright when looking into debates around technoscientific concerns. In studying public controversies, STS has also shown how the future is key in making an argument about whether or not to embrace a specific technology, or to act on specific kinds of scientific knowledge.

Discourses that speak to potential futures are everywhere around us, from Hollywood movies to the pages of popular science magazines, and are a central location where co-production happens. More specifically, they take part in bringing into being what Jasanoff and Kim (2009, 2015) have called 'socio-technical imaginaries'. As discussed in Chapter 2, section 2.1, such imaginaries connect visions of social order and technological and scientific developments. In any given society and at any given point in time, multiple imaginaries may co-exist, pointing to the different directions the future might go and – perhaps – creating frictions as they rub up against each other. It is then often up to the media, among other institutions of power, 'to elevate some imagined futures [and with this also specific kinds of knowledge] above others, according them a dominant position' (Jasanoff 2015: 4). Developing or being able to draw on a strong sociotechnical imaginary when communicating science creates preferred links between past and future, defines possible actions, and 'naturalize[s] ways of thinking about possible worlds' (Jasanoff 2015: 24).

Addressing elements of wider sociotechnical imaginaries in the analysis of science communication thus calls for reflection upon the shared and stabilised elements of narratives on science and society, as well as on efforts to share and stabilise them.

This is often connected with specific ways of plotting stories about technoscientific developments. In fact, as Appadurai (2013) has argued, modernity tends to be trapped in the idea that everything develops along a trajectory, always 'assum[ing] that there is a cumulative journey from here to there, more exactly from now to then' (ibid.: 223). Even though the connection between pasts and futures might in reality prove to be more complex, we tend to squeeze them into a linearity that fits this dominant way of thinking. This trope of the inevitable trajectory (Appadurai 2013) allows the creation of a specific image of the past and uses it to credibly anticipate a future that may demand action from responsible citizens.

Science communication often features new and emerging technologies, and in this way helps bring them into being. In Chapter 8 Szymanski examines how one emerging biological entity, synthetic yeast, is produced in media texts. She shows how the societal future of a technoscientific object depends on its relation to a familiar present.

The notion of temporality further makes us aware that any plot or storyline developed in the context of science communication is about a development in time. Very often communication is triggered by an event, something that broke the frame of the expected (a disaster, a public relations crisis, a new discovery). It is captured as a moment in time in which something specific was realised, something that is viewed as important enough to be narrated. Stories of scientific breakthroughs (Felt 1993) are such typical temporal narratives. They plot a history of a past in which we did not foresee a specific development, in order to capture that moment (sometimes a moment can last quite a long time) that has culminated in something new, leading to the unexpected future that just opened up. The development of the gene-editing technique CRISPR Cas 9 would be an excellent example of this kind of narrative. This development allowed scientists and communicators to tell a story about basic research leading to an unexpected application that would revolutionise specific areas of research in biology as well as society itself. Using time as a lens to unpack science communication both helps us to notice these narratives and to explore their effects in terms of what they co-produce (an imagination of basic research as having societally useful outputs, for instance).

Time also comes into play in Horst and Michael's (2011) conceptualisation, discussed in Chapter 2, of science communication as an 'event'. This view means that we think of communication as something that is assembled, connecting human and non-human elements – different actors, objects, experiences – at a specific moment in time. This again connects to a notion we encountered at the beginning of this chapter: situatedness. Analysing science communication thus calls for temporal contextualisation of an event, and for trying to capture what happened in the immediate temporal environment and which potentially participated in the shaping of the communication event.

Finally, time also comes in as a feature of the very act of communication and is related to questions of ownership and availability of time. What is the time needed – or is imagined as being needed – to engage with science in a museum, an article, a webpage, or any other form of communication? Who can afford this amount of time, given different situations in life? Time in communication therefore becomes a question of power and justice, and of who is able to participate and engage with science communication (Dawson 2014).

What do these points mean for the kinds of questions that should be considered when analysing and carrying out science communication?

- We can ask: what *trajectories* are presented in an instance of science communication, implicitly or explicitly, and *what work do those trajectories perform*? Asking this question means that we will explore the kinds of futures and pasts that are constructed in science communication and how they get connected.
- We can further *explore the temporalities of a piece of science communication itself.* How is it assembled and dis-assembled, and over what timescale does it operate? How much time do communicators expect people to invest in the communication effort?
- What *wider imaginaries about the co-evolution of science and society* are produced in the context of science communication? How does the construction of futures come to matter?

3.8 ATMOSPHERES OF COMMUNICATION: HOW VALUES AND AFFECT MATTER

The final sensitivity we want to discuss draws together several of the other perspectives we have described, in particular those concerned with space, time, and materiality. We can think these things together through the notion of atmosphere – the affective experience of space. Atmosphere is the intangible aspect, an 'excess effect' (Luhmann 2000: 112), that emerges out of the constitution of space (Löw 2016), in our case communicative spaces.

Atmosphere builds on space in that the effort of connecting elements in specific ways creates an 'atmosphere' that is constituted by the subjective experience of the arrangements we encounter. An understanding of space developed solely with reference to physical substance grasps the visible world of things but fails to cover aspects such as affect or other expressions of valuation. Atmosphere thus captures the often intangible ways that emotions, spaces, objects, and bodies work together to produce a particular effect.

Looking at science communication through this lens allows us to ask new forms of questions. For example, it invites us to move away from asking cognitive questions such as 'did people understand the science?' and instead encourages us to look into how participants experience communication and interaction (Davies 2015; Harvey 2009; Kimura 2017). What are people's feelings when they engage with science and technology? What role does the emotional part of these settings play, how are those emotions triggered, and how do participants productively use them in relating to the issue at stake? Taking such an approach invites us to look into how images, sounds, objects, and other parts of a science communication 'event' come together to produce a particular effect and to make space for emotional attachments.

Irwin and co-authors (2018), in the case of environmental communication, point towards the need to consider how values and affect are communicated, both explicitly and implicitly. But they also highlight the need 'to examine how values can be mobilised to communicate' about a specific subject (ibid.: 19). Not doing so, and trying to solely argue with scientific evidence, might miss connecting people to the wider issues at stake, as the values that are in question are rendered invisible. This process of opening up issues and values is essential given that public communication is often tied to questions of responsibility or controversy, for instance in cases such as genetic modification, climate change, or potentially powerful future technologies such as synthetic biology. This approach thus asks about the sets of values that communicators, actors in an issue space, and publics share and where they potentially diverge.

Oliver Marsh's account of the Facebook page IFLScience (Chapter 9) shows that only certain emotions are seen as appropriate in the context of online interactions based around science. The case study points us to the way in which a combination of particular structures and forms of expression creates a specific 'atmosphere', which shapes users' experiences of the page.

This links us back to the question of physical space. As we have argued, it is vital to consider how the specific physical location in which communication happens matters for what is regarded as appropriate or as 'out of place' behaviour (Gieryn 2000). This is important given that much discussion of science communication makes implicit judgements about what, and how much, emotion is adequate in what kind of communicative settings. Which emotions are seen as appropriate, and which are viewed as out of place? We know from research on focus groups on health-related issues (Felt et al. 2008) that, for example, affected people are granted more leeway in expressing radical positions or openly expressing emotions than is the case for people regarded as 'ordinary participants'. We can thus ask which sets of values and emotions are framed as suitable for a particular setting. For example, as much as amazement has its place in a science museum environment, in a debate about a scientific controversy it might be seen as naïve admiration or as a lack of critical scrutiny of scientific expertise. In a similar move, we have seen feelings of fear or anger judged as a sign of irrationality in cases of science communication around disasters or technological accidents (Kimura 2017). Furthermore, specific locations of engagement with science might also lead to people forming 'emotional, sentimental bonds' (Gieryn 2000: 481). Such 'place attachments', as Gieryn continues to argue, 'result from accumulated biographical experiences: we associate places with the fulfilling, terrifying, traumatic, triumphant, secret events that happened' (ibid.: 481). This would also count for encounters with science and technology. In short, the space defines to a certain degree how the 'reasonable' and rational participant/member of the public should perform his/her role in the setting of science communication.

It can be hard to study atmospheres (Wetherell 2012). Indeed, part of how we have defined them, in the text above, is their intangibility. But there are at least some questions we can ask as researchers in order to try to access how space, affect, and materialities work together to produce specific effects.

- First, we can use our own bodies and experiences as data-collecting devices and ask: how does an instance of science communication *make me feel*, and *how do I feel about those feelings*? Such experiences will not be universally shared, but interrogating our own emotions can help give insight into the atmospheres that circulate around science communication and the way in which they are normalised or rendered 'out of place'. Such an approach is also an important reminder of our presence as part of our research. As discussed in Chapter 2, we cannot neutrally study the emotions and values of others, but need to acknowledge our own stance and experiences.
- We also need to ask more generally: *what emotions are made present*, whether through representations or performances? How do specific choreographies used in science communication make use of and seek to trigger emotions, and what efforts are required from addressees? How are pleasure and playfulness put at the centre of communication?
- Finally, when studying spaces of science communication, it is relevant to grasp *which emotional expressions are perceived* as 'in place' or even expected in a specific setting. It is essential to be attentive to acts of self-censuring – for instance, when people hesitate to contest specific ways in which science depicts the world.

3.9 CONCLUSION

Our discussion in this chapter has sought to guide the reader through some of the (potential) practicalities of studying and thinking about science communication through the lens of an STS approach. We have described seven sensibilities, or sensitivities, that we see as central. It is useful to be attentive to *how publics are made* in and through science communication, and to examine the specific ways in which *facts are made* in public spaces alongside matters of public concern. *Expertise, evidence*, and *authority* are central ways to unpick the work that is done by science communication. *Materiality* is key to public communication of science: this might mean looking at objects, but also at emerging digital infrastructures and practices or at the role of visuals and images. Similarly, *space* structures and shapes science communication, whether this is the immediate space of a courtroom or park, or wider cultural or national spaces. *Temporality, timescales, futures, and anticipatory work* are commonly intertwined with public articulations of science and society, and open up possibilities for exploring how science communication may take a role in co-constructing new and emerging science and technology. Finally, we have suggested that the notion of *atmosphere* can be used as a way to explore what is often left intangible within experiences of communication: emotions, values, attachments.

We are aware that, as a whole, the chapter has raised many questions. We have aimed to point multiple ways forward for those who want to study or reflect upon the practice of science communication, in all its forms. The next part of the book therefore seeks to help ground the reader by offering a series of eight studies of science communication that mobilise an STS approach. In a short introduction to each of these studies, we highlight some of the key concepts described in this and the preceding chapter that are used within it. We hope, then, that what follows offers (even more) inspiration to anyone who wants to think of science communication in new ways.

REFERENCES

Adam, Barbara. 1998. *Timescapes of Modernity: The Environment and Invisible Hazards*. Abingdon and New York: Routledge.

Adam, Barbara and Groves, Chris, 2007. *Future Matters: Action, Knowledge, Ethics*. Leiden, Boston, MA: Brill.

Appadurai, Arjun. 2013. *The Future as Cultural Fact*. London: Verso.

Bennett, Tony. 2004. *Pasts beyond Memory: Evolution, Museums, Colonianism*. Abingdon: Routledge.

Borup, Mads, Nik Brown, Kornelia Konrad, and Harro Van Lente. 2006. 'The Sociology of Expectations in Science and Technology'. *Technology Analysis and Strategic Management* 18 (3–4): 285–298. https://doi.org/doi:10.1080/09537320600777002

Böschen, Stefan, Karen Kastenhofer, Ina Rust, Jens Soentgen, and Peter Wehling. 2010. 'Scientific Nonknowledge and Its Political Dynamics: The Cases of Agri-Biotechnology and Mobile Phoning.' *Science, Technology & Human Values* 35 (6): 783–811. doi: 10.1177/0162243909357911.

Brown, Nick, and Mike Michael. 2003. 'A Sociology of Expectations: Retrospecting Prospects and Prospecting Retrospects'. *Technology Analysis & Strategic Management* 15 (1): 3–18.

Callon, Michel, Pierre Lascoumes, and Yannick Barthe. 2009. *Acting in an Uncertain World: An Essay on Technical Democracy*. Translated by Graham Burchell. Cambridge, MA: The MIT Press.

Clarke, Adele. 1998. *Disciplining Reproduction: Modernity, American Life Sciences, and 'the Problems of Sex'*. Berkeley, CA: University of California Press.

Davies, Sarah R. 2016. 'Participation as Pleasure: Citizenship within Public Engagement with Science'. In Jason Chilvers and Matthew Kearnes (eds.), *Remaking Participation: Science, Democracy and Emergent Publics*, pp. 162–177. Abingdon: Routledge-Earthscan.

Dawson, Emily. 2014. '"Not Designed for Us": How Science Museums and Science Centers Socially Exclude Low-Income, Minority Ethnic Groups'. *Science Education* 98 (6): 981–1008. https://doi.org/10.1002/sce.21133.

Dewey, John. 1927. *The Public and Its Problems*. New York: Holt.

Dudley, Sandra H. (ed.). 2009. *Museum Materialities: Objects, Engagements, Interpretations*. London: Taylor and Francis.

Dumit, Joseph. 1999. 'Objective Brains, Prejudicial Images'. *Science in Context* 12 (1): 173–201.

Felt, Ulrike. 1993. 'Fabricating Scientific Success Stories'. *Public Understanding of Science* 2 (4): 375–390.

Felt, Ulrike. 1999. 'Why Should the Public "Understand" Science? A Historical Perspective on Aspects of the Public Understanding of Science'. In Meinolf Dierkes and Claudia Von Grote (eds.), *Between Understanding and Trust: The Public, Science and Technology*, pp. 7–38. Amsterdam: Harwood Academic Publishers.

Felt, Ulrike, Kay Felder, Theresa Ohler, and Michael Penkler. 2014. 'Timescapes of Obesity: Coming to Terms with a Complex Socio-Medical Phenomenon'. *Health* (London) 18 (6): 646–664. doi: 10.1177/1363459314530736.

Felt, Ulrike, and Maximilian Fochler. 2008. 'The Bottom-Up Meanings of the Concept of Public Participation in Science and Technology'. *Science and Public Policy* 35 (7): 489–499.

Felt, Ulrike, and Maximilian Fochler. 2010. 'Machineries for Making Publics: Inscribing and De-Scribing Publics in Public Engagement.' *Minerva* 48 (3): 219–238. https://doi.org/10.1007/s11024-010-9155-x.

Felt, Ulrike, and Maximilian Fochler. 2013. 'What Science Stories Do: Rethinking the Multiple Consequences of Intensified Science Communication'. In Patrick Baranger and Bernard Schiele (eds.), *Science Communication Today: International Perspectives, Issues and Strategies*, pp. 75–90. Paris: CNRS Editions.

Felt, Ulrike, Maximilian Fochler, Astrid Mager, and Peter Winkler. 2008. 'Visions and Versions of Governing Biomedicine: Narratives on Power Structures, Decision-making and Public Participation in the Field of Biomedical Technology in the Austrian Context.' *Social Studies of Science* 38 (2): 233–255.

Felt, Ulrike, Maximilian Fochler, and Peter Winkler. 2010. 'Coming to Terms with Biomedical Technologies in Different Technopolitical Cultures: A Comparative Analysis of Focus Groups on Organ Transplantation and Genetic Testing in Austria, France, and the Netherlands'. *Science, Technology & Human Values* 35 (4): 525–53. https://doi.org/10.1177/0162243909345839.

Felt, Ulrike, Rayvon Fouché, Clark A. Miller, and Laurel Smith-Doerr (eds.). 2017. *Handbook of Science and Technology Studies*. Cambridge, MA: The MIT Press.

Felt, Ulrike, Brian Wynne, Michel Callon, Maria Eduarda Gonçalves, Sheila Jasanoff, Maria Jepsen, Pierre-Benoît Joly, Zdenek Konopasek, Stefan May, Claudia Neubauer, Arie Rip, Karen Siune, Andy Stirling, and Mariachiara Tallacchini. 2007. *Taking European Knowledge Society Seriously*. Luxembourg: Office for Official Publications of the European Communities.

Fleck, Ludwik. 1979 [1935]. *Genesis and Development of a Scientific Fact*. Chicago, IL, and London: University of Chicago Press.

Gabrys, Jennifer, Helen Pritchard, and Benjamin Barrat. 2016. 'Just Good Enough Data: Figuring Data Citizenships through Air Pollution Sensing and Data Stories'. *Big Data & Society* 3 (2): 1–14. doi: 10.1177/2053951716679677.

Gieryn, Thomas F. 1999. *Cultural Boundaries of Science: Credibility on the Line*. Chicago, IL: University of Chicago Press.

Gieryn, Thomas F. 2000. 'A Space for Place in Sociology'. *Annual Review of Sociology* 26: 463–496.

Gieryn, Thomas F. 2002. 'What Buildings Do'. *Theory and Society* 31 (1): 35–74.

Gross, Matthias, and Linsey McGoey (eds.). 2015. *Routledge International Handbook of Ignorance Studies*. Abingdon: Routledge.

Grundmann, Reiner. 2017. 'The Problem of Expertise in Knowledge Societies'. *Minerva* 55 (1): 25–48. doi: 10.1007/s11024-016-9308-7.

Hajer, Maarten A. 2009. *Authoritative Governance: Policy-Making in the Age of Mediatization*. Oxford: Oxford University Press.

Hansen, Anders. 2016. 'The Changing Uses of Accuracy in Science Communication'. *Public Understanding of Science* 25 (7): 760–774.

Haraway, Donna. 1988. 'Situated Knowledges: The Science Question in Feminism and the Privilege of Partial Perspective'. *Feminist Studies* 14 (3): 575–599. https://doi.org/10.2307/3178066.

Harvey, Matthew. 2009. 'Drama, Talk, and Emotion: Omitted Aspects of Public Participation'. *Science, Technology & Human Values* 34 (2): 139–161.

Hilgartner, Stephen. 1990. 'The Dominant View of Popularization: Conceptual Problems, Political Uses'. *Social Studies of Science* 20 (3): 519–539.

Hilgartner, Stephen. 2000. *Science on Stage: Expert Advice as Public Drama*. Stanford, CA: Stanford University Press.

Horst, Maja, and Alan Irwin. 2010. 'Nations at Ease with Radical Knowledge: On Consensus, Consensusing and False Consensusness'. *Social Studies of Science* 40 (1): 105–126.

Horst, Maja, and Mike Michael. 2011. 'On the Shoulders of Idiots: Re-Thinking Science Communication as "Event"'. *Science as Culture* 20 (3): 283–306.

Irwin, Alan. 2001. 'Constructing the Scientific Citizen: Science and Democracy in the Biosciences'. *Public Understanding of Science* 10 (1): 1–18.

Irwin, Alan, Massimiano Bucchi, Ulrike Felt, Melanie Smallman, and Steven Yearly. 2018. *Re-Framing Environmental Communication: Engagement, Understanding and Action*. Stockholm: MISTRA.

Irwin, Alan, and Mike Michael. 2003. *Science, Social Theory and Public Knowledge*. Maidenhead: Open University Press.

Irwin, Alan, and Brian Wynne. 1996. *Misunderstanding Science? The Public Reconstruction of Science and Technology*. Cambridge: Cambridge University Press.

Jasanoff, Sheila. 1995. *Science at the Bar: Law, Science, and Technology in America*. Cambridge, MA: Harvard University Press.

Jasanoff, Sheila. 2004. 'The Idiom of Co-Production'. In Sheila Jasanoff (ed.), *States of Knowledge: The Co-Production of Science and Social Order*, pp. 1–12. Abingdon and New York: Routledge.

Jasanoff, Sheila. 2005. *Designs on Nature: Science and Democracy in Europe and the United States*. Princeton, NJ, and Oxford: Princeton University Press.

Jasanoff, Sheila. 2015. 'Future Imperfect: Science, Technology, and the Imaginations of Modernity'. In Sheila Jasanoff and Sang-Hyun Kim (eds.), *Dreamscapes of Modernity: Sociotechnical Imaginaries and the Fabrication of Power*, pp. 1–47. Chicago, IL: University of Chicago Press.

Jasanoff, Sheila, and Sang-Hyun Kim. 2009. 'Containing the Atom: Sociotechnical Imaginaries and Nuclear Power in the United States and South Korea'. *Minerva* 47 (2): 119–46. https://doi.org/10.1007/s11024-009-9124-4.

Jasanoff, Sheila, and Sang-Hyun Kim (eds.). 2015. *Dreamscapes of Modernity: Sociotechnical Imaginaries and the Fabrication of Power*. Chicago, IL: University of Chicago Press.

Kerr, Anne, Sarah Cunningham-Burley, and Richard Tutton. 2007. 'Shifting Subject Positions: Experts and Lay People in Public Dialogue'. *Social Studies of Science* 37 (3): 385–411.

Kimura, Aya H. 2018. Fukushima ETHOS: Post-Disaster Risk Communication, Affect, and Shifting Risks, *Science as Culture* 27 (1): 98–117. doi: 10.1080/09505431.2017.1325458

Knorr-Cetina, Karin D. 1981. *The Manufacture of Knowledge: An Essay on the Constructivist and Contextual Nature of Science*. Oxford: Pergamon Press.

Latour, Bruno. 1983. 'Give Me a Laboratory and I Will Move the World.' In Karin D. Knorr-Cetina and Michael Mulkay (eds.), *Science Observed: Perspectives on the Social Study of Science*, pp. 141–170. Thousand Oaks, CA: Sage.

Latour, Bruno. 2004. 'Why has Critique Run Out of Steam? From Matters of Fact to Matters of Concern'. *Critical Inquiry* 30 (Winter): 225–248.

Latour, Bruno, and Steve Woolgar. 1986. *Laboratory Life: The Construction of Scientific Facts*. Princeton, NJ: Princeton University Press.

Law, John. 2017. 'STS as Method'. In Ulrike Felt, Rayvon Fouché, Clark Miller, and Laurel Smith-Doerr (eds.), *The Handbook of Science and Technology Studies*, pp. 31–57. Cambridge, MA: The MIT Press.

Lezaun, Javier, and Linda Soneryd. 2007. 'Consulting Citizens: Technologies of Elicitation and the Mobility of Publics'. *Public Understanding of Science* 16 (3): 279–297.

Limoges, Camille. 1993. 'Expert Knowledge and Decision-Making in Controversy Contexts'. *Public Understanding of Science* 2 (4): 417–426.

Löw, Martina. 2016. *The Sociology of Space: Materiality, Social Structures, and Action*. New York: Palgrave Macmillan.

Luhmann, Niklas. 2000. *Art as a Social System*. Stanford, CA: Stanford University Press.

Lynch, Michael, and Simon Cole. 2005. 'Science and Technology Studies on Trial: Dilemmas of Expertise'. *Social Studies of Science* 35 (2): 269–311.

Mager, Astrid 2009. 'Mediated Health: Sociotechnical Practices of Providing and Using Online Health Information'. *New Media & Society* 11 (7): 1123–1142. doi: 10.1177/1461444809341700.

Marres, Noortje. 2005. 'No Issue, No Public: Democratic Deficits after the Displacement of Politics.' PhD dissertation, Amsterdam School for Cultural Analysis (ASCA).

Marres, Noortje, and Javier Lezaun. 2011. 'Materials and Devices of the Public: An Introduction'. *Economy and Society* 40 (4): 489–509. https://doi.org/10.1080/03085 147.2011.602293

Michael, Mike. 1996. 'Knowing Ignorance and Ignoring Knowledge: Discourses of Ignorance in the Public Understanding of Science'. In *Misunderstanding Science? The Public Reconstruction of Science and Technology*. Cambridge: Cambridge University Press.

Michael, Mike. 2002. 'Comprehension, Apprehension, Prehension: Heterogeneity and the Public Understanding of Science'. *Science, Technology & Human Values* 27 (3): 357–378.

Mitchell, W. J. Thomas 1994. *Picture Theory: Essays on Verbal and Visual Representation.* Chicago, IL: University of Chicago Press.

Nelkin, Dorothy. 1995. *Selling Science: How the Press Covers Science and Technology.* New York: W. H. Freeman.

Nerlich, Brigitte (ed.). 2018. *Science, Politics and the Dilemmas of Openness: Here Be Monsters.* Manchester: Manchester University Press.

Nowotny, Helga, Peter Scott, and Michael Gibbons. 2001. *Re-Thinking Science: Knowledge and the Public in an Age of Uncertainty.* Cambridge: Polity Press.

Oudshoorn, Nelly. 2003. *The Male Pill – A Biography of a Technology in the Making.* Durham, NC: Duke University Press.

Parthasarathy, Shobita. 2010. 'Breaking the Expertise Barrier: Understanding Activist Strategies in Science and Technology Policy Domains.' *Science and Public Policy* 37 (5): 355–367. doi: 10.3152/030234210x501180.

Porter, Theodore M. 1995. *Trust in Numbers. The Pursuit of Objectivity in Science and Public Life.* Princeton, NJ: Princeton University Press.

Rose, Hartmut. 2003. 'Social Acceleration: Ethical and Political Consequences of a Desynchronized High-Speed Society'. *Constellations* 10 (1): 3–33.

Ruppert, Evelyn, Engin Isin, and Didier Bigo. 2017. 'Data politics.' *Big Data & Society* 4 (2): 1–7.

Secord, James A. 1989. 'Extraordinary Experiments: Electricity and the Creation of Life in Victorian England'. In David Gooding, Trevor Pinch, and Simon Schaffer (eds.), *The Uses of Experiment.* Cambridge: Cambridge University Press.

Selin, Cynthia. 2008. 'The Sociology of the Future: Tracing Stories of Technology and Time'. *Sociology Compass* 2 (6): 1878–1895. https://doi.org/10.1111/j.1751-9020.2008.00147.x.

Sismondo, Sergio. 2010. *An Introduction to Science and Techology Studies.* Chichester: John Wiley & Son.

Sloterdijk, Peter. 1989. *Eurotaoismus: Zur Kritik der politischen Kinetik.* Frankfurt am Main: Suhrkamp.

Star, Susan L., and James R. Griesemer. 1989. 'Institutional Ecology, "Translations" and Boundary Objects: Amateurs and Professionals in Berkeley's Museum of Vertebrate Zoology, 1907–39'. *Social Studies of Science* 19: 387–420.

Stimson, Garry V. 1986. 'Place and Space in Sociological Fieldwork'. *Sociological Review* 34: 641–656.

Stirling, Andy. 2008. '"Opening Up" and "Closing Down": Power, Participation, and Pluralism in the Social Appraisal of Technology'. *Science, Technology & Human Values* 33 (2): 262–294. https://doi.org/10.1177/0162243907311265.

Van Dijck, José, 1998. *Imagenation: Popular Images of Genetics*. Houndmills: Palgrave Macmillan.

Weingart, Peter, and Lars Guenther. 2016. 'Science Communication and the Issue of Trust'. *Journal of Science Communication* 15 (5): C01.

Wetherell, Margaret. 2012. *Affect and Emotion: A New Social Science Understanding*. London: Sage.

Wynne, Brian. 2006. 'Public Engagement as Means of Restoring Trust in Science? Hitting the Notes, but Missing the Music'. *Community Genetics* 9 (3): 211–220.

PART II
MOBILISING STS CONCEPTS AND SENSITIVITIES: THE CASE STUDIES

Reflections and Connections

The core of this chapter – by Karin Tybjerg, Louise Whiteley, and Sarah Davies – follows a gene gun to a number of sites where it was meant to engage in communication with different audiences. We are thus invited to engage with the *material practices* of science communication and with the role *objects* can play in it. Tybjerg et al. use the notion of an object biography, a concept that nicely captures the fact that life (as told in a biography) is never simply out there but needs be written or told, performed, in order to come into being. It also makes us aware of how much a biography is shaped by the different spaces and moments in which life happens.

The chapter further points to the unstable nature of a seemingly robust object when it starts to travel across time and space. It highlights the plasticity of (this) object, but also its multiplicity as it is *assembled* in different ways in different spaces.

This biography of the gene gun therefore sensitises readers to the crucial role of *space* in science communication. They are taken to four different sites: a hackerspace, a museum, a public debate, and an art-science venue. In each of them, specific performances of the gene gun become visible, while others are made impossible.

Space, and the prevailing *atmosphere* that comes with a particular space, are key to making different publics. These are in turn expected to do specific things and to engage with the issue at stake in particular ways and not others. This also includes the feelings that are regarded as adequate and acceptable in any given setting. For example, having the gene gun in a public debate was seen as disruptive as it might trigger feelings of fear – which, in this context, was viewed as inappropriate.

4

OBJECT BIOGRAPHIES: THE LIFE OF A HACKED GENE GUN

KARIN TYBJERG, LOUISE WHITELEY AND SARAH R. DAVIES

4.1 INTRODUCTION

This chapter offers the notion of 'object biographies' as a tool to investigate science communication. We combine methods for following the 'lives' of material objects, coming from anthropology, museum studies and history of science, with STS ideas of science communication as a product of relations between people, objects, sites, and cultures, and of 'boundary objects', that is, objects that are adaptable to different environments and viewpoints while being robust enough to maintain identity across the different sites (see Chapter 2 and Star & Griesemer 1989: 387). We illustrate this approach by examining the life of a hacked gene gun as it moved between different science communication spaces: a hackerspace, a museum, a public debate, and an art-science venue.

A gene gun is a device for producing genetically modified or transgenic cells, that is, cells containing foreign DNA. It works by 'shooting' metal dust containing foreign DNA into cells, where it can be absorbed by existing strings of DNA. The foreign DNA is then replicated together with the cell's own DNA, and the cell becomes transgenic. The first gene gun was made out of a modified air pistol, so the 'gun' nomenclature is not purely metaphorical (Nelson 2012; Sanford 2000).

There are two specific gene guns at the heart of this paper. Both are hacked versions of the technology, made from cheap materials and using accessible techniques. The first was built in a hackerspace in Copenhagen as part of a collaboration with Medical Museion, a university museum at the University of Copenhagen. Its visible electronics were built onto a gun-shaped tree branch, resulting in a potent object that could appear both playful and provocative (Figure 4.1). This gene gun's efficacy was tested in a lab at the Danish Technical University (DTU), but failed to produce any results. A second version (Figure 4.2) was built using an old SodaStream machine and succeeded in firing genetic material into onion cells. Both versions of the gun were displayed as part of a hybrid lab/installation at Medical Museion (called *Biohacking: Do It Yourself!*) and were handled by visitors. The first gene gun, the tree branch version, was also the centrepiece of a public debate organised in collaboration with a synthetic biology research centre, and was almost excluded from the event because the communication staff at the research centre were worried about its potentially 'aggressive' message. After the project ended there were negotiations to acquire this tree branch gene gun for the museum's collection, which ultimately failed. It was kept by the hacker, although it was later exhibited at Ars Electronica (a centre for electronic art in Linz, Austria, which explores interlinkages between art, technology, and society), a collaborator of Medical Museion.

Figure 4.1 The first gene gun hack, mounted on a wooden branch shaped like a gun. This photo was taken for press and dissemination purposes, with the onion in the background referring to a simple DNA extraction activity available in the Medical Museion lab/installation. (Photo: Malthe Borch and Medical Museion)

As the first gene gun moved between these different spaces it took on a number of science communication guises. It was used as a tool for dissemination and science education, an embodiment of the hacker spirit, an invitation to engagement with the cultural contexts of hacking, the centrepiece for a debate on opportunities and risks, and as part of an artistic exploration of the social

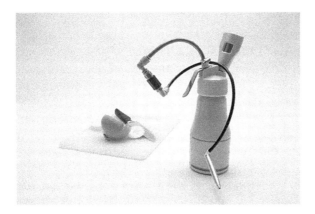

Figure 4.2 The alternative gene gun based on a SodaStream machine. This version functioned to produce transgenic cells in a laboratory at the Danish Technical University (DTU), but was not as hotly contested as the non-functional but more evocative branch-based gene gun. (Photo: Malthe Borch and Medical Museion)

and symbolic meanings of synthetic biology. The ways in which this material object travelled into different spaces, and the kinds of stories, social relations, ideas about the public, and science communication approaches it sparked into being, brings out both the flexibility and constraints of objects in science communication. Different participants related to this object differently, but public communication around the gene gun was not infinitely flexible. Its physical instantiation offered certain affordances while backgrounding other behaviours or interpretations (Hutchby 2001); at the same time, the practices of science communication surrounding it were themselves patterned around particular assumptions or models (Gregory & Lock 2008). We suggest that focusing on a shared material object is a powerful tool for illuminating such flexibilities and constraints. Different modes of science communication are assembled over time and as the gene gun travels to different spaces. The same object is thus understood as triggering, variously, the communication of basic science, engagement with scientific practice, engagement with the cultures of science, political critiques of science and industry, fear of new scientific possibilities, appreciation of societal benefits of science, and a broader integration of science in culture.

In our analysis we bring together literature from STS, anthropology, museum studies, and history of science, arguing that this can help us to think about how objects travel between scientific and public spaces. We offer two contributions to STS studies of science communication. By focusing on a particular physical object, we are responding to calls to focus on the materiality of science communication and thereby better notice how public encounters with science go beyond the discursive (Davies 2014; Marres & Lezaun 2011). Second, we suggest drawing on the notion of 'object biographies' or 'life histories' (Alberti 2005;

Daston 2000; Kopytoff 1986), as such object biographies can reveal the chang-ing function, relations, status, use, and meaning of an object used in science communication over time. Just as a biography of a person might be used as a prism to explore their time or environment, we use the biography of an object as a prism for unpicking forms of science communication. And just as a person shapes and is shaped by time, places, and stories told about them, we seek to capture the plasticity of the object. We see the gene gun as a 'boundary object', thus as 'more than one but less than many' (Mol 2002: 55; Star & Griesemer 1989) – assembled differently in different groups and spaces, but maintaining some continuity.

Our chapter is therefore about the stories and relations that accrue to an object, and the way in which different aspects of these come to the fore at different sites and times. Our argument is that we can examine differing approaches to science communication by exploring the 'biography' of these accumulated stories and relations. Materiality matters, and so does history, in the shape of the accumulated accounts told about material objects that may be seen as making up their biographies. As we will see, space is also central to these dynamics: objects are done differently in different settings.

4.2 CASE AND EMPIRICAL MATERIAL

The gene gun and the empirical material analysed in this chapter stem from a collaboration between the university museum Medical Museion at the University of Copenhagen, biohackers associated with the hackerspace Labitat/Biologigaragen in Copenhagen, and a synthetic biology research centre. The collaboration ran from 2013 to 2015, was supported by the EU Creative Europe project Studiolab as part of a work package focusing on art, innovation, and synthetic biology, and resulted in the construction of the gene gun as well as associated activities such as public workshops, a hybrid lab/installation at Medical Museion, research publications, and online communication. The physical object of the gene gun thus emerged through different motivations. Medical Museion, through its involvement in the Studiolab project, was look-ing for a partner who could help to develop an exhibition built on notions of art-science, with a focus on craft practices in science, and within a public context. This constellation of interests led them to DIY biology and to the local group of biohackers. One of the biohackers in turn saw the collaboration as an opportunity for funding to help build a gene gun and to present it in public, something they were already interested in doing (more of the history behind the collaboration and the final exhibition development can be found in Davies et al. 2015).

Below, we will describe in more detail the construction, travels, and differ-ent uses of the gene gun, and how this affected the ways in which science communication was produced in the different spaces. Our empirical material includes interviews with those involved in the project (including two of the authors of this chapter): biohackers; Medical Museion curators who are also university researchers; science communication professionals from a synthetic biology research centre; and a curator from Ars Electronica. Of the authors of this paper, KT and LW were involved in the Medical Museion–biohacker collaboration in their dual roles as university researchers and museum curators; SRD is not affiliated to Medical Museion but carried out the interviews and has, with KT and LW, previously written about the project (Davies et al. 2015). One round of interviews was carried out during the process of setting up the lab/installation *Biohacking: Do It Yourself!* at Medical Museion, and a second after it was set up. We also draw on textual material produced to describe the gene gun and on our own experiences of the collaboration. The aim is to present a biography of the gene gun – to tell some of its 'life history'. Our approach is ethnographic in that we are centrally concerned with actors' meanings and stories (Hammersley & Atkinson 1995). It is auto-ethnographic in that we are attentive to our own roles in co-constructing those meanings and stories, and use our experiences and reflections as a central aspect of our data (see discussion in Anderson 2006). It is museological in the sense that we are particularly interested in objects, and, in STS terms, how these are assembled and stabilised. Overall, we hope to demonstrate that biographies of material objects can be a useful point of departure for investigating the role of different assemblages in science communication.

4.3 THE BIOGRAPHY OF OBJECTS

Before we recount the life of the gene gun we will lay out some relevant literature on the biography of objects from anthropology, museum studies, and history of science, and relate it to STS in order to clarify our notion of biography in the context of science communication.

A biography of an object can help to reveal how transformations of objects and persons over time are intertwined. Objects change during the period of their existence, and the significance of an object derives from its relations to persons and events (Gosden & Marshall 1999: 169–170) as well as its material form. The idea of object biographies was first developed by the anthropologist Kopytoff (1986), who suggested that if material objects are seen as having a 'life', we can ask similar questions to those posed about people: Where does the thing come from and who made it? What has been its career so far? What were its uses? How are the possibilities of the thing realised? What happens as the object ages? Kopytoff wrote that '[b]iographies of things can make salient what might otherwise remain obscure'. We may, for instance, understand the laws of inheritance in a foreign culture better by following the travels of objects than by a direct account of the laws themselves. When different cultures meet, we can follow the ways an object is culturally redefined and put to use (Kopytoff 1986: 66–67), which often reveals information different from that revealed through an analysis of discourse. In the case at hand – the gene gun – we might view the biohackers, research curators, and communicators from the synthetic biology research centre as part of different cultures, and the gene gun as being defined and redefined by these groups. Science communication in general necessitates a meeting of different cultures of scientists, communicators, publics, etc., and following the life history of a material object in science communication is one way to understand such meetings.

Following redefinitions and histories of concrete objects is an approach also gaining traction in the study of museum collections. Concrete objects are traced through changes in status, including the shift from being outside the museum to being inside the museum. This has often been seen as the end of 'active life', but more recently has been considered a new phase in an ongoing trajectory of reuse and redefinition. Sandra Dudley, for instance, points out that objects do not 'die' when they are removed from their original context. Instead of being de-contextualised, they are simply re-contextualised by the museum (Dudley 2012: 1–2; see also Alberti 2005; Pearce 1992). By analogy, a scientific object does not 'die' when it is removed from scientific use to be employed in science communication. Objects may thus be used to reflect on the role of different locations of science communication, and on the ways in which different spaces may enact different versions both of science and science communication.

While objects in museology are well-defined material entities, Lorraine Daston deals with more slippery scientific objects in *The Biographies of Scientific Objects* (2000). Her aim is to present an alternative to debates between realism and constructivism in history and philosophy of science. She wants to tread a line between, on the one hand, the classical realist, who holds that scientific objects are discovered and are real in the same sense as our everyday objects, and on the other, constructivist views which hold that scientific objects are created, that they are products of a given time and place and have histories that show them as changeable. By following the 'life' of scientific objects, the book suggests that objects can be both 'real' *and* have a history in which they are constructed by their situated lives and specific moments in time. Scientific objects come into being as scientific objects only to have their scientific status wane again after their time in the limelight.

Approaching relations between people and objects by following the life of material objects brings us to STS, where actor network theory (ANT) in particular has explored the complex networks of heterogeneous actants (human and non-human) that link science, technology, and society. ANT (often) takes a stronger view as to the agency of objects and non-human actants other than museum studies; it also dissolves clear boundaries between such actants by emphasising that what any actant 'is' is fluid rather than fixed, emerging from the way particular networks are configured at a particular moment and in a particular setting (Michael 2016). Ontology is therefore relational and temporary:

the nature of an object depends on the interconnections it currently has with the world around it. In the context of science communication, this has led to a view of public communication as an assemblage that brings together 'different elements through which novel relations and identities can emerge' (Horst & Michael 2011: 286).

Our approach mixes aspects from the theoretical landscape outlined above. Like the anthropological and museological approaches, we do not explicitly engage with the agency of the objects. We allow the gene gun a material identity and follow different phases in its life, its redefinitions, and changes in status and value, all as it moves through diverse spaces which constitute it in different ways. Following the gene gun allows us to follow relations between the gene gun and the different actors using it for science communication. As a 'boundary object' the gene gun is 'plastic enough to adapt to local needs and constraints of the several parties employing them, yet robust enough to maintain a common identity across sites' (Star & Griesemer 1989: 393). From Daston we take the idea that it is important to acknowledge not only the 'realness' of objects, but also the fact that they have a history, that is, that they are constructed as scientific objects and as objects of science communication. In the context of this project, we can follow the waxing and waning of different uses of the gene gun (as a scientific instrument, as an object of public engagement in science, as a risk, as an art piece) when we recount its biography. But we also see the material, in the shape of the physical whittled tree branch with electronics on it (Figure 4.1), as an important constraint in shaping the science communication surrounding it. We are thus sensitive to the co-production not just of nature and the social, or science and society, but of how science communication is articulated through specific configurations of objects, people, and spaces. What we gain is an approach to science communication that, without relinquishing the exploration of networks and sociopolitical contexts, also acknowledges that concrete objects are often central to communication. We suggest that the notion of an object biography – of following a material object as a stable point within shifting science communication assemblages – helps us tread this middle ground.

4.4 MOMENTS IN THE LIFE OF THE GENE GUN

There are many ways of structuring a biography. For this object biography we follow the gene gun roughly through time, focusing on four spaces it passed through: laboratory spaces where it was constructed and tested; the museum where it was displayed; a public debate arranged by the museum and a synthetic biology research centre; and finally, a gallery focusing on the interaction of art, technology, and society.

For each space we describe how the gene gun was framed and the ideas about science communication that this was prompted by or brought forth.

In brief, we identify four different articulations of the gene gun: it began its 'life' as a scientific object; became a contested symbol of engagement and collaboration; embodied a political statement of risk and conflict; and was lastly presented as an art object. Science communication itself was further co-produced along with the nature of the gene gun; the gene gun as science communication assemblage, then, brought together not just a specific object with a particular space and group of actors, but with different imaginations of what communication should be.

4.4.1 HACKERSPACE AND UNIVERSITY LABORATORY: THE PRODUCTION OF A SCIENTIFIC INSTRUMENT

The gene gun was constructed in a hackerlab, and was shortly afterwards tested in a university laboratory. During its early life the main focus was on its scientific aspects, and communication was mainly internal to the science and hacker environments. Although it was 'commissioned' for the project and thus created as a tool of communication, the biohackers' primary concern was to get it to work as a scientific instrument and make it cheaply out of materials at hand. The gene gun was constructed, designed, and tested to instantiate the hacker approach to science.

When devising the hack, the biohackers contacted the local hackerspace for help with the electronics. They described the collaboration as children playing together: you 'just go there and enjoy playing with the technology and stuff and just make things and it turns out that it works' (Hackers I: 6). The gun-shaped wooden branch on which the hack was mounted also carried associations of children at play. The hack was thus an embodiment of collaboration and a playful attitude to science.

One striking aspect of the gene gun is that it has no 'casing' around the electronics (Figure 4.1); it reveals the mechanisms that are often hidden in grey boxes on modern scientific instrumentation, where '[y]ou've some buttons to press and you are totally disconnected from what is inside' (Hackers I: 7). In this sense, the object is constructed as more scientific than science itself – more transparent and technically aware. The hack was designed to show both scientists and the public what science should really be like, and how to understand scientific instruments and recover the craft of making your own tools.

After the instrument was constructed in the hackerspace it was tested in a university laboratory. It is not permitted to produce transgenic cells in non-licensed labs, and work with the instrument could therefore not legally be done in a hacker lab. The first version of the gene gun – the instrument on the wooden branch – in fact turned out not to work. It was first tested in front of a journalist from a popular science magazine. The hacker explained, with a laugh, that they had said to the journalist '"I will demonstrate to you how it works" and then BARPH it broke' (Hackers I: 6). This did not bother the hacker. The failed instrument added to the image of opening up the process of instrumentation construction and of genuine experimental science. A second complete device was later constructed using a SodaStream machine (Figure 4.2). This was not as visually spectacular, but worked: the SodaStream gene gun was used to produce transgenic cells that were then photographed at the university lab, demonstrating that the instrument was functional. The hacker presented the result to university scientists who 'were like "wow, that's crazy"' (Hackers I: 5). Part of the attraction was that it is possible 'to actually do some scientific, real technology stuff' (Hackers I: 7).

Thus, both the process of making and designing the gene gun and its testing in the university laboratory mirror ideas about what the hacking approach to science is about. It produced scientific results, but at the same time it was more playful, collaborative, accessible, and truly experimental than science itself – especially as found in large university labs and industry. The gene gun simultaneously argued for demonstrable scientific status and participated in science communication about hacking, primarily with other scientists and hackers. Interestingly, the possibility of producing a gene gun for hacker labs was restricted, as transgenic work is only permitted in certified laboratories. Indeed, its testing within an institutional lab revealed the limitations of its 'call to arms' to do experiments at home. The potential of scientific openness was therefore a key message of the gene gun, albeit one that ignored moral questions about who should have access to potentially risky technologies.

In this way, the early life of the gene gun was about establishing a network inside scientific and hackerspaces and producing the gene gun as both a hack and a scientific instrument. The gene gun combined scientific functionality with playfulness, openness, and accessibility. When the gene gun was placed in the laboratory environments the science communication surrounding it took on a very traditional form. The journalist was called in to witness – in a manner that has a long history (Shapin 1994) – that it worked, and reported on it in a similar fashion to other technoscientific achievements, in part to gain support (Barry 1999).

4.4.2 MUSEUM EXHIBITION: DEFICIT AND ENGAGEMENT

After an early life in laboratories, both versions of the gene gun moved into a museum exhibition about biohacking and synthetic biology (Figure 4.3). No longer in active use as a scientific instrument, they were articulated as public objects through their presentation in a (particular kind of) public space. The move from the hackerspace into the museum required much negotiation about how the gene guns should be displayed and described (see Davies et al. 2015), and biohackers and museum curators revealed different approaches to science communication when describing the uses of the object.

Figure 4.3 The lab/installation space at Medical Museion in Copenhagen. The table with the two gene guns and the information board explaining how they might be used can be seen near the windows. (Photo: Malthe Borch and Medical Museion)

Being understood and presented by the hacker as a scientific instrument went hand-in-hand with a form of science communication seeking to mediate basic scientific principles to public audiences. The hacker thus brought the form of science communication prevalent from its early time in the lab into the new setting of the museum. The gene gun was used as a didactic tool, described as a vehicle for 'transporting' knowledge about genetics and hacking from the biohacker-scientist to the public: '...to transport this message that it actually works, you can do stuff if you really want to' (Hackers I: 7). Seeing the gene gun as a transporter of educational knowledge and of advocacy for people engaging with science reveals tensions within the role of the hacker as both scientist and an advocate for a new form of knowledge making. The hacker wanted to use the gun for traditional science communication with a strongly didactic slant – something perhaps influenced by their own ideas about the nature of museum spaces – and simultaneously to challenge institutional authority and traditional modes of scientific apprenticeship. Specifically, they were keen to support the role of the gene gun as an educational tool in the museum space by introducing didactic scientific placards into the exhibition. This material was, for instance, intended to communicate the central dogma of genetics – how genetic information is transcribed and turned into proteins in the cells – with the biohacker stating that they 'would have preferred to have some bigger charts of the actual biology like the set up of the cell and the DNA and so on' (Hackers II: 4). Similarly, they were anticipating more 'educational information, graphs and schematics and so on that are usually in the text books in the first chapters'; they 'sent it to the museum and expected them to print it huge and people could have them on the wall and point to them' (Hackers II: 5). For the biohacker, the main value of the object was as a scientific instrument and means of transmitting scientific facts.

The museum curators felt the exhibition should not necessarily explain the basics of genetics, but rather explain what biohacking and synthetic biology are about in a broader sense. The placard in the exhibition did not explain basic biology, but rather acted as a cartoon 'manual' for hacking: sketching the process of extracting DNA, separating relevant DNA strings, and shooting them into cells using the gene gun. The placard thus explained the science and hacking behind the use of the gene gun, but with much less detail and in a more 'friendly' style than is typical in scientific diagrams.

In one sense the curators and biohackers agreed: the gene gun should make people interested and excited about the possibilities of hacking and the power of engagement. They also shared a common desire for the object to be handled and used; for material 'engagement' that would help people understand or get a sense of how it worked (Figure 4.4). The fact that it couldn't actually be used for 'real' experiments during the participatory workshops, because the museum was not a certified lab, troubled the biohackers, as they hoped engagement with the process would actually recruit more biohackers; the hacked gene gun was meant to provide a cheap version of lab equipment to make experimentation available to everyone. For the museum staff, materially engaging with the idea of biohacking was a satisfactory outcome. The gene gun thus hovered between instrument and symbol, between engaging people in working with science and with 'how science works' – a tension that is found in many science engagement activities.

Figure 4.4 Visitors to the lab/installation at Medical Museion handling the branch-based gene gun. (Photo: Malthe Borch and Medical Museion)

When the gene gun entered the museum, it was framed by the biohackers as a scientific instrument and a tool for transferring scientific knowledge from science to the public. This aligns with the notion of science communication known as the deficit model, where a transfer of information from scientists to the public is expected to result in an increase in knowledge and more positive attitudes towards science (Irwin & Wynne 1996). Both hackers and curators were, however, also concerned with science communication as engagement. They wanted the gene gun, and the project as a whole, to trigger reflection and participation. In this respect, the gene gun instantiated a more recent emphasis on science communication as interactive and participatory (Davies et al. 2009). The prototype was seen as a potential inspiration, a means of sparking further actions, although this engagement was imagined differently by hackers and curators. While the hackers wanted to recruit new, active members into the hacker movement, the curators were more concerned with engaging audiences in debates about the role of craft and handiwork in science, about relations between science and the public, and about making scientific practices broadly available. In both cases, the gene gun became entangled with discourses that produced it as a trigger for further action: a starting point, rather than a finished instrument for display.

4.4.3 PUBLIC DEBATE: 'A FIRE IN THE DISCUSSION'?

In the laboratory and the exhibition, the gene gun was produced as a tool for science communication as education or engagement. But in other spaces it became an obstacle to science communication, something that should be removed or backgrounded in encounters between science and public audiences. This became particularly evident with regard to the public debate that was set up to explore the political and ethical questions associated with biohacking. These matters were not prioritised within the restricted zone of the exhibition text. Rather, the curators presented them at a live event, where the public and project participants met in person and were better able to negotiate challenges and possibilities of synthetic biology, including ethical and political questions embodied by the gene gun's mixture of dangerous and tamed technology.

In this setting, the gene gun – here the non-functional, tree branch version – met with strong criticism from the synthetic biology centre communications team. The gun was seen as associating the technology with danger and thereby potentially provoking public resistance, as seen in the case of GMO crops (the connection between the gene gun and the controversy surrounding genetically modified crops is particularly close as the gene gun technology was used in the production of GMOs in the late 1980s and 1990s; see Horlick-Jones et al. 2007 on the controversy). The professional communicators initially wanted the gun removed from the exhibition and excluded from the event. They believed that the museum had simply gone for a 'wow-effect' and was intentionally positioning the dangers of synthetic biology as the starting point of the debate. One said, 'In my world, the gene gun is the weapon that will start a fire in the discussion. It is not a meeting point; it is too provocative. ... There is going to be too many negative reactions to it' (Synthetic biology communication unit II: 11). Without the gun, the focus could be on the inspirational aspects of biohacking and synthetic biology: 'so that we can talk about synthetic biology and biohacking in a positive and inspiring way instead of talking about fear and what will happen if things go wrong' (Synthetic biology communication unit I: 3).

The museum resisted the removal of the gene gun, in part through an explicit discussion of the relation between openness and public trust. Disagreement about the presentation of a material object crystallised differences that might otherwise not have been elucidated. In the end, the team reached a compromise on the captioning of photographs on the webpage and the language used in the press release. After the debate, the communication people were surprised 'that people were so positive towards synthetic biology and towards biohacking. There weren't really any critics...'. They even voiced the idea that the team should have invited more critical voices to the debate: 'perhaps we should have done more to invite the people that were not exactly against synthetic biology or biohacking but perhaps in a slightly different segment' (Synthetic biology communication unit interview II: 2).

In moving from the slow medium of the exhibition, where disagreements about framing can be negotiated behind the scenes or on the level of individual visitors, to the more volatile assemblage of a live public debate, the gene gun changed its identity. It was seen as an obstacle to communicating science, as representing outdated technology, and, at best, as a point of departure for discussing risks and the handling of technologies. The biohacker used it to discuss the functions of hacking in society, and no longer to teach about genetics. In the new space of a public debate, the gene gun began to embody risk and controversy, becoming a symbol of public concern about biotechnology, rejection of emerging technologies, and fears of contemporary risks (Beck 1992; Horlick-Jones et al. 2007). It was seen by some project participants as inherently inflammatory and destructive; here, then, science communication was about damage control or public relations. Science communication became articulated as a process of mediation within a fundamentally damaged relationship between science and society.

4.4.4 ART GALLERY: BECOMING PART OF THE WIDER CULTURAL SPHERE

Initially, the gene gun hack was not described as sci-art by the biohacker. But it later entered an art-science context when the tree branch version was exhibited in the electronic arts gallery Ars Electronica in Linz as part of a show, *Yours Synthetically*, which brought together art-science projects on synthetic biology. The gene gun's display as an artistic object resonates with wider developments in science communication, and specifically an increasing emphasis on communication as not (only) education, participation, or risk management, but as an aspect of the wider cultural sphere. An influential 2014 report on 'The evolving culture of science engagement', for instance, argued that there was growing interest in 'mainstreaming science in the wider culture' (Kaiser et al. 2014: i), and suggested that mechanisms such as storytelling, artistic expression, and emotion were important in doing this. In these moves, and in the Ars Electronica exhibition, we see science communication performed as something else entirely.

The hacker who built the gene gun initially resisted the transformation of his hack into an art piece, feeling it might destabilise its status as a scientific object and his status as a serious scientist. This is mirrored in the text for the exhibit in Ars Electronica. The gene gun was introduced with the words 'A gene gun is a scientific instrument'. Within the art-science space the hack was thus returned to its original role as a scientific instrument and its promise of fully equipped home-labs and 'experimenting with new life forms'. The 'artist's talk' given by the biohacker at an event at the gallery was similarly concerned with how the gene gun worked and with the possibility of ordinary people constructing a gene gun at home. But in the context of the exhibition the gene gun performed a broader vision of science communication. The curator at Ars Electronica was interested in the symbolic and artistic value of the gene gun, as this added an aspect that they found was missing in much science communication: 'science communication often doesn't deal with symbolic meaning – art shows us what it means' (Ars Electronica I).

As part of this broader exploration of the meanings of the gene gun, the 'dangerous' aspects were explored in exactly the way that the communication staff at the research centre of synthetic biology had opposed. The idea of doing transgenic work at home was not problematised, and the curator stated that they wanted to bring out scary aspects: 'I love the symbolic value of shooting that stuff into the cells' (Ars Electronica I). Here, the symbolic meanings of the instrument were deliberately emphasised and explored, and controversy and fear were seen as encouraging rather than hindering debate.

By being exhibited in an art-science exhibition the gene gun gained symbolic value through being viewed as part of, and relevant to, a wider cultural sphere. It might seem that the hacker was less interested in this form of cultural value, as they continued to focus on the gene gun as a scientific instrument and the scientific possibilities it opened up. However, when the collaborative project drew to a close and Medical Museion wanted to keep both versions of the gene gun for their collections, the biohacker was only willing to part with the SodaStream gene gun. This was perhaps indicative of the aesthetic and cultural value of the hacked tree branch gene gun, enhanced by being displayed by institutions such as Medical Museion and Ars Electronica. The functioning SodaStream version was less spectacular, less illustrative of the childlike creative process of hacking. Following the path of the material object thus shows us a different set of values from the explicit discourse of the participants; a preference for the object that had accrued greater cultural value through its history of display and its particular material form. The Ars Electronica curator mirrored this, stating that they did not care that people said that the gene gun would blow apart if it was used and that it was 'badly made', because its main message was its non-sterile image of science.

In its latest iteration at Ars Electronica, the gene gun layered a series of different approaches to science communication. It was used didactically to explain the science of producing transgenic cells, it was used to engage gallery visitors in the possibility of building instruments, and it brought out the symbolic layers of fear and opportunity in the instrument. As the object aged, it accrued meanings and the communication surrounding it became more complex, simultaneously playing on different modes of science communication. Old age for the gene gun is about representing its broader significances rather than its functions. The point here is thus not only that the gene gun and science communication are assembled differently in (and because of) different spaces, but that they accrue meanings as they move through different contexts and temporal moments; the gene gun becomes ever more multiple (Mol 2002).

4.5 CONCLUSION

This chapter has followed a material object used in science communication, exploring the tensions between its production and reproduction in different spaces, the simultaneous co-production of science communication, and the history it accrues and which travels with it. The biography of the object takes seriously the role of the material object in STS and science communication and thus ties together social and material aspects of science communication, showing, for instance, that space plays a crucial role in how an object is framed and understood. Moreover, it pays attention to the development of the public role of the object over its life history, where it continuously acquired new layers of value as both a scientific instrument and as an object with wider cultural meanings.

The gene gun's life story – from a scientific instrument used for dissemination to a piece of art-science exploration – may be seen as loosely corresponding with a story that has been told about the 'biography' of science communication itself (Gregory & Lock 2008). Science communication can be framed as evolving from a process based out of scientific institutions and expertise to notions of 'engagement' and, lastly, as an eclectic, hybrid part of culture at large (Davies & Horst 2016; Whiteley et al. 2017). However, this is too simple a tale.

Different meanings and stories have always overlapped both temporally and conceptually (Felt et al. 2013; Irwin 2008) and, depending on where you look, didactics, engagement, and culture are always present when science meets the public. This was very noticeable in our object's biography. The gene gun was from the outset modelled on a gun-shaped branch to elicit discussions of risk, and both the hacker and the curators mixed didactics and engagement, even through to the hacker's didactic presentation in the art gallery context.

However, we want to suggest that there may be some development in the accumulated history of objects used in science communication. There is, in other words, a change in the tenor of science communication and the complexity of the relations surrounding it as an object 'matures'. As in the case of the gene gun, the didactic approach might be dominant early in the life of an object used in science communication, when the object is closely associated with scientific practice, while symbolic and cultural meanings increase in complexity and importance as the object moves to public spaces and gets re-contextualised as a public object. Broader cultural meanings become even more valuable than the scientific, as illustrated by the functioning SodaStream device becoming less coveted than the tree branch gene gun.

Methodologically, a biography-of-objects approach in science communication experiments with shifting the focus from analysis of different discourses to an analysis of the changes and layerings in the science communication surrounding an object, thereby combining a range of approaches developed in connection with museum objects, with STS, and with history of science approaches. The object provides a way to anchor the analysis while at the same time demonstrating how the object and the science communication surrounding it mutually construct each other, and thus how particular ways of defining the gene gun are co-produced with modes of science communication and with specific spaces.

More pragmatically, we found that collaborators made their views on science communication more explicit when talking about the gene gun than when speaking on their own behalf. This is related to an earlier observation from the project that concrete questions of how to use, describe, and display material objects force people to bring forth and reconcile differing positions (Davies et al. 2015). The observation that talking about objects is a fruitful way to bring out stories is also noted in a different context by Hoskins (1998), who found that she could elicit life-histories from informants when she asked about significant objects, but not when enquiring directly about their lives. The material object thus prompts different cultures of science communicators to express their mode of science communication when they express what the gene gun 'is'.

We hope to have demonstrated that material objects can be a useful point of departure for investigating relations between different modes of science communication, diverse communicators, and particular spaces. Objects in science communication, while produced differently at different moments, also have histories, and the accumulation of relations and meanings matters to how they, and the science communication around them, are enacted.

ACKNOWLEDGEMENTS

Thanks to the entire team behind *'Biohacking: Do It Yourself!'*, including our external collaborators and the Medical Museion staff who made this challenging experiment possible. The project was primarily funded by the European Commission Seventh Framework Programme in 2011 under the Studiolab network, and co-funded by Medical Museion and the Novo Nordisk Foundation Center for Basic Metabolic Research (CBMR).

REFERENCES

Alberti, Samuel J. M. M. 2005. 'Objects and the Museum'. *Isis* 96: 559–571.

Anderson, Leon. 2006. 'Analytic Autoethnography'. *Journal of Contemporary Ethnography* 35 (4): 373–395.

Barry, Andrew. 1999. 'Demonstrations: Sites and Sights of Direct Action'. *Economy and Society* 28 (1): 75–94.

Beck, Ulrich. 1992. *Risk Society: Towards a New Modernity*. London: Sage.

Daston, Lorraine (ed.). 2000. *The Biographies of Scientific Objects*, Chicago, IL: University of Chicago Press.

Davies, Sarah R. 2014. 'Knowing and Loving: Public Engagement beyond Discourse'. *Science and Technology Studies* 3: 90–110.

Davies, Sarah R., and Maja Horst. 2016. *Science Communication: Culture, Identity and Citizenship*. London: Palgrave Macmillan.

Davies, Sarah, Ellen McCallie, Elin Simonsson, Jane L. Lehr, and Sally Duensing. 2009. 'Discussing Dialogue: Perspectives on the Value of Science Dialogue Events that Do Not Inform Policy'. *Public Understanding of Science* 18 (3): 338–353.

Davies, Sarah R., Karin Tybjerg, Louise Whiteley, and Thomas Söderqvist. 2015. 'Co-Curation as Hacking: Biohackers in Copenhagen's Medical Museion'. *Curator* 58: 117–131.

Dudley, Sandra H. 2012. 'Encountering a Chinese Horse: Engaging with the Thingness of Things'. In Sandra H. Dudley (ed.), *Museum Objects: Experiencing the Properties of Things*, pp. 1–15. Abingdon: Routledge.

Gosden, Chris, and Yvonne Marshall. 1999. 'The Cultural Biography of Objects'. *World Archaeology* 31 (2): 169–178.

Gregory, Jane, and Simon J. Lock. 2008. 'The Evolution of "Public Understanding of Science": Public Engagement as a Tool of Science Policy in the UK'. *Sociology Compass* 2 (4): 1252–1265.

Hammersley, Martyn, and Paul Atkinson. 1995. *Ethnography*. Abingdon: Routledge.

Horlick-Jones, Tom, John Walls, Gene Rowe, Nick Pidgeon, Wouter Poortinga, Graham Murdock, and Tim O'Riordan. 2007. *The GM Debate: Risk, Politics and Public Engagement*. New York: Routledge.

Horst, Maja, and Mike Michael. 2011. 'On the Shoulders of Idiots: Re-Thinking Science Communication as "Event"'. *Science as Culture* 20 (3): 283–306.

Hoskins, Janet. 1998. *Biographical Objects: How Things Tell the Story of People's Lives.* Abingdon: Routledge.

Hutchby, Ian. 2001. 'Technologies, Texts and Affordances.' *Sociology* 35 (2): 441–456.

Irwin, Alan. 2008. 'Risk, Science and Public Communication: Third Order Thinking about Scientific Culture'. In Massimiano Bucchi and Brian Trench (eds.), *Handbook of Public Communication of Science and Technology*, pp. 199–212. Abingdon and New York: Routledge.

Irwin, Alan, and B. Wynne. 1996. *Misunderstanding Science: Public Reconstructions of Science and Technology*. New York: Cambridge University Press.

Kaiser, David, John Durant, Thomas Levenson, Ben Wiehe, and Peter Linett. 2014. 'Report of Findings: September 2013 Workshop'. MIT and Culture Kettle. www.cultureofscienceengagement.net

Kopytoff, Igor. 1986. 'The Cultural Biography of Things'. In Arjun Appadurai (ed.), *The Social Life of Things: Commodities in Cultural Perspective*, pp. 64–91. Cambridge: Cambridge University Press.

Marres, Noortje, and Javier Lezaun. 2011. 'Materials and Devices of the Public: An Introduction'. *Economy and Society* 40 (4): 489–509.

Michael, Mike. 2016. *Actor Network Theory: Trials, Trails and Translations*. London: Sage.

Mol, Anne Marie. 2002. *The Body Multiple: Ontology in Medical Practice*. Durham, NC: Duke University Press.

Nelson, Nicole. 2012. 'Shooting Genes, Distributing Credit: Narrating the Development of the Biolistic Gene Gun'. *Science as Culture* 21 (2): 205–232.

Pearce, Susan M. 1992. *Museums, Objects, and Collections*. Washington, DC: Smithsonian Books.

Sanford, John C. 2000. 'Turning Point Article – The Invention of the Biolistic Process'. *In Vitro Cellular & Developmental Biology – Plant* 36: 303–308.

Shapin, Steven. 1994. *A Social History of Truth: Civility and Science in 17th Century England*. Chicago, IL: University of Chicago Press.

Star, Susan, and James Griesemer. 1989. 'Institutional Ecology, "Translations" and Boundary Objects: Amateurs and Professionals in Berkeley's Museum of Vertebrate Zoology, 1907–39'. *Social Studies of Science* 19 (3): 387–420.

Whiteley, Louise, Karin Tybjerg, Bente V. Pedersen, Adam Bencard, and Ken Arnold. 2017. 'Exhibiting Health and Medicine as Culture'. *Public Health Panorama* 3 (1): 59–68.

Reflections and Connections

Marcus Owens, in the chapter that follows, focuses on a kind of space that is rarely thought of as involving science communication: public parks. Through two case study parks – one in San Francisco and one in Berlin – he explores how these landscapes have been designed to embody particular imaginations of nature, communicate certain ecological visions, and *make specific kinds of publics*.

He is particularly concerned with the making of what he calls 'ecological publics'. The design and physical structure of these parks function to frame their audiences in particular ways. For instance, the San Francisco park was heavily reliant on volunteer labour for its construction. Its publics had to be active, comprised of enthusiastic recruits who would participate in the making and maintenance of the park, but also, importantly, take the ecological practices they had learned into their own homes and lives. On the other hand, some aspects of these parks constrained audiences through boardwalks or signage that defined how they could move, configuring them as observers within a kind of natural museum.

Owens is obviously concerned with a specific kind of space, and with the behaviours and emotions that are normalised there. In this respect, we can view his study as telling us something about how *spaces*, *atmospheres*, *emotions*, and *knowledge* are made together. Particular versions of ecology are mobilised in these parks, shaping not only what one can know about nature, but also how one should feel about and interact with it.

5

PUBLIC SCIENCE AND PUBLIC SPACE: COMMUNICATING ECOLOGIES THROUGH LANDSCAPE DESIGN

MARCUS OWENS

5.1 INTRODUCTION

The space of the museum has long been a focus for analysis of public communication of science, particularly when it comes to communicating topics related to nature (Agassiz 1862; Bennett 1995; Berkowitz & Lightman 2017; Conn 2000; Haraway 2013a; Hooper-Greenhill 1992; Macdonald 1998; Murray 1904). However, the public parks that often surround these museums are under-examined sites for studying science communication. This chapter considers how public parks co-evolve with both museological and urban planning practices, suggesting that this co-evolution reveals insights about changing practices of engagement with publics and the communication of nature and ecology. The focus is on the second half of the 20th century, tracing the significance of communication in ecological planning and management as reflected in the innovation of the Visitor's Center by the US National Park Service (NPS), and the ways in which this is translated into the urban contexts of San Francisco and Berlin.

The central argument is that, as scientific expertise became increasingly contested throughout the 1970s (Fischer 2018), parks emerged as spaces that promoted interactive engagements with preserved or regenerated urban landscapes and thus brought into being what I want to call 'ecological publics'. However, as ecological communication moved from the NPS Visitor Center into the landscape of the park, the design of user experiences in these sustainability- and ecology-oriented spaces at times led to a 'museumification of nature' (Gobster 2007). By examining how landscape architecture, ecological knowledge, and publics have been co-produced through park design, the overall aim is to suggest that science communication scholarship can benefit from exploring how public knowledge – in this case, of concepts of nature – relates to the design of public spaces. The chapter thus builds on STS scholarship exploring how knowledge and social orders are intertwined in the context of cities (Lachmund 2013), the materiality of representational practices (see Chapter 3.4), the work that specific kinds of spaces and places are able to do (Gieryn 2000), and the ways in which publics are made in the processes and settings of engagement (Felt & Fochler 2010).

The chapter begins with a brief description of the shared history of parks and museums, providing the context of the development of the NPS Visitor's Center, a key turning point for ecological communication within environmental planning. The core of the chapter focuses on the ways in which the modernist logic underpinning the NPS Visitor Center was destabilised through the urban environmental and social movements of the 1970s. These developments are expanded upon through two key case studies of ecological parks: Crissy Field in San Francisco and the *Gleisdreieck* in Berlin, which both include similar contemporary responses to the 'museumification of nature'.

5.2 THE MUSEUM, THE LANDSCAPE, THE (NATIONAL) PARK

The development of both museums and landscape design intersects with the development of objectivity as a way of seeing (Bennett 1995; Macdonald 1998; Mitchell 1991; Rudwick 1992). As Peter Galison and others have argued, objectivity became increasingly prominent by the middle of the 19th century (Dalston & Galison 2007; Galison & Jones 1998). Accordingly, Natural History Museums and Universal Exhibitions sought to order and organise the world through detached, objective representations (Mitchell 1991). The objective presentation of the world-as-picture links both the formation of the modern Natural History Museum and the public park that often surrounded it.

As both forms developed, however, an interesting point of contrast emerged. While the museum aimed to create an objective view of the world-as-picture that the public spectator could observe from the *outside*, by the middle of the 19th century an emerging class of professional landscape architects mobilised the sentimental English Landscape Garden style as the form of the public park, aiming to create the illusion of stepping *into* a picture (Conway 1991).

In both cases, however, a logic of Victorian improvement dominated, conceiving the public as a medium to be crafted through exposure to narratives of evolutionary progress and technological advancement (Bennett 1995; Griffiths & Robin 1997; Pratt 2007; Rudwick 1992).

The relationship between the visual culture of the museum and of the public park is complicated with the advent of the National Park as a 'natural museum' (Mason 2004) in the United States in the aftermath of its Civil War. Conceptualising the National Park as a natural museum was predicated on the objective representation of the landscape through the 'scientific' medium of photography, conceived as the workings of a 'nature machine' (Grusin 2008). This focus on photographs and other forms of media and communication adds nuance to narratives of the formative years of the US National Parks, which have often been preoccupied with the prominence of aesthetics and myth, presupposing an opposition between the formation of environmental science and the 'unscientific' preservation of nationalist scenic beauty in the late Victorian era (Cronon 1996). In fact, this use of a scientific visual culture – in the shape of photography – in the early national parks foreshadows the rise of expert interpretation in the 20th century (Galison & Jones 1998). This is epitomised by John Muir, steward of Yosemite Valley and advocate for the National Parks in the late 19th century, who emerged as an early progenitor of park interpretation (Gross & Zimmerman 2002). Understanding the landscape as a valuable artefact of natural history, albeit a specimen too large to be transported to a museum, park concessioners soon hired guides to communicate natural history to visitors through campfire talks, nature walks, and instruction in plant identification (Wirth 1980).

Despite these early efforts at landscape interpretation, even after the institutional apparatus of the NPS was established in 1916, formal interpretative services were scant. In the early years of the Park Service, there was a clear understanding that education programmes should expand beyond what concessioners were offering if they were to receive federal rather than local support (Carr 2007). The first comprehensive effort to systematically interpret the National Parks for a mass audience would not occur until 1956 and the 'Mission 66' programme. Developed in tandem with the American Automobile Association and the Federal Highway Act, mass automobility was a major factor in the Mission 66 programme, which anticipated 80 million visitors (roughly half the US population at the programme's onset in 1956) by the 50th anniversary of the agency in 1966 (Kim 2004). NPS director Conrad Wirth saw the extent to which visitor numbers could safely increase as being directly dependent upon an effective programme of information and interpretation – hence the development of the Mission 66 Visitor Center.

The NPS Visitor Centers brought the museum, and its interpretative techniques, into the park in new ways. Concerned that an increasingly 'city-bred' population with higher education levels and exposure to sophisticated media presented a challenge to park interpreters, National Park Service officials deployed new media technologies to reach an increasing number of visitors with only moderate increases in staff. The visitor centre evolved from small park museum-type buildings that presented broad instruction on natural and cultural history into modern structures of open design mobilising the latest media and design technologies (Wirth 1980).

Moreover, by the end of the Mission 66 programme, a new approach to nature, public parks, and science communication had taken hold. The institution of wilderness areas with the passage of the Wilderness Act of 1963 allowed National Parks to more fully evolve into 'nature laboratories' or research sites for ecological study (Benson 2010; Kupper 2016; Sellars 2009). Scientific attitudes, knowledge, and authority thus began to more forcefully shape and legitimise park management practices, with designers and media communications professionals called upon to fill the widening gap between experts and publics through didactic information provided in visitor centres. In this way, popular demands for 'unspoiled wild nature' of the older, romantic variety dovetailed with scientific demands for laboratory-like conditions, both of which required effective scientific communication to the public so that they would accept restricted access (Kupper 2016). In the words of Park Service director Conrad Wirth, 'the principal purpose of such a program is to help the park visitor enjoy the area, and to appreciate and understand it, which leads directly to improved protection through visitor cooperation in caring for the park resources' (Wirth 1980: 258).

5.3 FROM LANDSCAPE INTERPRETATION TO INTERACTIVITY

Underpinning the transformation of parks into nature laboratories was a philosophy of nature derived from the 'climax' ecology of the time, in which ecosystems develop along a linear path towards an ideal, static state (Botkin 1990; Latour 2004). As Bruno Latour and others have shown, the climax ecosystem concept built upon a division of nature and culture that structured a modernist constitution of neatly delineated subjects and objects (Haraway 2013b; Latour 2004). In terms of architecture, this modernist constitution can be seen as culminating in the manifestos of the Congrès internationaux d'architecture modern (CIAM) and the logic of the functional city with its 'machines of living' (Farías & Blok 2017). In a similar vein, the late-modernist style of Mission 66 architecture is tasked with distancing the visitor from the park, ensuring the integrity of the ecological laboratory of the park wilderness.

However, just as it would appear that the Mission 66 programme and the Wilderness Act had succeeded in leveraging the Visitor's Center multimedia technologies in tandem with ecosystem monitoring practices that reconfigured the National Parks into a kind of public ecological laboratory, these same technologies began to unravel the division of nature and culture that structured the park-as-laboratory. The Mission 66 Visitor's Center in fact marks the beginnings of a transition from interpretation to interactivity in scientific culture, just as Muir's efforts had heralded a departure from objectivity to interpretation.

Architectural historians of the end of the post-war period have described this transition as a second modernism (Dutta et al. 2013), as design fields began to respond to transformations of the public and private sphere associated with mass automobility, television, air-conditioning, and other automations of productive and reproductive life (Colomina 2013). These developments were characterised by the mobilisation of the social and cognitive sciences towards 'user-centered design' that reconceives the environment in terms of media and information communication acting upon both individual experience and perceptions of the city as subjects of designerly improvement (Krieger & Saunders 2009; Martin 2005).

The newly dynamic figure of the user exerting influence on the modernist designer corresponds to a decentring of technocratic expertise in favour of deliberative planning practices that increasingly placed communication and interaction with the public at the forefront of the design process (Arnstein 1969; Innes 1998; Schön 1991). These developments were at times politicised in the context of opposition to a variety of modernist projects perceived as technocratic and 'top down', from urban renewal and urban highway construction to nuclear proliferation and American involvement in Vietnam (Castells 1983; Clavel 1986). However, as the term 'second modernism' (Dutta et al. 2013) or Ulrich Beck's concept of 'reflexive modernity' (Beck 1994) implies, deliberation and interactivity were firmly rooted in the project of modernity itself, growing out of previous scientific practices of objectivity and interpretative expert judgement. Late 20th-century enthusiasm for interactivity should therefore be understood not only as oppositional – triggered through protest and resistance to technical knowledges – but as a product of modernist logics that promote the creative scientific abilities of the individual citizen (Barry 1998; Lee 2013).

In this sense, the NPS Visitor Center, with its use of interactive media technologies to educate park visitors, provided a template for planners and designers to attempt to open up the 'black box' of technocratic urban planning to the public. In the context of science and technology, innovations such as the science shop aimed to challenge hegemonic techno-scientific epistemologies through participatory research models (Lachmund 2013; Leydesdorff & Ward 2005). Public planning procedures facilitated by non-governmental organisations (NGOs) through the 1980s and 1990s similarly sought to open up urban design to a variety of forms of knowledge and expertise (Joassart-Marcelli et al. 2011; Wolch 1990). The remainder of this chapter examines how these developments played out in ecological communication and park design, examining two sites where science communication, ecological knowledge, and museology were closely intertwined in the formation of new kinds of parks.

5.4 THE EXPLORATORIUM AND CRISSY FIELD

The first case is the relationship between San Francisco's Exploratorium, the prototypical example of an interactive science centre (Hein 1990), and Crissy Field, part of the Golden Gate National Recreation Area. The Exploratorium, founded in 1968 by Manhattan Project physicist Frank Oppenheimer, is well known for its aim to catalyse understandings of science through interaction with technical equipment rather than through the passive presentations of collections of historical objects traditionally found in science and technology museums (Ogawa et al. 2009). Housed in the Palace of Fine Arts, the sole pavilion remaining from the 1912 Panama–Pacific International Exhibition, the Exploratorium moved beyond the Natural History Museum's objective displays, or the NPS Visitor Centers' reliance on interpretative media spectacle. Rather, it sought to provide an interactive pedagogical approach conceived as a 'library of experiments' (ibid.: 285), mobilising experiential phenomena to accomplish 'educational objectives that were not possible in school classrooms, or through books, films or television programs' (ibid.: 282). The new public engendered by the Exploratorium – one that was active in uncovering knowledge of scientific principles for themselves (Barry 1998) – corresponded to transformations in the landscape surrounding the Exploratorium, and to a re-conceptualisation of the visitors.

As a 'new kind of national park' (Rothman 2004), the Golden Gate National Recreation Area has roots in Mission 66-era visitor studies which revealed a failure to adequately serve inner-city populations. In response, the Bureau of Outdoor Recreation generated proposals to create a system of National Recreation Areas in major urban areas, beginning with obsolete harbour defence facilities in New York and San Francisco. While the initial studies were primarily oriented around urban recreation, by the time the project was implemented over the course of the 1970s, ideas about urban open space increasingly emphasised ecological 'survival' (Futrell 1976). Designs for the transformation of urban military landscapes into national parks therefore not only used what were then new forms of deliberative planning, but also hinged on communicating this new risk-based relationship to nature.

In tandem with a developing ecological awareness among the general public, new institutions emerged from the deliberative planning process as San Francisco activists demanded more agile public relations than a cumbersome federal agency could provide (Benton-Short 1998). Both the Golden Gate National Park Conservancy (GGNPC) and later the Presidio Trust developed into prototypical non-profit environmental organisations, pioneering the design, communications, and marketing strategies necessary for producing an 'urban national park experience' (Goldsmith & Eggers 2005). Their activities included leveraging outside funding to transform spaces such as Alcatraz Penitentiary into some of San Francisco's premier tourist attractions over the 1970s and 1980s, and later developing the first NPS park website and independent brand identity, to the consternation of Federal Officials (Benton-Short 1998; Rothman 2004). In particular, the reconstruction of Crissy Field between 1994 and 2001, with numerous intersections and convergences with the Exploratorium and financed by the GGNPC (rather than the federal or local government), illustrates these new dynamics of scientific communication in landscape design.

As a former bay shore wetland first filled in to make space for the 1912 Panama–Pacific International Exhibition, Crissy Field was paved by the military for use as an early airfield and railyard after the First World War. By the end of the 1930s, the approach to the Golden Gate Bridge bisected the field, which became derelict and overgrown by the 1960s. The first alternative plans began to emerge in the early 1980s, when Michael Painter, a landscape architect and Exploratorium board member, ventured onto the roof of the Palace of Fine Arts to devise a plan to expand the Exploratorium's programming to the surrounding waterfront. Over the course of the 1980s, the GGNPC rallied the public for a redesigned landscape that eventually featured both the historic aspects of the airfield dating from the 1920s and a restored wetland (Meyer & Delehanty 2006; Rothman 2004). Notably, the conversion of Crissy Field into an 'outdoor classroom' (Meyer & Delehanty 2006) occurred as the Exploratorium was institutionalising its outdoor museological activities through the Exploratorium Studio for Public Spaces, which staged site-specific Exploratorium-style science communication events in the urban landscape.

A key aspect of the project was its educational component, which was centred on a hands-on youth environmental education facility, the Crissy Field Center. According to park managers, stewardship programmes would allow 'urban residents to rediscover ecological processes and wild places hidden in the urban environment and to play a role in their preservation' (Cranz & Boland 2004: 114). Beyond seeking to catalyse a broader appreciation for the landscape (as in the case of Muir's interpretative methods, or even the mid-century NPS Visitor's Center), the Crissy Field Center also played a crucial role in soliciting volunteers for the labour-intensive ecological restoration that was the core of the larger project's design. Further, the aspiration of this park model was not only to solicit volunteers to (re-)construct 'nature', by doing the work of ecological restoration and minimising vandalism and graffiti within the park, but also to inspire visitors to implement ecological practices outside the park, in everyday life (Cranz & Boland 2004). To this end, Crissy Field and the Golden Gate National Park Conservancy became notable in their use of branding and advertising to augment the reach of education and interpretative facilities (Meyer & Delehanty 2006). The 'ecological publics' produced by the Crissy Field Center's activities are therefore active evangelists for the ecological knowledge and practices it communicates.

Hargreaves Associates, the designers of Crissy Field, also sought to communicate ecology to the public through the landscape itself. Native plants and landforms evoke the dune landscape that once proliferated across most of western San Francisco, but which, due to urban conditions, no longer naturally forms. Even the wetland, which is the signature feature of the restoration project, is representational rather than functional, since tidal flows were not compatible with maintaining the historic airfield or adjacent streets (M'Closkey 2013). While the wetland required mechanical dredging, and the dunes were created by volunteers and donations rather than the movement of water, wind and soil, park managers believe there is value in these representative forms in their communicative capacity, as a 'material rhetoric' or ability to 'educat[e] the public about ecological process in the urban environment' (Cranz & Boland 2004: 117). However, this representation of a pre-industrial landscape required the efforts of thousands of volunteers, private funds, and a major media advertising campaign, suggesting contradictions in the goals and methods of deliberative planning and sustainability predicated on both material self-sufficiency and designs directed by authentic democratic discourse. Cranz and Boland acknowledge these contradictions, arguing that sustainability is a social concept rather than a technical or biological one, since 'humans are responsible for the ecological crisis' (ibid.: 105) For this reason, while a 'truly sustainable' park would not require human labour, a sustainable park that is 'both ecologically self-sufficient and culturally satisfying still requires human care in planting and maintenance' (ibid.: 111).

The story of Crissy Field offers insight into both the historical development of science museums and the ways in which landscapes are themselves designed as communicative tools. Emerging from Mission 66 studies of user profiles, the Golden Gate National Recreation Area's focus on public engagement heralded a more general turn towards interaction with the public in the National Park Service. The delegation of power and decentring of expertise reflects a profound change from the conceptualisation of the National Park as natural museum, as depicted by 'objective' glass plate photographs or through Muir's expert interpretation. As an outdoor classroom, designs for Crissy Field share more in common with the Exploratorium's strategies for communicating scientific principles through tactile engagement. Interactivity is also a financial strategy, where the costly labour of ecological restoration is performed by volunteers solicited through an advertising and branding campaign. However, once the bulk of the ecological restoration is complete, fenced-off zones for protected flora and fauna replicate the natural museum of the 19th century or the park-as-laboratory of the Mission 66 era. What we observe, then, is a move from interpretation to interactivity back into interpretation.

5.5 COMMUNICATING URBAN ECOLOGY IN BERLIN

Like the founding of the Exploratorium and the development of Crissy Field in San Francisco, university restructuring in Germany in the late 1960s reflected critiques of scientific institutions and expertise (Lachmund 2013). This restructuring helped bring about the Berlin School of Urban Ecology, which operated as a 'science shop', collaborating with emerging environmental community activist groups (Leydesdorff & Ward 2005). In particular, activities of the Berlin School of Urban Ecology in the *Gleisdreieck* (rail triangle) area of Berlin, around what would become the German Museum of Technology, form the basis of a second case of public science communication in urban environments through museum landscapes.

The development of the Berlin School of Urban Ecology was tied to the practicalities of research in post-war Berlin. The difficulty of leaving West Berlin and the proliferation of rural landscapes due to stalled post-war reconstruction meant that Berlin-based ecologists began to evaluate the ecological value of everyday vacant spaces in the city, framing the overgrown urban wilderness landscapes of divided Berlin as a 'fourth nature' – 'first nature' being 'wild'; 'second nature' describing functional agricultural landscapes; 'third nature' denoting pleasure gardens; and 'fourth nature' describing novel ecosystems that emerge to reclaim vacant urban space (Kowarik 1995). As a result, urban landscapes were explicitly reconstituted as places of knowledge (Lachmund 2013) and harnessed by urban environmental activists opposed to the city's development plans (Kowarik & Langer 2005). Like the Crissy Field marsh, public communication around this ecological research had to deal with the fact that 'a rotting carcass swarming with maggots is integral to ecology but not normally considered an aesthetic experience that has any relation to the culture of nature as a source of pleasure' (Gandy 2013: 1309). Through careful framing, fallen trees or rotting wood became part of a 'scientifically-enriched public culture' (ibid.: 1309), an approach that underpinned the development of a 'Berlin school' of landscape design, in which everything is designed to look as if it was found (Geiger & Hennecke 2015: 236). While the aesthetic of emergent urban wilderness was less dependent on volunteer labour than the ecological restoration at Crissy Field, activist scientists and designers nonetheless turned to user-oriented design and mobilised media communications. Rather than designing a landscape *per se*, they aimed to develop an 'ecological public' by catalysing a new environmental consciousness in the public audiences of landscape design.

Key forums for communicating this new ecological landscape perspective to the public included the 1985 *Bundesgartenschau* (BUGA) and 1987 International Building Exhibition (IBA) in West Berlin. In the case of the former, an 'emergent vegetation' section presented swaths of land cleared five and two years prior as a means of communicating the value of the biodiversity that existed in liminal spaces around the city (Sukopp & Launhardt 1985). Additionally, promotional literature encouraged visitors to replace their own manicured lawns with more ecologically valuable spontaneous vegetation (Bundesgartenschau Berlin 1985). This intersection between urban environmental communication and landscape design foreshadowed a similar campaign at the International Building Exhibition 1987 (IBA), also known for showcasing public engagement (Akcan 2018), including the mobilisation of residents of inner-city tenements to maintain gardens in their courtyards (Heinze & Jäger 1987). However, perhaps the most crucial venue for this new approach to the urban landscape emerged from the construction of a new German Museum of Technology (DTM), influenced by the Exploratorium and planned during the IBA for the *Gleisdreieck*.

Part of a larger railyard bombed during the Second World War, the *Gleisdreieck* was an important site for the production of ecological knowledge for the Berlin School of Urban Ecology. These scientists were then drawn into political conflicts when residents organised against post-war reconstruction plans that called for a highway known as the 'West-Tangent' through the railyard corridor. By the end of the 1970s, scientists were publicising the high species counts of the *Gleisdreieck*, arguing that it was more valuable than traditional green spaces such as the *Tiergarten*. A collective of activists and researchers formed the *Bürgerinitiative Westtangente* (citizens' movement West-tangent) to oppose highway construction, becoming one of Germany's most important environmental movements in the process (Engelke 2011). A major feature of *Bürgerinitiative Westtangente* and related movements was the use of alternative media and handmade zines, which featured counter-designs for the *Gleisdreieck* area, ecological survey results, and protest art (Häußermann 1976; Markham 2005; Westtangente 1976). Once plans for the highway were shelved, activists and ecologists fought against the reactivation of the railyard, advocating for a reclassification of the area as nature conservation zones, park spaces, and green corridors (Behrens et al. 1982). In a nod to this social movement, the designers of the landscape around the DTM drew on ecological evaluations conducted by researchers at the Technical University of Berlin and blended redundant infrastructure and technological artefacts with novel emergent vegetation, highlighted by signage that repositioned the landscape as part of an exhibition display (Göhler 1991). The *Museumspark* surrounding the DTM served as an important precedent for subsequent designs for nature parks in the surrounding wastelands along the larger defunct rail corridor.

The continuation of these development activities was organised by *Grün Berlin GmbH*, a state-owned non-profit that facilitated public engagement and ecological management of Berlin's large green spaces following the unification of Germany (Liebold & Liebold 1991). While *Grün Berlin GmbH* emerged under somewhat different conditions from the NGOs involved in the Crissy Field case, it carried out similar communicative functions of performing public engagement and framing the value of 'messy ecosystems' (Nassauer 1995) – both activities deemed beyond the capacity of the conventional state apparatus. *Grün Berlin* facilitated the planning and design of a larger park at the *Gleisdreieck*, as well as a nature park at the *Süd Gelände* (the southern end of the railyard corridor; Mohrmann 2002). The latter's re-zoning as a nature protection area triggered debates between ecologists, who wanted to manage the vegetation to maximise biodiversity and therefore to restrict access to the area, and activists, who saw this as 'fascist ecology' (Gandy 2013) and wished to allow unimpeded growth, even if this would ultimately stabilise into a less biodiverse ecotope. Opening the museum into the urban landscape as an outdoor laboratory or demonstration landscape thus relied on designing spaces that could mediate between these competing valuations of 'fourth nature'. Just as at Crissy Field, where design functioned as a material rhetoric to highlight 'natural processes at work', conflict over managing emergent vegetation in Berlin reveals a 'disjuncture between scientific understandings of urban space and mediated discourses of nature for consumption or recreation' (Gandy 2013: 1307).

In the end, *Grün Berlin GmbH* insisted on more public access and a balance between overgrowth and ecological management. For the opening of the *Süd-Gelände* park, as part of a sustainability showcase at the Expo 2000, industrial artists from a studio adjacent to *Süd-Gelände* created a 'walkable sculpture' out of steel that divided the landscape up into different areas of use, with signage describing the different weedy yet protected emergent ecosystems (Grün Berlin GmbH 2000). The use of the sculpture also underscores the increasing importance of art and cultural production in place-based ecological communication – another way the museum may be thought to have extended into the landscape.

The two cases therefore present contrasting conceptions of urban nature, from the 'Berlin-school' of landscape design, with its emphasis on messy emergent ecosystems, and the labour- and capital-intensive restoration of Crissy Field. However, both cases evidence the ways that design and the communication of science in public space coalesced within the new urban environmental political dynamics of the late 20th century. Each case shows the importance of interactivity in the production of urban nature, and the ways that questions about access versus protection may slip into the interpretative visual regime of the museum. The exhibition-style staging of the landscape found in Crissy Field or the *Gleisdreieck* thus contributes to a dilemma dubbed the 'museumification of nature', defined as a process in which aspects of the everyday world are transformed such that people think and act as if they were within a museum (Gobster 2007). Museumification thus includes ecological design tactics such as boardwalks that direct movement through a site, fencing that provides a physical or symbolic barrier, or labelling plants in ways that imply the site is more a botanical collection than a living ecosystem. In both of the case studies discussed here, park managers are developing methods for dealing with the problem of museumification, and therefore seeking to actively expand methods for communicating science to the public in ecological parks. These moves, as I discuss in the next section, continue to reconfigure the body as the site of ecological knowledge, drawing even further on the interactive model of science communication pioneered by the Exploratorium (Barry 1998).

5.6 RESPONSES TO THE MUSEUMIFICATION OF NATURE

In San Francisco, a key instance of managing 'museumification' can be seen in plans for the New Presidio Parkway, an extension of the 1997 Crissy Field marsh project. This new park space includes a 'learning landscape', framed as an 'active' landscape and linking the Crissy Field Center and the restored marsh (James Corner Field Operations 2015). This learning landscape is available on a drop-in basis and acts as an adjunct to more structured environmental education programming. The design aims to provide a 'place-based experience and play environment' and 'high-quality, immersive environmental education' (Rayes 2017: n.n.). Within it, pathways link different spaces – 'rooms' – that can support the addition of 'environmental and place-based educational, play installations and features' where children and families can gather to 'learn, discover, gather and create' (James Corner Field Operations 2015: 124). These rooms sit within a larger 'cohesive dune landscape' that surrounds a botanical garden and examples of coastal, prairie, and wildflower habitats (ibid.). According to Presidio Trust landscape architects, 'kids learn when they are allowed to play freely … putting out signs and exhibitory is not how kids will be able to learn' (Rayes 2017: n.n.). The aim is thus to give children 'full body' experiences through which they can learn how to take risks, with the landscape becoming increasingly risky as they move outwards (ibid.). The design aims to be relatively free from parental supervision, permitting children to graduate from one level of risk to the next on their own.

In Germany, landscape architects have developed the *Naturerfahrungsraum* (or nature experience space, NER) as a response to museumification (Stopka & Rank 2013). Reflecting the 'Berlin-school' landscape aesthetic, 'nature' in this space is determined not by the presence (and labelling) of specific species but by an impression of 'real nature' which emerges spontaneously (Reidl et al. 2003). The roots of NERs can be traced to post-war Europe and the development of adventure or junk playgrounds (Kozlovsky 2008). By the end of the 1960s, adventure playgrounds had been embraced by communities interested in unstructured play (Cooper 1970). However, beyond the pedagogical emphasis of the Adventure Playground, where the primary goal is the facilitation of imaginative experiences, the NER is specifically grounded in the ecological objectives of the sustainable urban park. This includes fostering biodiversity and support for urban climate measures through developing environmental consciousness (Rink & Herbst 2011; Schemel 2004).

While the idea of the NER emerged out of research on nature pedagogy and through gradual refinements in Adventure Playground design, the context of its implementation in the urban landscape speaks to the contradictions of the museumification of nature. The first NER in Berlin is located in the *Gleisdreick Park* adjacent to the DTM's *Museumsgarten*. The larger Gleisdreieck Park's central location is critical, since its development as a park space began in the late 1990s as ecological compensation for the nearby *Potsdamer Platz* mega urban redevelopment project. Due to its proximity to the urban centre, and anticipated high visitor numbers, the designers opted against preserving wide swathes of biotopes. Rather than the prohibition signs associated with nature conservation, they aimed for an environmental graphic schema intended to solicit desire – signs that read, for instance, 'Discover Me!' – which they saw as appropriate to an open and public urban environment (Grosch et al. 2016). While some 'urban wilderness' areas are fenced off from the public and annotated with environmental graphics in a way that evokes the notion of the ecological park as a natural museum or 'outdoor laboratory' (Kupper 2016), the NER ameliorates this distancing from nature by providing a nature experience for children in the renovated and accessible park.

The development of the learning landscape at Crissy Field and the NER at the *Gleisdreick* reflect current responses to the museumification of nature. While aspects of both landscapes remain 'museumified', making use of signage and guided experiences, these new spaces simulate or recreate the tactile experiences that were involved in the production of the parks in the 1990s and 2000s. These efforts can therefore be read not so much as a demuseumification, or a move away from interpretation, but as a more explicit incorporation of continuous and expanded notions of interactivity within an interpretative strategy.

5.7 CONCLUSION

This chapter has outlined some of the intertwined developments in ecological science, public participation, and park design. It has described shifts in museums towards a 'science centre' model and the transfer of museological techniques of communication and education into public parks. We have observed the ways in which the construction of new parks and museums, through their spatial arrangements and distinctive materialities, produced specific kinds of 'ecological publics' framed as actively interested in, and practitioners of, urban ecology. These cases thus offer a key opportunity that allows us to observe the ways in which spaces, publics, and public knowledges (and knowledge-based behaviours) are made together.

These new kinds of public spaces and concomitant new ideas of nature as urban also came with a transfer of responsibility from the state to new actors, non-governmental organisations (in the cases presented, the Golden Gate National Park Conservancy and *Grün Berlin GmbH*). The establishment of these institutions and the formalisation of specific ideas of urban nature revealed a new set of problems. Preserving an 'urban wilderness' inevitably means restricting access, resulting in 'museumification'. As a return to a more explicitly interpretative visual regime, this could be considered a way of constructing the landscape as an image for detached observation in the Victorian tradition of the Natural History Museum. Standing in contrast with the ideal of an environment for immersive interaction, this flattening of the landscape runs counter to the aims of those who seek to reveal the ecologies of risk embodied in the post-industrial landscape (Meyer 2007). Both the 'learning landscape' of Crissy Field and the *Naturerfahrungsraum* reflect this shift from interaction to interpretation and back to interaction again. The final materialisation of interaction, however, is a simulated and planned engagement with nature that seeks to communicate, in a carefully controlled manner, embodied familiarity with environmental risk.

While beyond the scope of this chapter, the ways in which landscape interactivity is designed into and simulated within the *Naturerfahrungsraum* and the Learning Landscape also parallels the adoption by park NGOs of digital applications for participating in park design and engaging in citizen science research (Owens & Wolch 2019). One important area for further research is thus the ways in which these forms of digital interactivity intersect with engagement with parks as physical spaces, and how these intersections serve to further constitute ecological publics. However, it is notable that both the *Naturerfahrungraum* and Learning Landscape are seen in part as antidotes to screen addiction and the widespread proliferation of digital technologies in everyday life. While the various derivations of the adventure playground seem adequate to address the problem of park managers desiring a 'hands-on nature experience' for their young constituents, the environmental prerogatives of the next generation of ecological citizens remains to be seen. Time will tell how landscapes, public engagement with nature, and ecological citizens are co-produced, and their relations negotiated, in these latest experiments.

ACKNOWLEDGEMENTS

The author would like to thank the editors of this volume for their insightful feedback and the Berkeley Institute for European Studies and the Presidio Archives and Records Center for supporting the underlying research.

REFERENCES

Agassiz, Louis 1862. 'On the Arrangement of Natural-History Collections'. *Annals and Magazine of Natural History* 9 (53): 415–419.

Akcan, Esra. 2018. *Open Architecture: Migration, Citizenship, and the Urban Renewal of Berlin-Kreuzberg by IBA-1984/87*. Boston, MA: Birkhauser.

Arnstein, Sherry R. 1969. 'A Ladder of Citizen Participation'. *Journal of the American Institute of Planners* 35 (4): 216–224.

Barry, Andrew. 1998. 'On Interactivity: Consumers, Citizens and Culture'. In Sharon MacDonald (ed.), *The Politics of Display: Museums, Science, Culture*, pp. 85–102. Abingdon: Routledge.

Beck, Ulrich. 1994. *Reflexive Modernization: Politics, Tradition and Aesthetics in the Modern Social Order*. Palo Alto, CA: Stanford University Press.

Behrens, M., B. Hühn, and E. Karbowski. 1982. 'Naturschutz in Der Stadt Berlin-Gleisdreieck'. *Landschaftsentwicklung Und Umweltforschung* 14: 163–228.

Bennett, Tony. 1995. *The Birth of the Museum: History, Theory, Politics* (Culture: Policies and Politics series). Abingdon and New York: Routledge.

Benson, Etienne. 2010. *Wired Wilderness: Technologies of Tracking and the Making of Modern Wildlife*. Baltimore, MD: Johns Hopkins University Press.

Benton-Short, Lisa. 1998. *The Presidio: From Army Post to National Park*. Lebanon, NH: University Press of New England.

Berkowitz, Carin, and Bernard Lightman. 2017. *Science Museums in Transition: Cultures of Display in Nineteenth-Century Britain and America*. Pittsburgh, PA: University of Pittsburgh Press.

Botkin, Daniel B. 1990. *Discordant Harmonies: A New Ecology for the Twenty-First Century*. Oxford: Oxford University Press.

Bundesgartenschau Berlin. 1985. *Wie die Natur es will: Spontanvegetation auf der Bundesgartenschau*. Berlin: Bundesgartenschau Berlin 1985.

Carr, Ethan. 2007. *Mission 66: Modernism and the National Park Dilemma*. Amherst, MA: University of Massachusetts Press.

Castells, Manuel. 1983. *The City and the Grassroots: A Cross-Cultural Theory of Urban Social Movements*. Berkeley, CA: University of California Press.

Clavel, Pierre. 1986. *The Progressive City: Planning and Participation, 1969–1984*. New Brunswick, NJ: Rutgers University Press.

Colomina, Beatriz. 2013. 'Multi-Screen Architecture'. In Chris Berry, Janet Harbord and Rachel O. Moore (eds.), *Public Space, Media Space*, pp. 41–60. Basingstoke: Palgrave Macmillan.

Conn, Steven. 2000. *Museums and American Intellectual Life, 1876–1926*. Chicago, IL: University of Chicago Press.

Conway, Hazel. 1991. *People's Parks: The Design and Development of Victorian Parks in Britain*. Cambridge: Cambridge University Press.

Cooper, Clare. 1970. *The Adventure Playground: Creative Play in an Urban Setting and a Potential Focus for Community Involvement*. Center for Planning and Development Research. Working Paper, no. 118. University of California, Berkeley.

Cranz, Galen, and Michael Boland. 2004. 'Defining the Sustainable Park: A Fifth Model for Urban Parks'. *Landscape Journal* 23 (2): 102–120.

Cronon, William. 1996. 'The Trouble with Wilderness: Or, Getting Back to the Wrong Nature'. *Environmental History* 1 (1): 7–28.

Daston, Lorraine, and Peter Galison. 2007. *Objectivity*. New York: Zone Books.

Dutta, Arindam, Stephanie Marie Turek, Michael Kubo, Jennifer Yeesue Chuong, and Irina Chernyakova (eds.). 2013. *A Second Modernism: MIT, Architecture, and the 'Techno-Social' Moment*. Cambridge, MA: The MIT Press.

Engelke, Peter. 2011. 'Green City Origins: Democratic Resistance to the Auto-Oriented City in West Germany, 1960–1990.' Dissertation, Georgetown University, Washington, DC.

Farías, Ignacio, and Anders Blok. 2017. 'STS in the City'. In Ulrike Felt, Rayvon Fouché, Clark A. Miller, and Laurel Smith-Doerr (eds.), *The Handbook of Science and Technology Studies*. Cambridge, MA: The MIT Press.

Felt, Ulrike, and Maximilian Fochler. 2010. 'Machineries for Making Publics: Inscribing and De-Scribing Publics in Public Engagement'. *Minerva* 48 (3): 219–238.

Fischer, Frank. 2018. 'Environmental Democracy: Participation, Deliberation and Citizenship'. In Magnus Boström and Debra J. Davidson (eds.), *Environment and Society*, pp. 257–280. London: Palgrave.

Futrell, J. William. 1976. 'Parks to the People: New Directions for the National Park System'. *Emory Law Journal* 25: 255.

Galison, Peter, and Caroline A. Jones (eds.). 1998. *Picturing Science, Producing Art*. New York: Routledge.

Gandy, Matthew. 2013. 'Marginalia: Aesthetics, Ecology, and Urban Wastelands'. *Annals of the Association of American Geographers* 103 (6): 1301–1316.

Geiger, Annette, and Stefanie Hennecke. 2015. 'Gleisdreieck: A Modern Volkspark?' In Flavia Mameli and Andrea Lichtenstein (eds.), *Gleisdreieck: Parklife Berlin*, pp. 222–238. Bielefeld: Transcript.

Gieryn, Thomas F. 2000. 'A Space for Place in Sociology'. *Annual Review of Sociology* 26 (1): 463–496.

Gobster, Paul H. 2007. 'Urban Park Restoration and the "Museumificatio" of Nature'. *Nature and Culture* 2 (2): 95–114.

Göhler, Hans. 1991. *Gleisdreieck Morgen: Sechs Ideen Für Einen Park; Dokumentation*. Cottbus: Bundesgartenschau 1995.

Goldsmith, Stephen, and William D. Eggers. 2005. *Governing by Network: The New Shape of the Public Sector*. New York: Brookings Institution Press.

Griffiths, Tom, and Libby Robin (eds.). 1997. *Ecology and Empire: Environmental History of Settler Societies*. Seattle, WA: University of Washington Press.

Grosch, Leonard, Amy Klement, Constanze A. Petrow, and Leonard Grosch. 2016. *Designing Parks: Berlin's Park Am Gleisdreieck or the Art of Creating Lively Places*. Berlin: Jovis.

Gross, Michael P., and Ron Zimmerman. 2002. 'Park and Museum Interpretation: Helping Visitors Find Meaning'. *Curator: The Museum Journal* 45 (4): 265–276.

Grün Berlin GmbH. 2000. *Vor Einfahrt: Halt: ein neuer Park mit alten Geschichten: der Natur-Park Schöneberger Südgelände in Berlin*. Berlin: Jaron.

Grusin, Richard. 2008. *Culture, Technology, and the Creation of America's National Parks* (1st edition). Cambridge: Cambridge University Press.

Haraway, Donna J. 2013a. *Primate Visions: Gender, Race, and Nature in the World of Modern Science*. New York: Routledge.

Haraway, Donna J. 2013b. *Simians, Cyborgs, and Women: The Reinvention of Nature*. New York: Routledge.

Häußermann, Hartmut. 1976. 'Verkehr Und Stadtplanung'. In Bürgerinitiative West-Tangente Berlin (eds.), *Stadtautobahnen. Ein Schwarzbuch Zur Verkehrsplanung*.

Hein, Hilde S. 1990. *The Exploratorium: The Museum as Laboratory*. Washington, DC: Smithsonian Institution Press.

Heinze, Barbara, and Ruth Jäger. 1987 *Grün gegen Grau: Hofbegrünung in der Luisenstadt; ein Bericht aus Berlin-Kreuzberg*. Berlin: STERN.

Hooper-Greenhill, Eileen. 1992. *Museums and the Shaping of Knowledge*. Abingdon: Routledge.

Innes, Judith E. 1998. 'Information in Communicative Planning'. *Journal of the American Planning Association* 64 (1): 52–63.

James Corner Field Operations. 2015. 'New Presidio Parklands Project Concept Design.' Prepared for the Presidio Trust.

Joassart-Marcelli, Pascale, Jennifer Wolch, and Zia Salim. 2011. 'Building the Healthy City: The Role of Nonprofits in Creating Active Urban Parks'. *Urban Geography* 32 (5): 682–711.

Kim, Jeannie. 2004. 'Mission 66.' In Jeannie Kim and Beatriz Columina (eds.), *Cold War Hothouses: Inventing Postwar Culture, from Cockpit to Playboy*. New York: Princeton Architectural Press.

Kowarik, Ingo. 1995. 'Unkraut Oder Urwald? Natur Der Vierten Art Auf Dem Gleisdreieck'. *Bundesgartenschau Berlin*, pp. 45–55.

Kowarik, Ingo, and Andreas Langer. 2005. 'Natur-Park Südgelände: Linking Conservation and Recreation in an Abandoned Railyard in Berlin'. In Stefan Körner (ed.), *Wild Urban Woodlands*. pp. 287–299. Berlin: Springer.

Kozlovsky, Roy. 2008. *Adventure Playgrounds and Postwar Reconstruction*. New Brunswick, NJ: Rutgers University Press.

Krieger, Alex, and William S. Saunders. 2009. *Urban Design*. Minneapolis, MN: University of Minnesota Press.

Kupper, Patrick. 2016. 'Nature's Laboratories: Exploring the Intersection between Science and National Parks'. In Adrian Howkins, Jared Orsi, and Mark Fiege (eds.), *National Parks beyond the Nation: Global Perspectives on 'America's Best Idea'*, pp. 114–134. Norman, OK: University of Oklahoma Press.

Lachmund, Jens. 2013. *Greening Berlin: The Co-Production of Science, Politics, and Urban Nature*. Cambridge, MA: The MIT Press.

Latour, Bruno. 2004. *Politics of Nature*. Cambridge, MA: Harvard University Press.

Lee, Pamela M. 2013. *New Games: Postmodernism after Contemporary Art*. Abingdon: Routledge.

Leydesdorff, Loet, and Janelle Ward. 2005. 'Science Shops: A Kaleidoscope of Science–Society Collaborations in Europe'. *Public Understanding of Science* 14 (4): 353–372.

Liebold, Edda, and Rolf Liebold. 1991. 'Was Bleibt von Der BUGA 1995?' *Grünstift Forum*, October.

Macdonald, Sharon. 1998. *The Politics of Display: Museums, Science, Culture*. New York: Routledge.

Markham, William T. 2005. 'Networking Local Environmental Groups in Germany: The Rise and Fall of the Federal Alliance of Citizens' Initiatives for Environmental Protection (BBU)'. *Environmental Politics* 14 (5): 667–685.

Martin, Reinhold. 2005. *The Organizational Complex: Architecture, Media, and Corporate Space*. Cambridge, MA: The MIT Press.

Mason, Kathy S. 2004. *Natural Museums: U.S. National Parks, 1872–1916*. East Lansing, MI: Michigan State University Press.

M'Closkey, Karen. 2013. *Unearthed: The Landscapes of Hargreaves Associates*. Philadelphia, PA: University of Pennsylvania Press.

Meyer, Amy, and Randolph Delehanty. 2006. *New Guardians for the Golden Gate: How America Got a Great National Park*. Berkeley, CA: University of California Press.

Meyer, Elizabeth K. 2007. 'Uncertain Parks: Disturbed Sites, Citizens, and Risk Society'. In Julia Czerniak and George Hargreaves (eds.), *Large Parks*, pp. 58–85. New York: Princeton Architectural Press.

Mitchell, Timothy. 1991. *Colonising Egypt*. Berkeley, CA: University of California Press.

Mohrmann, Rita. 2002. 'Beitrag Der Landschaftsplanung Zur Städtischen Freiraumgestaltung: Beispiel Natur-Park Schöneberger Südgelände in Berlin'. *Landschaftsplanung in Der Praxis–Stuttgart: S*, pp. 328–354.

Murray, David. 1904. *Museums, Their History and Their Use: With a Bibliography and List of Museums in the United Kingdom* (Vol. 1). Glasgow: J. MacLehose and Sons.

Nassauer, Joan Iverson. 1995. 'Messy Ecosystems, Orderly Frames'. *Landscape Journal* 14 (2): 161–170.

Ogawa, Rodney T., Molly Loomis, and Rhiannon Crain. 2009. 'Institutional History of an Interactive Science Center: The Founding and Development of the Exploratorium'. *Science Education* 93 (2): 269–292.

Owens, Marcus, and Jennifer Wolch. 2019. 'Media Ecologies of Re-Wilding Cities'. In Natolie Pettorelli (ed.), *Re-Wilding*. Cambridge: Cambridge University Press.

Pratt, Mary Louise. 2007. *Imperial Eyes: Travel Writing and Transculturation*. New York: Routledge.

Rayes, Rania. 2017. 'Interview with Rania Reyes'. San Francisco.

Reidl, Konrad, Hans-Joachim Schemel, and E. Langer. 2003. 'Naturerfahrungsräume Im Städtischen Bereich. Konzeption Und Erste Ergebnisse Eines Anwendungsbezogenen Forschungsprojekts'. *Naturschutz Und Landschaftsplanung* 35 (11): 325–331.

Rink, Dieter, and Harriet Herbst. 2011. 'From Wasteland to Wilderness – Aspects of a New Form of Urban Nature'. In Matthias Richter and Ulrike Weiland (eds.), *Applied Urban Ecology: A Global Framework*, pp. 82–92. Oxford: Blackwell.

Rothman, Hal. 2004. *The New Urban Park: Golden Gate National Recreation Area and Civic Environmentalism*. Lawrence, KS: University Press of Kansas.

Rudwick, Martin J. S. 1992. *Scenes from Deep Time: Early Pictorial Representations of the Prehistoric World*. Chicago, IL: University of Chicago Press.

Schemel, Hans-Joachim. 2004. 'Emotionaler Naturschutz – zur Bedeutung von Gefühlen in naturschutzrelevanten Entscheidungsprozessen'. In *Natur und Landschaft*, Jg. 79, Heft 8.

Schön, Donald A. 1991. *The Reflective Practitioner: How Professionals Think in Action*. Abingdon: Routledge.

Sellars, Richard West. 2009. *Preserving Nature in the National Parks: A History*. New Haven, CT: Yale University Press.

Stopka, Irma, and Sandra Rank. 2013. *Naturerfahrungsräume in Gross Städten: Wege Zur Etablierung Im Öffentlichen Freiraum*. Bundesamt für Naturschutz.

Sukopp, H., and Martin Launhardt. 1985. 'Spontanvegetation Im Berliner Stadtgebiet Und Auf Der Bundesgartenschau'. *Gartenpraxis* 5: 16–18.

Westtangente, Bürgerinitiative. 1976. *Stadtautobahnen. Ein Schwarzbuch Zur Verkehrsplanung*. Self-published.

Wirth, Conrad Louis. 1980. *Parks, Politics, and the People*. Norman, OK: University of Oklahoma Press.

Wolch, Jennifer R. 1990. *The Shadow State: Transformations in the Voluntary Sector*. New York: The Foundation Center.

Reflections and Connections

Dorothea Born's chapter brings together three key aspects of science communication: popular science magazines, climate change communication, and the use of images and visuals. She is further concerned with an issue that is central to our discussions in Chapters 2 and 3, and to the volume as a whole: that of how particular scientific facts may be gradually *assembled and stabilised* through public communication. In this case, she looks at how the controversial topic of climate change became established as factual within the 'knowing space' of *National Geographic* magazine.

The chapter therefore offers a case study of how images can be investigated and the ways in which they work, in combination with text, to *make 'scientific facts' public*, thus establishing them as public facts. Born's detailed examination of images (from graphs to schemes and photos) in *National Geographic* shows that over time they perform climate science in different ways: earlier graphics can be read as depicting scientific uncertainty, allowing one to understand climate change as a 'natural' occurrence. In later years, human-induced climate change is stabilised as a fact within the space of the magazine. It is 'unnatural' – and therefore the focus shifts to showing its consequences, rather than discussing climate change itself. This shift also results in different *values* being at play. If climate change is induced by human activity, then the issue of responsibility can be addressed. The construction of climate change as factual therefore allows for particular kinds of political and moral arguments: about blame, responsibility, or the need for action.

Born thus nicely shows how science and social worlds are co-produced in climate change communication. She also charts the way in which science is depicted through *National Geographic*'s imagery and text. It is, she suggests, frequently framed as a puzzle-solving activity, which entails the idea that *uncertainty or non-knowledge* is only a temporary condition, which can in principle be remedied as new insights are produced.

6

VISUAL CLIMATE COMMUNICATION: MAKING FACTS AND CONCERNS IN POPULAR SCIENCE MAGAZINES

DOROTHEA BORN

6.1 INTRODUCTION

In November 2015, a whole issue of *National Geographic*, one of the most widely read and influential popular science magazines (Whitley & Kalof 2014), was devoted to the topic of climate change. The cover was adorned with the iconic 'blue marble', an image of earth as seen from outer space, and upon it, written in white letters, the simple message: 'Cool it.'

Climate change is here presented as a fact, connected to an explicit call to proceed against its causes and mitigate its consequences. In the US context, where many Republican Party members are still vehemently committed to denying (at least the anthropogenic causes of) the phenomenon, and at a time when Donald Trump was soon to be elected as president, this could certainly be regarded as a political message. Yet employees of *National Geographic*, with whom I talked just a few months later, would deny that their climate change reporting is political. Climate change, they would argue, is simply a scientific fact and thus of concern for the American public.

National Geographic's claims of the facticity of climate change, therefore, are situated in a highly contested political space, and are simultaneously tied to imaginations of science being 'objective' and above political controversies. Yet the debate over the facticity of anthropogenic climate change is itself visible within the historic development of *National Geographic*'s climate change discourse. So how has this controversially debated issue become a 'scientific fact' in this popular science magazine?

With its self-proclaimed educational mandate to generate a 'planet in balance',[1] primarily targeting a middle-class readership, *National Geographic* holds a position to participate in the shaping of public imaginations of science, nature, and culture (Lutz & Collins 1993), and thus constitutes an important communicative space where issues such as climate change are shaped, framed, and negotiated. This chapter explores the discourse on climate change within *National Geographic*, and in particular the way in which debates about anthropogenic climate change became settled within this magazine. Drawing on articles published over 20 years, I show how climate change was discursively established and stabilised as a 'scientific fact', as well as transformed and solidified as a 'public fact' within the communicative space of this popular science magazine.

As contemporary science communication is heterogeneous (see Section 2.4 in this volume) and increasingly relies on interrelated modes of representation (audio, visual, textual) to create meaning (Davies & Horst 2016), I follow the approach of multimodal critical discourse analysis (MCDA) (Machin & Mayr 2012) to study the interactions and choreographies of the visual and the verbal within *National Geographic*'s climate change discourse.

I start by looking at the specificities of popular science magazines as spaces for science communication and the importance of the visual within these magazines. Next, I introduce my case study, explaining how I employed MCDA to reconstruct *National Geographic*'s climate change discourse. Using selected visual material, I then show how, over time, anthropogenic climate change was gradually transformed into an unquestionable scientific fact and that at the same time changes in climate were increasingly framed as 'unnatural' and thus human-induced. I further discuss how these two discursive strategies allow for different ways of doing politics and display specific rationales for how public claims can be made. Stressing the importance of the visual, I show that the way the discourse is built provides a particular narrative framework that enables a certain way of storytelling. By conceptualising popular science magazines as specific 'knowing spaces' (Law 2017: 47), I also look at what practices of looking and reading, what imaginations of science, and what publics are co-produced (Jasanoff 2004) within the knowing spaces of these magazines.

---

[1] See: www.nationalgeographic.org/about-us/

6.2 SCIENCE COMMUNICATION AND POPULAR SCIENCE MAGAZINES

Popular science magazines are particularly interesting spaces within the 'eco-system of science communication' (Davies & Horst 2016: 5) because they are located between scientific journals and the mass media (Stöckel et al. 2009). They follow the logics of media production, while also being committed to the scientific community in how they present, reproduce, and thus produce knowledge. Those creating these magazines often conceive their role as trans-mitters of science, leading to particular logics in the production of articles (Born 2018b). Specific research topics or discoveries are turned into appealing stories, and scientific knowledge is not only selected but also re-contextualised (Pramling & Säljö 2007), transformed, synthesised, and visualised (Hommrich & Isenkenmeier 2016), creating the distinct literary genre of popular science (Jurdant 1993). Popular science magazines can be understood as a particular kind of 'knowing space' (Law 2017: 47; also see Chapter 2 in this volume), where popular-scientific knowledge is produced, by following specific rules and practices con-cerning how knowledge claims can be discursively established and stabilised.

During the earlier days of scientific journals there was no clear boundary between 'scientific' and more 'popular' science writings. But with the increas-ing sophistication of science during the 19th century, science stories became more complex and were written for more specialised audiences (Bazerman 1988). Many popular science magazines were established during that time, often developing out of scientific journals (Bowler 2009), which explains why popular science magazines are often conceived as being obliged to report 'true scientific facts'. This self-imposed credo of scientificity (i.e., being as scienti-cally correct as possible) is manifest in the production processes of popular science magazines – for instance, through rigorous fact-checking or basing articles on original scientific papers – as well as being expected by readers of these magazines (Born 2018b).

Audiences of popular science magazines are diverse, ranging from research-ers who want to stay up to date about scientific developments outside their immediate specialisation (Ricci 2010) to interested amateurs looking for sci-ence news and entertainment (Bowler 2009). This is a specific and rather specialised public, a public both real and imagined. Journalists and publish-ers behind popular science magazines often commission audience reception surveys or reader interviews and study sales statistics and web-commentar-ies in order to adapt the magazines' communication strategies accordingly. While popular science magazines create their publics through each issue, they are also shaped by the opinions and purchasing practices of their read-ers (Felt & Fochler 2010). Being thus co-created with their publics, these magazines can also be regarded as laboratories where certain socio-scientific knowledge can be tested in order to withstand public opinions and scrutiny (Oudshoorn 2003).

6.3 SCIENCE COMMUNICATION AND THE IMPORTANCE OF THE VISUAL

While images and visualisations are an intrinsic part of scientific knowledge production (Coopmans et al. 2014), they have also become 'a vital part of almost any kind of science communication' (Davies & Horst 2016: 162). As our contemporary 'visual culture' is characterised both by the social creation of the visual and the visual creation of the social (Mitchell 2002), it is important to consider what visions of science are co-produced with what imaginations of society (Hüppauf & Weingart 2008). Images are never innocent nor arbitrary but are used with the intention of achieving specific ends (Schneider & Nocke 2014), such as evoking strong emotional reactions (Joffe 2008). These intentions are, however, often concealed by the idea of 'photographic truth', whereby images are seen as portraying objective reality (O'Neill & Smith 2014). This powerful concept needs active and reflexive deconstruction (Clarke 2005) through investigating the 'visual logics' (Burri 2012: 55) of images in their social context, asking what kind of work they do and how it is achieved.

Even if clearly deployed as a strategic means of communication, images also have a life of their own. They have multiple meanings (O'Neill & Smith 2014) and can be understood as spaces of negotiation, within which different forms of knowledge can be presented in parallel. Their final meanings are made through an interplay of the images themselves, their sites of production and circulation, and the views and interpretations of their audiences (Rose 2016).

Within popular science, visuals perform important tasks. They not only serve to provide information and enable understanding of complex scientific matters, but also have to be aesthetically appealing and communicate emotions and feelings (Hommrich & Isenkenmeier 2016). While their selection and production are highly complex, entailing negotiation processes between photographers, photo editors, and layout designers (Lutz & Collins 1993), they themselves can become a selection criterion for certain stories: if a topic cannot be visualised, it will simply not be told (Born 2018b).

In the context of climate change communication, images provide powerful but also challenging tools. Because of the issue's complexity – it involves different scientific disciplines and political actors, global scales as well as intricate temporalities – knowledge about climate change is difficult to communicate. Images and visualisations offer helpful resources to make this abstract issue more tangible (O'Neill & Smith 2014). But climate change visuals can also pose challenges as the issue's future consequences should (ideally) be prevented and therefore cannot yet be shown (Doyle 2011).

These difficulties also become evident when looking at *National Geographic*'s different strategies to visually communicate climate change. One strategy was to build up the icon of the polar bear as a figure of identification (Born 2018a). But polar bears are just one aspect of the highly complex visual and verbal climate change discourse in *National Geographic*. As I will show, within this discourse, images and visualisations played an important role in establishing climate change not only as a matter of fact, but also as a matter of concern (Latour 2004b).

6.4 THE CASE STUDY AND RESEARCH APPROACH

National Geographic was founded in 1888 as the official magazine of the National Geographic Society. Originally intended as a scientific journal, it was formed to support the establishment of geography as a distinct scientific discipline (Pauly 1979), but gradually developed into a more 'middlebrow' magazine (Lutz & Collins 1993: 20). The increasing publication of images, which was enabled by a reduction in the costs for photo engraving after 1900, further supported this development, as more images left less space for articles within the magazine's pages (Hawkins 2010). *National Geographic* therefore has a long and special relation to the visual. Self-defined as a 'visual magazine', it has been called a 'generator of icons' (ibid.: 1) and is assumed to influence the American public's popular consciousness and national imagination (Lutz & Collins 1993). Its broad influence and large readership (*National Geographic* has a global circulation of about 6.7 million, of whom 3.5 million are based in the US) make it a key space in which to study the visual communication of climate change and how this controversial topic has been (visually) stabilised as a public fact.

This research uses a framework of multimodal critical discourse analysis (MCDA; Machin & Mayr 2012). MCDA analyses the specific qualities as well as interplays of different modes (e.g., verbal, visual, auditory) of meaning-making within discourses, thereby critically investigating the interrelations between discourses, power, and ideology (ibid.). Discourses are defined as 'context-dependent semiotic practices ... situated within specific fields of social action', being 'socially constructed and socially constitutive' (Meyer & Wodak 2015: 27).

As the 'principle of triangulation' encourages the use of various methods (Reisigl & Wodak 2015: 26), I further designed my own analytical toolbox. Following Keller (2005), I primarily analysed texts using grounded-theory coding (Charmaz 2006) but also paid attention to how linguistic devices create meaning (Reisigl & Wodak 2015: 33). I attended to tropes and specific semantic rhetorical figures, such as metaphors, irony, metonymies, or synecdoches (Gouthier & Di Bari 2003), and their role in naming and discursively constructing the issue of climate change. Another important linguistic device I analysed was the use of topoi – common viewpoints from which arguments can be built.

The analysed material comprises all feature articles on climate change published in *National Geographic* between 1990 and 2012. This sample was retrieved using The Complete National Geographic DVD Collection and comprises 31 articles, including over 400 images. After writing memos for each article, I summarised the different themes and shifts of the discourse. Based on this analysis, I selected 13 articles,[2] which cover topical and qualitative shifts within the discourse particularly well, for closer analysis.

This final sample contained heterogeneous material consisting of headings, running text, picture captions, and 227 visualisations, of which the majority were photographs but which also included maps, charts, graphs, and illustrations. Adapting Müller-Doohm's type-building approach (Müller-Doohm 1996), I synthesised this large number of images: proceeding in chronological order of publication, I grouped the images of each article regarding their primary messages, the depicted objects or persons, and their stylistic features. I then selected representative images, paying attention to their distribution over time. In this way, I could discern the 'iconography of climate change' (Manzo 2010: 96) within *National Geographic* over time. Finally, I conducted comparative single-image analyses with visualisations published at different points in time that best captured the changes of the visual discourse, following Van Leeuwen's combination of semiotics and iconography (Van Leeuwen 2000). I further analysed the article's text in a second round of focused coding. Yet in order to analyse the choreography of the different modes of representation, it proved essential to view the various forms of text and images in conjunction. My final analysis thus evolved out of the combination and synthesis of these different analytical methods.

6.5 ANALYSIS: CLIMATE CHANGE IN *NATIONAL GEOGRAPHIC*

Analysing the chronological development of the climate change discourse in *National Geographic*, I could discern fundamental changes in the verbal and visual framing of the issue, whereby changes in one mode are always reflected in the other. Overall, I distinguish two distinct phases of the discourse. Phase 1 lasts from May 1998 until September 2004, with articles predominantly concerned with establishing the science of climate change, during which the dominant iconography to visualise climate change is also built up: melting glaciers, smoking factory chimneys, burning forests, and dried-up soil. I demarcated this first phase as capturing the process whereby climate change is discursively stabilised as a 'scientific fact' within the particular 'knowing

---

[2] The full list of articles as well as those selected for more detailed analysis are available on the web resource Phaeidra: https://phaidra.univie.ac.at/view/o:976124

space' of *National Geographic*. As I will show in my analysis, while in a feature from 1998 the anthropogenic causes of climate change are still contested, over following articles the level of scientific certainty about anthropogenic climate change gradually increases. Finally, in February 2004, an article explicitly acknowledges it as a fact and marks what I describe as the 'turning point' within *National Geographic*'s climate change discourse.

After 2004, I observed a shift in discourse towards showing the effects of climate change, focusing on affected animals, regions, or people, which I have defined as the second phase of the discourse, lasting from 2005 until the end of the dataset (2012). In this second phase, single aspects of the iconography are taken up, for example in stories on retreating glaciers or Inuit hunters. Here images play an important role in further solidifying the 'factictiy' of climate change by showing evidence for it. Furthermore, from 2007 there is an additional thematic diversification of the discourse. Climate change becomes connected to larger issues such as world population, food security, and energy consumption. These serve both as the backdrop to articles as well as a discursive resource to undergird argumentative claims.

It is striking that issues that were contested in the beginning of the discourse are framed as factual in more recent articles. In order to trace this process of how (anthropogenic) climate change became discursively established as a fact, I now want to zoom into the first phase of contestation and stabilisation.

6.6 FROM TENTATIVE TREND TO SCIENTIFIC FACT – ESTABLISHING CLIMATE CHANGE (1998-2004)

The increasing facticity attributed to anthropogenic climate change is achieved by the deployment of two discursive strategies: first, through the topos of scientific uncertainty, and second, through gradually changing the framing of climate change from natural to more and more human made – what I call unnaturalising climate change. In what follows, I demonstrate these two discursive strategies by recounting the development of the discourse. In particular, I focus on articles published in 1998 and 2004, comparing and contrasting the verbal and visual rhetoric deployed at the beginning and end of this first phase of *National Geographic*'s climate change discourse.

6.6.1 THE PUBLIC MAKING OF SCIENTIFIC CERTAINTY

In a feature article in *National Geographic* from May 1998, called 'Unlocking the Climate Puzzle', the Intergovernmental Panel on Climate Change (IPCC) report from 1995 is quoted: 'The amount of that [human] influence … is unknown because of "uncertainties in key factors" …. It may take a decade or more of additional research to resolve those uncertainties' (Suplee 1998: 44).

In the article, the author acknowledges the non-knowledge in this research area, in order to not make definite statements about the human causes of climate change. Instead, he argues that more scientific research is needed in order to definitely answer the question of what causes climate change. This topos of scientific uncertainty thus reveals a strong reliance on scientific research that will allow us to finally know, showing how science and scientificity are highly held virtues within the editorial department of *National Geographic*. The strong position attributed to science within verbal and visual discourse is specific to *National Geographic* and differentiates it from the mass media (O'Neill 2013). This is not only reflected in the rigorous fact-checking of the magazine's research department, but also in the way images of scientists as well as scientific visualisations support the 'scientificity' of the discourse. Furthermore, the scientific graphs also make visual arguments regarding the certainty or uncertainty of anthropogenic climate change.

Let me explore this in some depth by analysing the representation shown in Figure 6.1. Published in 1998, it shows past temperature variations (represented by a blue to orange line) based on oxygen isotope measurements retrieved from an ice-core. The yellow line displays the amount of solar radiation reaching earth. As a whole, the graph is superimposed on an image of the ice core from which these measurements are taken. The older the ice is, the more it becomes compressed over time, leading to a non-linear temporal axis from left to right. While this representation allows the viewer to link past and present changes, it also renders the interpretation of the information quite complex.

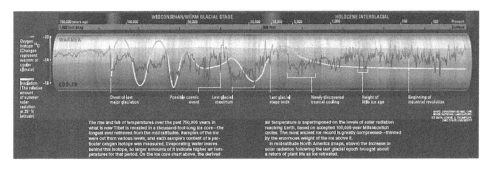

Figure 6.1   Graph from *National Geographic*, 'Unlocking the Climate Puzzle', published in May 1998. Courtesy of National Geographic Creative

Although the present period seems relatively warm – indicated by the orange and red colour – the temperature increase does not seem very pronounced. This impression is created by the non-linear time axes along which the data are presented. Past temperature variations appear very pronounced, since they cover longer time periods in smaller spaces of the graph, while recent temperature increases are more spread out and thus seem less dramatic. Showing these developments over time allows a construction of variations in climate as 'natural' and as having always occurred: present temperature increases, according to this visualisation, can be seen as part of a long natural cycle. The close observer may, however, notice that while in the past higher solar radiation has correlated with higher temperatures, towards the end of the time axis solar radiation is not increasing while temperatures are, which could indicate that the current warming trend is not part of a natural cycle. However, this is not mentioned in the picture caption; the visualisation, then, offers an alternative reading that slightly differs from the description of the graph in the text, which does not mention that current temperature increases are not correlating with increasing solar radiation.

Polysemy – diversity of meaning – within both visual and verbal modes are characteristic of the whole article from 1998, which aligns with the strategy of telling 'both sides of the story' (Nelkin 1995) typical of media coverage of climate change in the US (Boykoff & Boykoff 2004). Yet some things remain uncontested, including the trend towards warming. The seemingly balanced approach thus in fact contains a specific view in which some issues are taken for granted. This also includes an irrevocable trust in science to solve the 'climate puzzle'.

While in 1998 the topos of scientific uncertainty is evoked to argue that crucial information for solving the question of the causes for climate change is missing, this has changed by 2004. In February 2004, in 'The Case of the Missing Carbon', in *National Geographic*, the author states: 'Each year humanity dumps roughly 8 billion metric tons of carbon into the atmosphere, 6.5 billion tons from fossil fuels and 1.5 billion from deforestation. But less than half that total, 3.2 billion tons, remains in the atmosphere to warm the planet. Where is the missing carbon?' (Appenzeller, 2004: 94). The article is narrated as a detective story, in which scientists have to tackle the question of where this excess carbon is going. The topos of scientific uncertainty and the puzzle metaphor of the article from 1998 are taken up again, which creates continuity, while in the meantime one puzzle has been solved: humans are indeed seen as responsible for climate change. This article thus marks the 'turning point' within the climate change discourse, since it is the first article that explicitly links climate change to human burning of fossil fuels.

This now-established public fact is also visible in the scientific graphs used within *National Geographic* at the end of the first phase of the climate change discourse. Figure 6.2, published as part of three feature articles on climate change in September 2004, displays a very different level of certainty about climate change and its causes. It shows a correlation between carbon dioxide (CO_2) concentrations and average Northern Hemisphere surface temperatures.

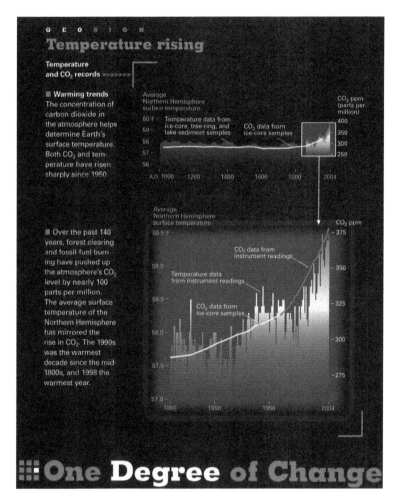

Figure 6.2 Graph from *National Geographic*, 'GeoSigns', published in September 2004. Courtesy of 5W Infographics

In contrast to Figure 6.1, the time line is not compressed and only covers the last 1000 years, leading to the graph's familiar 'hockey stick' form. The right-hand part of the graph (the heel and toe of the hockey stick) is enlarged in the lower part of the page, which depicts only the past 50 years, making the increasing temperatures of the past years even more visible. The picture captions not only explicitly state a correlation between atmospheric CO_2-concentrations and surface temperatures but also explain that 'forest clearing and fossil-fuel burning have pushed up the atmosphere's CO_2 level by nearly 100 parts per million' (*National Geographic* 2004: 20).

While the graph in Figure 6.1 from 1998 is based on a single data source, the graph in Figure 6.2 contains data from several sources, including ice-cores, tree-rings, or lake sediments. The 'scientific fact' of the correlation of CO_2 concentrations and temperature increase is thus tied into a network of arguments, problems, and data. These data are linked to many of the photographs published throughout the three feature articles from September 2004. We see a man drilling a hole into a tree, another holding an ice core, or a person taking sediment samples. These images represent the scientists retrieving the data later shown in the graphs. The choreography of images and graphs throughout these three articles suggests a direct link between the scientists in the pictures and the scientific graphs and illustrations, and reveals the interplay of the different visuals. The pictures of the scientists at work prove the 'realness' of the data and underline the scientificity of the graphs. The graphs and illustrations, in turn, complement these photos by visualising the end product: scientific evidence. *National Geographic* thus not only verbally explains the science, but also visualises the scientificity on which the whole argumentative structure of the climate change discourse is built. Moreover, this puts forward a conception of scientists as mediators between nature and culture (Latour 2004a) as scientists are depicted to observe nature, retrieve 'facts' from it, and thus make it understandable. Interestingly, such images of scientists disappear after climate change is established as a fact and are replaced by images of nature, such as comparisons of melting glaciers over time. Thus, as long as the controversy continues, we seem to need images of scientists trying to find the truth in nature, but once the controversy is settled, nature becomes the 'ultimate referee' (Latour 1987: 97).

Although the messages of the compared articles from 1998 and 2004 are different, the conception of science as the 'solver of the puzzle', implicitly referring to Kuhn's concept of 'normal science' (Kuhn 1996 [1962]), remains stable. In the mystery story, the murder happens at the beginning and it is for the detectives to uncover the truth, which at the end seems quite obvious from all the evidence collected. Anthropogenic climate change is discursively established as a scientific fact in a similar way. Who or what causes climate change is framed as a mystery, but one where scientists have now collected all the evidence such that anthropogenic climate change can no longer be challenged.

This demonstrates the important role attributed to science and scientificity within *National Geographic*'s climate change discourse. Climate change is established and stabilised as a scientific fact, using the topos of scientific uncertainty, which is based on a specific conception of science as 'solving the puzzle' and delivering evidence. Climate change can be discursively stabilised as an important concern because it is framed as 'scientifically true'. However, this does not straightforwardly allow for making moral arguments about the importance of caring for the environment. This is tackled separately through addressing and negotiating the relation between nature and culture. It is to this that I turn next to examine in more detail.

6.6.2 NATURAL CYCLES AND HUMAN INTERVENTION

The 'naturalness' or 'unnaturalness' of climate change is hotly debated during the first phase (1998–2004) and is linked to the question of human responsibility: if observed warming trends occur naturally, then nothing can be done about them; however, if they are a consequence of human activities, then humans should take responsibility. Highly moral considerations thus get linked to the outcome of efforts to answer a scientific question.

An important rhetorical figure in this debate is the trope of the 'natural cycle', which is used to (partly) explain observed warming trends by attributing them to natural cycles of climate variations. This trope imagines nature as a balanced system, which is disturbed through human interference, reinforcing a classical, modern divide between nature and culture (Latour 1993). This is not only visible in many of the photographs, which display either 'nature' or 'culture', but also in illustrations that depict this 'natural cycle'.

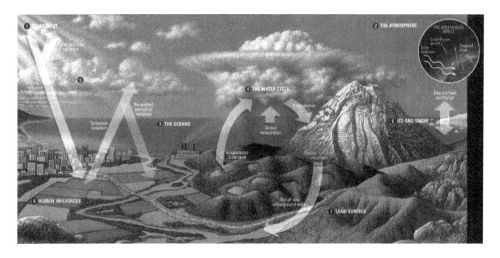

Figure 6.3 Illustration from *National Geographic*, 'Unlocking the Climate Puzzle', published in May 1998. Courtesy of Edward Gazsi/National Geographic Creative

The illustration in Figure 6.3, published in 1998 and titled 'What drives climate change?', presents a schematised version of the earth's climate system, which 'is influenced by innumerable interacting variables' (*National Geographic* 1998: 50–51). Eight factors are listed, with 'human influences' being the last on the list and the accompanying text implying overall complexity and ambiguity. While order and balance indicate that humans only minimally influence the natural system, the caption's explanation of 'human influences' acknowledges that 'human activities magnify warming effects' but also states 'aerosols … have temporary, localized cooling effects'. Overall, the page's composition points to a complex and still poorly understood global climate system where natural factors seem to predominantly matter (if we follow the list of influences). However, under close inspection, many traces of 'human influences' are visible within the illustration, such as roads leading into the mountains or forest clearances, suggesting that this category subsumes a large number of quite serious human interventions into the natural environment. The visual again allows for more multi-layered meanings than the text alone.

In the turning-point article 'The Case of the Missing Carbon' (February 2004), the author uses the previously established theme of the 'natural cycle' to argue that human interferences are bringing it 'out of balance'. The illustration in Figure 6.4 displays one such natural cycle – the carbon cycle – yet attributes a role to human interference quite different from that shown in Figure 6.3. The larger circle contains diverse forms of carbon, with the captions describing how carbon changes from one state into another. Animals blend into differently textured surfaces and photographic elements, with the various carbon deposits represented in harmonious colours. Cogwheels refer to the complexity of this interconnected system and imply a mechanistic and clockwork-like idea of these natural processes – referred to in the text as the 'finely calibrated gearing'. Most striking, however, is the separate cogwheel to the left of the main circle. In its middle is a running human figure: it is striking that this human figure is clearly gendered male. *National Geographic* thereby buys into a long tradition of using male bodies as the standard to represent humanity, as seen, for instance, in anatomy textbooks (Lawrence & Bendixen 1992) or popular depictions of scientists (Chimba & Kitzinger 2010). This cogwheel is titled 'human activity' and its spikes are connected to the cogwheel at a point titled 'coal, oil, gas deposits'. The sparks around this connection and the running figure indicate a dynamic, a turning of the wheels, an intervention into the well-functioning machinery, while additionally symbolising friction. Furthermore, the running figure also connotes speed and a possible acceleration of the system. Placing the human outside the natural cycle reinforces the nature–culture divide of earlier articles, but here the phenomenon of climate change is framed as caused by humans and therefore as 'unnatural'.

We thus witness the establishment of anthropogenic climate change as a public fact through framing it as a phenomenon caused by the human disruption of natural cycles. While in the first years of the climate change discourse in *National Geographic* observed changes in climate were attributed to the realm of nature, and humans could thus not be held accountable for it, they now verbally and visually deploy the trope of 'nature out of balance', shifting the phenomenon of climate change to the realm of culture. The powerful rhetorical figure of 'the natural cycle out of balance' is also taken up in later articles, serving to stabilise and reinforce anthropogenic climate change as a public fact.

Both these framings of climate change are based on the same conception of nature and culture as two separate realms. However, framing climate change as 'natural' marginalises cultural influences, while in the 'unnatural' framing,

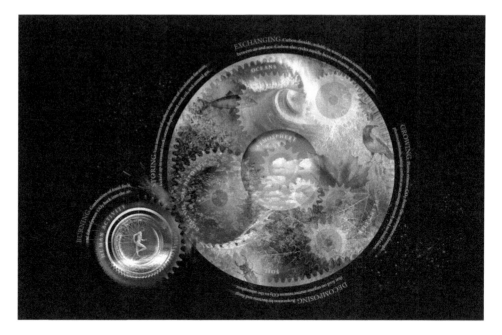

Figure 6.4 Illustration from *National Geographic*, 'The Case of the Missing Carbon', published in February 2004. Courtesy of Alicia Buelow/National Geographic Creative

humanity's impact on global climate change is used to make a moral argument for human responsibility. In other words, framings of nature and the natural are used to put forward moral statements about how humans should relate to nature.

6.7 DISCUSSION

6.7.1 POPULAR SCIENCE MAGAZINES AS POLITICAL SPACES

Zooming in on the first phase of climate change discourse in *National Geographic*, I have shown how climate change was discursively established as a scientific fact within the magazine, and thus stabilised as a public fact. This was achieved using two different discursive strategies, which were deployed through a choreography of visual and verbal modes. These discursive strategies allow for particular political arguments, and therefore also exemplify *National Geographic*'s ways of doing politics.

Stressing the scientificity of a phenomenon – and staging it as a not yet fully solved puzzle – is an argumentative strategy to depoliticise an issue. This strategy is based on a conceptualisation of science and politics as separate, where science delivers 'true facts' about nature while politics debates values (Latour 2004a). Framing climate change as a public scientific fact thus seemingly detaches it from opinion and political debates. In the US, where climate change remains controversial, building climate change stories exclusively around scientific results can be seen as a strategy to forestall anticipated critique. It also aligns with *National Geographic*'s long-standing editorial claim to report 'true and objective stories' (Lutz & Collins 1993).

Yet this strategy of 'depoliticising' climate change by framing it as a scientific puzzle also inhibits moral arguments. The latter are enabled through the second discursive strategy. Framing climate change as unnatural – induced and accelerated through human intervention – allows calls for responsibility and action, and thus also makes moral claims.

Both discursive strategies can be seen as different ways of doing politics within *National Geographic*. On the one hand, the topos of scientific uncertainty frames questions around climate change as simply in need of more scientific fact-finding. Putting scientific expert opinion at the centre, and giving little to no space to other arguments, could thus be interpreted as an effort to close a political controversy (Jasanoff 2011). On the other hand, describing climate change as 'unnatural' serves as a prerequisite for making explicit moral arguments and thus renders the topic a political concern. What both discursive strategies have in common is that they gain validity through stable conceptualisations of science, nature, and culture. They reflect and reproduce a shared understanding of the relation of science and politics that is present within US culture and that 'places science above values and preferences' (Jasanoff 2011: 135). Furthermore, they are based on a modern dichotomy of nature and culture as two realms ultimately set apart (Latour 1993). Thus, both discursive strategies also pursue ontological politics (Mol 2002) in that they make alternative conceptions of nature and culture, science, and politics invisible.

6.7.2 POPULAR SCIENCE MAGAZINES AS KNOWING SPACES

National Geographic can be regarded as a communication space that reflects wider public debates on climate change in the US, while simultaneously contributing to and intervening in these discourses. My analysis of *National Geographic*'s climate change discourse has shown how the magazine produces popular scientific knowledge, which becomes public facts. Popular science magazines thus constitute 'knowing spaces' (see Chapter 2 in this volume) which follow particular epistemic logics of claim-making, and which thereby entail particular conceptions of science, nature, culture, and their relations. There are three aspects of claim-making in these knowing spaces that are of particular note.

The first is the importance attributed to the visual in *National Geographic*. The discursive strategies I have discussed were achieved through using visuals to establish climate change as a scientific fact. The special qualities of the visual prove to be discursively powerful: their interpretative openness allows for more complex arguments than text alone, while the possibility of making climate change 'visible' by showing the effects of and thus evidence for climate change underlines its 'facticity'. The visualisations used to establish climate change evoke two different but complementary truths: photographic truth, with photos apparently showing what is 'really happening', and scientific truth, here found in scientific graphs and deemed to represent 'scientific facts'. But neither photographs nor scientific graphs are innocent representations of an external reality. Rather, they are shaped by various actors, entailing complex negotiation, selection, and production processes (Burri 2012; Lutz & Collins 1993). In return, they produce a specific reality based on the paradigm of 'seeing is believing'.

A second feature of claim-making in *National Geographic* is the imagination of science as a puzzle solver. In articles where anthropogenic climate change is still contested, many pieces of the puzzle are depicted as in place, but more are needed to put the final picture together. Through this narrative, a compelling argument for anthropogenic climate change can be made in a second step: now that all the pieces are on the table, climate science can put them together and thus solve the mystery. This reflects and reproduces Kuhn's concept of 'normal science', where scientists work together to add pieces to a specific puzzle – a scientific problem, which can be solved following the rules of the dominant paradigm (Kuhn 1996 [1962]: 35). This imagination of science as getting closer and closer to the truth through the accumulation of knowledge also applies to *National Geographic's* own practices of producing popular scientific knowledge. The narrative of puzzle-solving allows for the (retrospective) creation of a linear discourse, whereby single articles build on each other so that over time certain issues can be framed as being solved and become stabilised as facts within the magazine. As with scientific knowledge production, established facts become a 'black box' (Latour 1987: 11) upon which later articles can build in order to make new claims. The knowledge created in the magazine accumulates over time, while what is accepted as given shapes what can be further discussed or contested. This narrative further reflects and (re)produces a trajectorism typical of Western thought, 'which assumes ... a cumulative journey ... from now to then' (Appadurai 2013: 223). The conception of science as a puzzle solver retrospectively assigns a telos to the whole narrative, which evokes the impression that the story could not have ended differently. Alternative stories or contingent versions and visions of reality are deleted from the narrative. For instance, framing climate change as an explicitly political and moral question from the start could have enabled earlier calls for action, even before the 'puzzle' had been 'solved'.

Third, the internal logics of *National Geographic* also reflect a particular imagination of readers, who are implicitly conceptualised as long-term subscribers who follow developments in discussions about climate change over time. Throughout its coverage of climate change *National Geographic* develops a specific iconography for visualising climate change, the construction of which relies on and is established through a readership that continuously (re)views these images. The epistemic logics of claim-making thus depend on and (re)produce certain practices of looking and reading: an 'educated gaze' (Hawkins 2010: 22). Readers are imagined as a 'thought collective' (Fleck, 1979 [1935]) who know how to read images and put them into context, building up their knowledge as the knowledge is built up in the magazine. Thus, popular scientific knowledge and (imagined) readers and consumers of the magazine are co-created in this knowing space.

6.8 CONCLUSION

In sum, analysing climate change discourse in *National Geographic* shows how the magazine constitutes a knowing space that has its own practices of claim-making and knowledge production. The overarching credo of scientificity implies that stories have to be based on scientific research. In addition, the conception of science as a puzzle-solving entity is transferred to the magazine's own logics of meaning making: the narratives produced in and communicated through the magazine over time build on each other to create a coherent discourse of popular-scientific knowledge, thereby producing climate change as a public fact. This in turn assembles a public that not only exhibits high trust in science, but also follows this accumulation of knowledge over time.

These practices further entail specific conceptions of science, nature, and culture, and enable certain ways of doing politics. My analysis has tried to reveal some of the 'heterogeneous arrays' (Law 2017: 47) of these claim-making practices. They imply that science produces true facts about the world, while politics has to deal with their consequences. Scientists are the mediators between the separate realms of nature and culture and thus gain the authority to make scientific truth claims about the natural world (Latour 2004a). Such imaginations mobilise the specific knowing space of laboratory science and perform climate change as a reality because it is an indisputable 'scientific fact'. But these specific practices of producing scientific certainty also make other knowing spaces invisible, from lay people's embodied experiences with their changing environments to conceptions of nature and culture as ultimately entangled and co-produced. As public and political controversy on climate change continues, one might wonder how different communication practices, which do not solely rely on scientific truths for claim-making, could lead to different public understandings of climate change.

ACKNOWLEDGEMENTS

Many thanks go to all the staff at *National Geographic* who shared their insights and expertise with me, especially Denis Dimmick and Kurt Mutchler. Also, thanks to Gina Martin, who helped with the images copyright, and to 5W Infographics, who allowed the use of their material. I further want to thank everyone who read and commented on this chapter in its various forms and versions, including the anonymous reviewer. And finally, my greatest thanks to Ulrike and Sarah for all the thoughts and time they invested in my chapter.

REFERENCES

Appadurai, Arjun. 2013. *The Future as Cultural Fact: Essays on the Global Condition.* London and New York: Verso Books.

Appenzeller, Tim. 2004. 'The Case of the Missing Carbon'. *National Geographic* 204 (2): 88–117.

Bazerman, Charles. 1988. *Shaping Written Knowledge: The Genre and Activity of the Experimental Article in Science.* Madison, WI: Wisconsin Press.

Born, Dorothea. 2018a. 'Bearing Witness: Polar Bears as Icons for Climate Change Communication in National Geographic'. *Environmental Communication.* Advance online publication. https://doi.org/10.1080/17524032.2018.1435557

Born, Dorothea. 2018b. 'The Making of Popular Science: Imagining and Producing the German Popular Science Magazine GEO'. Manuscript submitted for publication.

Bowler, Peter J. 2009. *Science for All: The Popularization of Science in Early Twentieth-Century Britain.* Chicago, IL: University of Chicago Press.

Boykoff, Maxwell T., and Jules M. Boykoff. 2004. 'Balance as Bias: Global Warming and the US Prestige Press'. *Global Environmental Change* 14 (2): 125–136. https://doi.org/10.1016/j.gloenvcha.2003.10.001

Burri, Regula V. 2012. 'Visual Rationalities: Towards a Sociology of Images'. *Current Sociology* 60 (1): 45–60. doi: 10.1177/0011392111426647.

Charmaz, Kathy. 2006. *Constructing Grounded Theory: A Practical Guide through Qualitative Analysis.* Thousand Oaks, CA: Sage.

Chimba, Mwenya, and Jenny Kitzinger. 2010. 'Bimbo or Boffin? Women in Science: An Analysis of Media Representations and How Female Scientists Negotiate Cultural Contradictions'. *Public Understanding of Science* 19 (5): 609–624. doi: 10.1177/0963662508098580.

Clarke, Adele. 2005. *Situational Analysis: Grounded Theory after the Postmodern Turn.* Thousand Oaks, CA, and London: Sage.

Coopmans, Catelijne, Janet Vertesi, Michael E. Lynch, and Steve Woolgar. 2014. *Representation in Scientific Practice Revisited.* Cambridge, MA: The MIT Press.

Davies, Sarah R., and Maja Horst. 2016. *Science Communication: Culture, Identity and Citizenship.* London: Palgrave Macmillian.

Doyle, Julie. 2011. *Mediating Climate Change, Environmental Sociology.* Burlington, VT: Ashgate.

Felt, Ulrike, and Maximilian Fochler. 2010. 'Machineries for Making Publics: Inscribing and De-Scribing Publics in Public Engagement'. *Minerva* 48 (3): 219–238. https://doi.org/10.1007/s11024-010-9155-x

Fleck, Ludwik. 1979 [1935]. *Genesis and Development of a Scientific Fact.* Chicago, IL: University of Chicago Press.

Gouthier, Daniele, and Marcello Di Bari. 2003. 'Tropes, Science and Communication'. *Journal of Science Communication* 2 (1): 1–15. https://doi.org/10.22323/2.02010202

Hawkins, Stephanie L. 2010. *American Iconographic: National Geographic, Global Culture, and the Visual Imagination*. Charlottesville, VA: University of Virginia Press.

Hommrich, Dirk, and Guido Isenkenmeier. 2016. 'Visual Communication, Popular Science Journals and the Rhetoric of Evidence'. *Journal of Science Communication* 15 (2): 1–8. https://doi.org/10.22323/2.15020304

Hüppauf, Bernd R., and Peter Weingart. 2008. *Science Images and Popular Images of the Sciences*. New York: Routledge.

Jasanoff, Sheila. 2004. 'The Idiom of Co-Production'. In Sheila Jasanoff (ed.), *States of Knowledge: The Co-Production of Science and Social Order*, pp. 1–12. Abingdon and New York: Routledge.

Jasanoff, Sheila. 2011. 'Cosmopolitan Knowledge: Climate Science and Global Civic Epistemology'. In John S. Dryzek, Richard B. Norgaard & David Schlosberg (eds), *The Oxford Handbook of Climate Change and Society*, pp. 129–143. Oxford: Oxford University Press.

Joffe, Hélène 2008. 'The Power of Visual Material: Persuasion, Emotion and Identification'. *Diogenes* 55 (1): 84–93. https://doi.org/10.1177/0392192107087919

Jurdant, Baudouin. 1993. 'Popularization of Science as the Autobiography of Science'. *Public Understanding of Science* 2 (4): 365–373. https://doi.org/10.1088/0963-6625/2/4/006

Keller, Reiner. 2005. 'Analysing Discourse: An Approach from the Sociology of Knowledge'. *Forum Qualitative Sozialforschung/Forum: Qualitative Social Research* 6 (3). http://dx.doi.org/10.17169/fqs-6.3.19

Kuhn, Thomas. 1996 [1962]. *The Structure of Scientific Revolutions* (3rd edition). Chicago, IL: University of Chicago Press.

Latour, Bruno. 1987. *Science in Action: How to Follow Scientists and Engineers through Society*. Cambridge, MA: Harvard University Press.

Latour, Bruno. 1993. *We Have Never Been Modern*. Cambridge, MA: Harvard University Press.

Latour, Bruno. 2004a. *Politics of Nature: How to Bring the Sciences into Democracy*. Cambridge, MA: Harvard University Press.

Latour, Bruno. 2004b. 'Why Has Critique Run out of Steam? From Matters of Fact to Matters of Concern'. *Critical Inquiry* 30 (2): 225–248. https://doi.org/10.1086/421123

Law, John. 2017. 'STS as Method'. In Ulrike Felt, Rayvon Fouché, Clark Miller, and Laurel Smith-Doerr (eds.), *The Handbook of Science and Technology Studies*, pp. 31–57. Cambridge, MA: The MIT Press.

Lawrence, Susan C., and Kae Bendixen. 1992. 'His and Hers: Male and Female Anatomy in Anatomy Texts for U.S. Medical Students, 1890–1989'. *Social Science & Medicine* 35 (7): 925–934. https://doi.org/10.1016/0277-9536(92)90107-2

Lutz, Catherine, and Jane L. Collins. 1993. *Reading National Geographic*. Chicago, IL, and London: University of Chicago Press.

Machin, David, and Andrea Mayr. 2012. *How To Do Critical Discourse Analysis: A Multimodal Introduction*. Los Angeles, CA: Sage.

Manzo, Kate. 2010. 'Imaging Vulnerability: The Iconography of Climate Change'. *Area* 42 (1): 96–107. doi: 10.1111/j.1475-4762.2009.00887.x.

Meyer, Michael, and Ruth Wodak. 2015. *Methods of Critical Discourse Studies* (3rd edition). Thousand Oaks, CA, and London: Sage.

Mitchell, William J. T. 2002. 'Showing Seeing: A Critique of Visual Culture'. *Journal of Visual Culture* 1 (2): 165–181. https://doi.org/10.1177/147041290200100202

Mol, Annemarie. 2002. *The Body Multiple: Ontology in Medical Practice*. Durham, NC: Duke University Press.

Müller-Doohm, Stefan. 1996. 'Die kulturelle Kodierung des Schlafens oder: Wovon das Schlafzimmer ein Zeichen ist'. *Soziale Welt* 47 (1): 110–123. www.jstor.org/stable/40878132.

Nelkin, Dorothy. 1995. *Selling Science: How the Press Covers Science and Technology*. New York: W. H. Freeman.

O'Neill, Saffron J. 2013. 'Image Matters: Climate Change Imagery in US, UK and Australian Newspapers'. *Geoforum* 49: 10–19. https://doi.org/10.1016/j.geoforum.2013.04.030

O'Neill, Saffron J., and Nicholas Smith. 2014. 'Climate Change and Visual Imagery'. *Wiley Interdisciplinary Reviews: Climate Change* 5 (1): 73–87. https://doi.org/10.1002/wcc.249

Oudshoorn, Nelly. 2003. *The Male Pill: A Biography of a Technology in the Making*. Durham, NC: Duke University Press.

Pauly, Philip. 1979. 'The World and All that Is In It: The National Geographic Society, 1888–1918'. *American Quarterly* 31 (4): 517–532. doi: 10.2307/2712270

Pramling, Niklas, and Roger Säljö. 2007. 'Scientific Knowledge, Popularisation, and the Use of Metaphors: Modern Genetics in Popular Science Magazines'. *Scandinavian Journal of Educational Research* 51 (3): 275–295. https://doi.org/10.1080/00313830701356133

Reisigl, Martin, and Ruth Wodak. 2015. 'The Discourse-Historical Approach (DHA)'. In Michael Meyer and Ruth Wodak (eds.), *Methods of Critical Discourse Studies*, pp. 23–61. Thousand Oaks, CA, and London: Sage.

Ricci, Oscar. 2010. 'Technology for Everyone: Representations of Technology in Popular Italian Scientific Magazines'. *Public Understanding of Science* 19 (5): 578–589. https://doi.org/10.1177/0963662509104724

Rose, Gillian. 2016. *Visual Methodologies: An Introduction to Researching with Visual Materials* (4th edition). Thousand Oaks, CA, and London: Sage.

Schneider, Birgit, and Thomas Nocke. 2014. *Image Politics of Climate Change: Visualizations, Imaginations, Documentations, Image*. Bielefeld: transcript Verlag.

Stöckel, Sigrid, Wiebke Lisner, and Gerlind Rüve. 2009. *Das Medium Wissenschaftszeitschrift seit dem 19. Jahrhundert*. Stuttgart: Steiner.

Suplee, Curt. 1998. 'Untangling the Science of Climate'. *National Geographic* 193 (5): 38–70.

Van Leeuwen, Theo. 2000. 'Semiotics and Iconography'. In Theo van Leeuwen and Carey Jewitt (eds.), *The Handbook of Visual Analysis*, pp. 92–118. Thousand Oaks, CA, and London: Sage.

Whitley, Cameron T., and Linda Kalof. 2014. 'Animal Imagery in the Discourse of Climate Change'. *International Journal of Sociology* 44 (1): 10–33. https://doi.org/10.2753/IJS0020-7659440102

Reflections and Connections

The following chapter, by Ulrike Felt, is centrally concerned with how obesity is *assembled* in public (media) spaces. It explores how anecdotes are used in news media accounts of obesity, analysing the functions that these communicative devices have in such accounts.

One central effect that anecdotes have is to incorporate moral and value judgements into seemingly straightforward personal stories. For instance, the dominance of emotions of guilt, shame, lack of control, and even self-hatred speaks not only to the sense that obesity is a moral failing, but that responsibility for dealing with this 'problem' lies at the individual level. Felt therefore shows how *public facts* about obesity are made alongside *public values*.

Indeed, we can say that public knowledge about obesity is here being co-produced with a particular model of society, one in which the individual is the central agent of change and where little attention is given to collective action or structural factors. Anecdotes similarly transmit and normalise specific visions of how (good) citizens' bodies should be. Stories of 'not fitting into' the world – from café seats to a 'normal' weight on the bathroom scales – reinforce norms and standards concerning what is the 'right' kind of body.

Anecdotes have the power to do these things because they contain a very specific kind of *evidence*. In telling 'real' stories of mundane life with obesity, they have an evidential weight connected to their portrayal of lived experience. While this gives them a particular kind of authority, one that is different from that of statistics, scientific facts, and scientific expertise, it also means that they are not open to wider questioning, debate, or critique. This in turn raises the question of the politics of claim-making based on anecdotal evidence, of tacit governance of the ways we live in the world and, in the end, of *responsible communication*.

7

PUBLIC HEALTH COMMUNICATION: ANECDOTAL EVIDENCE AND RESPONSIBILITY IN PRINT MEDIA ACCOUNTS OF OBESITY

ULRIKE FELT

7.1 INTRODUCTION

I sit and nibble again dry crisp bread. What can be yummy about that? Admittedly, it is healthy! And full of nutrients. But otherwise? How yummy would it be to just eat a tiny little piece of nougat chocolate? Hmmm, this idea made my mouth water. But my diet program knows no mercy: special separation diet, sport and a strict prohibition of any sweets. Isn't that cruel? But do you know what's even more cruel? Despite all this torture, the last two weeks I did not lose a single kilo. What would have happened, if I simply had eaten normally? Would I be rolling through this door?

The next day I meet my super slim friend for coffee. While I boringly sip my coffee without sugar, Gloria treats herself with a cappuccino topped with whipped cream and eats with pleasure a brownie with chocolate sauce. How does she manage? Does she train all night? I, in contrast, already gain weight, just by watching Gloria gourmandising.

Enough! The next day I take a diet break, even chocolate is permitted. And to my astonishment, I do not gain weight! Eventually I am again motivated to nibble my carrots! And maybe, one never knows, one day I will also become a slim gourmet.

(*Neue Kronen-Zeitung* 2009/01/26, 25, all translations are the author's own)

This is a short stand-alone personal story which appeared under the headline 'Frustration with diets and lust for chocolate' in the most popular Austrian tabloid *Neue Kronen-Zeitung*. It is one of numerous anecdotes that readers encounter in mass media reporting on issues relating to obesity and being overweight. The story refers to hard work, emotion, willpower, and disappointment in the context of struggles with body weight – even cruelty and torture find their place. Healthiness and pleasure are depicted as difficult to combine, at least for the protagonist's body. But bodies also appear to be different. Some can afford alimentary pleasures without obvious consequences, while others operate under severe constraints. A moment of weakness is shown – the 'diet break' – where the rules are broken, but, in the end, responsibility is reassumed. The anecdote closes with the hope that maybe things might become different ('...one day I will also become a slim gourmet').

Many people – particularly those who have been or are struggling with body weight, or are close to anybody doing so – will recognise the tropes present in this short story. While such anecdotes can be regarded as part of wider narratives that tell of obesity as a major health threat to contemporary societies, it is relevant to ask what kind of work these short, personal accounts – these anecdotes – do in the wider context of mass media health communication. The analysis offered in this chapter will therefore focus on the anecdote as a specific communicative form. As I will discuss, anecdotes fulfil a number of purposes: they provide a specific kind of personalised evidence for people's struggles with their bodies and lives; ground obesity in everyday life experiences and practices; reflect the material aspects of bodily experiences and struggles; and address issues of agency, morality, and responsibility. The chapter thus addresses a series of questions. How do anecdotes contribute to assembling obesity as a phenomenon? In what ways can they be seen as moments and places of making obesity real? What kinds of evidence do anecdotes create and circulate? And how are values expressed and responsibility distributed through them?

In what follows I start by exploring the very notion of the anecdote, reflecting on what their analysis can offer to science communication and science and technology studies, and positioning them in the wider context of a mediatised world (e.g., Livingstone & Lunt 2014; Petersen et al. 2010; Rödder et al. 2012). After describing the corpus and research design, the chapter will then engage in a multidimensional analysis of anecdotes in media accounts of obesity. The central conclusion relates to the need to move away from seeing anecdotes as innocent short stories that illustrate everyday life situations to understanding them as political spaces, in which specific kinds of evidence are brought into being and tacitly used to create situated knowledge and understanding of a health phenomenon.

7.2 THE ANECDOTE AS COMMUNICATIVE DEVICE

What qualifies as an anecdote? Going to *Webster's Collegiate Dictionary*, we find it defined as 'a usually short narrative of an interesting, amusing, or biographical incident'. Generally, anecdotes are meant to reveal some form of wider argument beyond what the brief tale in itself might suggest. They refer to a wider discourse, in our case on the importance of body shape and weight, including its tensions and contradictions. In addition, anecdotes often invite – or even demand – action by those addressed through the anecdote. Anecdotes thus try to connect the individual to the collective, creating dense relational networks without necessarily making them explicit.

In the analysis I offer, I understand anecdotes as a *communicative device* that 'assembles and arranges the world in specific social and material patterns' (Law & Ruppert 2013: 230). In doing so they are 'an openly ambiguous textual form: combining the real and the constructed, holding them in tension' (Michael 2012: 19). They are written as they are experienced, offering some slice of life as it was lived by the narrator, yet always being selective and choreographed in specific ways. Anecdotes are thus narrative 'happenings of the social that are, for all their apparent "intimacy", more or less readily convertible into public (social scientific) goods that can be put into circulation' (ibid.: 28). Anecdotes also compress extended timescales of life into a short moment of reflection, bringing dispersed actors, events, and feelings together in a single story.

In the context of newspaper articles, anecdotes are employed by the article writers to have specific effects: to focus or shift the readers' attention, provoke particular responses, raise questions, disrupt straightforward and unproblematic assumptions, or offer alternative perspectives. A good anecdote is supposed to 'touch, move or teach us' (Ely et al. 1997: 70). In this respect, they are part of what Wright and Harwood (2009) have called bio-pedagogical practices in media narratives on obesity. Indeed, the anecdote allows us 'to start from a specific [often rather small and seeming insignificant] incident and explore its complex and constitutive range of associations without ever seeing this exploration as uncomplicatedly representational, nor regarding it as exhaustive' (Michael 2012: 27). The power of an anecdote therefore consists of its capacity to promote a specific understanding of a complex phenomenon, while at the same time never being open to scrutiny on empirical grounds. Anecdotes are 'to be valued for other than factual-empirical or factual-historical reasons' (Van Manen 1989: 119).

Even though anecdotes are denied the power to furnish a rational argument, they provide experiential knowledge and are thus a useful tool for accounts of 'the social'. Indeed, while traditionally anecdotes are not acknowledged as a reliable source of knowledge about social life or health, they might be understood in a similar way as myths, always containing both fact and fiction, expressing values, and capturing lived experience, while escaping the burden of generalisation and proof. Anecdotes allow moving 'the extraordinary moment' to the centre of attention, which then 'serves in the illumination of the ordinary flow of events' (Michael 2012: 28). In short, anecdotes sensitise us to the differences, contradictions, and tensions that populate the complex worlds of obesity.

These features of anecdotes invite us to investigate them as 'discursive assemblages' (Felt et al. 2015), as a set of heterogeneous interconnected components that are configured to represent a specific version of reality. Assemblages are thus to be understood as always fluid and situated configurations aimed at achieving specific effects. Such assemblages, in the context of accounts of obesity, contain a broad range of human and non-human components: obese people; healthcare systems; food production and consumption; (health) economies; standards (relating to bodies and their environments); all kinds of measuring devices; and ideas of the good life, morals, and responsibilities, to name but a few. At the same time, connections between the components are important: for example, body weight, eating habits, and public health become connected in specific ways, allowing us to value people's behaviour as adequate or tacitly to express expectations of different ways of life. Here I follow Deleuze, who reminds us 'that what counts are not the terms or the elements, but what there is "between," the between, a set of relations which are not separable from each other' (Deleuze & Parnet 2007: viii). Focusing on this 'between-ness' will thus allow us to reflect on the roles that anecdotes play in wider narratives of obesity and on what makes them powerful actors in constructing and communicating specific visions and versions of obesity, obese people, and obese societies.

Studying anecdotes as discursive assemblages will thus mean being attentive both to the components that make up a specific assemblage and to the relations between them. We will open up anecdotes by reflecting on the material and semiotic interventions that bring them into being, and by examining the many forces that shape them. This will help focus our attention on the materiality of obese bodies and the life worlds they are part of, on embodied emotions and sensations, as well as on values, moralities and responsibilities that tie elements together. Such analysis will allow us to understand the specific kinds of experiential evidence created concerning the wider phenomenon at stake and simultaneously confront us with the multiple realities of obesity (Mol 2002) that co-exist. But it will also show how anecdotes are a space where the co-production of specific ways of knowing and of living with obesity (Jasanoff 2004; see Chapter 2) takes place and can be witnessed.

7.3 OBESITY IN A MEDIATISED WORLD

Over the past decades we have witnessed the emergence of a growing body of literature diagnosing a medialisation/mediatisation of contemporary societies. Mass media are considered as being deeply entangled with all parts of technoscientific, social, and cultural life. This has led to 'an institutionalization of attention to mass media coverage and an internalization of media criteria' (Petersen et al. 2010: 865). In a mediatised world, the analysis of reporting on obesity and related issues is of particular interest because as such it is a hybrid space in which the epistemic, social, and political are deeply entangled, and where we can observe obesity being assembled.

Since the 1990s, obesity has had a prominent place in both public debate and on public health agendas (Gard & Wright 2005). One of the most pervasive framings of the problem at stake has been through narratives about rising numbers of obese people, and projections of where this might lead contemporary societies. Such statements about rising numbers, and the trajectorial thinking they build on (Felt et al. 2014), are not only 'tickets into specific discourse forums and forms' but have been shown to 'be a fruitful means of disciplining our own and others' thinking about the world' (Sætnan et al. 2011). The use of statistics allows for the creation of a shared understanding of the threat that obesity represents for contemporary societies, while in the same move being an excellent tool for holding people accountable for personal body weight.

Media have been a particular focus for critical obesity studies (Atanasova et al. 2012; Raisborough 2016). In investigating different national contexts, these analyses have pointed to the globalisation of obesity discourses and simultaneously to important national and cultural differences. Feminist perspectives, especially, have highlighted the creation and distribution of specific body images and the stigmatisation of fat (Inthorn & Boyce 2010; Saguy & Gruys 2010). Effort has also been devoted to showing the ideological nature of much media reporting (Campos 2004; Oliver 2006), often by making arguments about 'misrepresentation'. The distribution of blame and responsibility within media articles on obesity has attracted attention, indicating a trend of making individuals responsible, while neglecting more collective dimensions (Boero 2007; Felt et al. 2014; Shugart 2013). Finally, such collective dimensions are often captured by narrating the obesity epidemic as evidence for 'Western decadence' (Gard & Wright 2005: 2) and moral decline.

While an analysis of the rich body of writing on obesity as a cultural phenomenon would go beyond the scope of this chapter, it is essential to understand the media as collectively producing 'a first draft of history' (Garde-Hansen 2011: 3), giving shape to an imaginary that ties together a worryingly high number of obese people, a threatening future when it comes to public health and related costs, and a set of interventions that appear unavoidable if 'we' want to act in a responsible manner. Indeed, while rising body weight is staged as a 'matter of fact', proliferating media accounts connect these facts to specific lifestyles, broader politico-economic choices, and moral decline, thus transforming obesity into a 'matter of concern' in need of being addressed (Latour 2005). In short, public debate about obesity has opened the door to 'biopolitical struggles over appropriate forms of individual and collective life' (Penkler et al. 2015: 315), with the average body weight of citizens related to their height – namely, the body mass index – becoming the key indicator of conformity to the ideal.

Mass media are central sites for producing and distributing sense-making narratives in contemporary societies. Following David Silverman's introduction to Czarniawska (2004: viii), in assuming that 'an observer's ability to see regularities in "everyday life" depends upon a complex body of linguistically mediated interactions', makes a careful analysis of anecdotes, as one narrative device featured within media accounts, a promising approach. Because of the ways in which anecdotes are crafted in order to assemble a specific version of lived obesity, they are key bio-pedagocial sites that 'bring together the idea of biopower and pedagogy in ways that help us understand the body as a political space' (Wright & Harwood 2009: 79). Analysis of anecdotes will also invite us to reflect how these short stories are potentially 'influencing beliefs, behaviours, and health and educational policies' (ibid.: 15) – how, in short, they affect the (self-) governance of bodies in contemporary societies. In what follows, the analysis will focus on how obesity is assembled in anecdotes and on the work performed by anecdotes in media accounts of obesity.

7.4 MATERIAL

The analysis examines a sample of articles published in six Austrian daily newspapers and two weekly news magazines between 2005 and 2015. The starting date for this sample is one year before the publication of the first Austrian obesity report (Kiefer 2006), which coincided with an increase in media attention. Newspapers and magazines were chosen to represent national and regional papers with differing political leanings and target audiences: *Neue Kronen-Zeitung* (circulation 930,000), the country's largest tabloid and, in relation to 8 million inhabitants of the country, reaching a large number of Austrians; *Kurier* (211,000), a nationwide daily in the middle of the political spectrum; the liberal-left *Der Standard* (109,000) and the conservative *Die Presse* (103,000), Austria's two widest-circulated broadsheets; and *Oberösterreichische Nachrichten* (138,000) and *Salzburger Nachrichten* (91,000), two regional dailies with nationwide circulation. Two magazines were also part of the corpus: *NEWS* (222,000), a glossy magazine that in addition to politics and high society covers public health and wellness; and *Profil* (90,000), a weekly with regular specials on health issues, tailored to a readership with higher levels of education.

The articles were drawn from the electronic database of German language media articles WISO using the search terms 'obesity', 'obese', 'weight', 'weight loss', 'fat', 'slim', 'chubby', 'kilo', 'diet', 'nutrition', and 'eating' (in German). Only longer articles were selected in order to obtain fully fledged accounts that contained more complex narrative elements, and which would thus potentially use anecdotes. Finally, to limit the material collected, every second year between 2005 and 2015 was searched for anecdotes. The result was a corpus of 126 anecdotes used as a basis for the following analysis.

A first analysis showed that the use of anecdotes is distributed quite unequally across the print media investigated. The strongest use was made in *Kurier*, followed by *Neue Kronen-Zeitung* and *NEWS*, all belonging to a segment with the highest readership or to the tabloid segment. This already points to anecdotes being used where a classical, fact-heavy health communication approach might be seen as less prone to success in terms of getting the readers' attention. The number of anecdotes also decreased over the period under study, which could be connected to the fact that public discourse on obesity became less prominent and frequent, perhaps because 'the obesity problem' has become a widely accepted trope and has therefore lost some of its newsworthiness. The gender of the person central to the anecdote was quite balanced, with 43% stories having a female main protagonist. I can say much less about other socioeconomic or age criteria, as this information is present in only some of the anecdotes and varies largely.

The anecdotes were then analysed (as a corpus, not differentiating between different publications), focusing on the structure and main elements of the story, the choreography, and the kinds of evidence performed. I look at the findings through three functions that anecdotes perform: (1) they describe the mundane technologies for measuring and surveilling (obese) bodies and for materialising obesity; (2) they recommend specific kinds of 'body work', from tracking food consumption to defining 'good' and 'bad' foods; and (3) they co-produce moralities, value judgements, and material practices of eating and food.

7.5 FINDINGS: ANECDOTES AS SPACES FOR CREATING OBESITY ASSEMBLAGES

7.5.1 MATERIALISING OBESITY: MEASURING AND SURVEILLANCE TECHNOLOGIES

Most media articles reporting on the obesity problem conceptualise and narrate it as a collective phenomenon, often expressed through some reference to statistics (Sætnan et al. 2011). This allows for a broader narrative of dissatisfaction with wider societal developments and constructing the imagination of the 'societal body' (Penkler et al. 2015) that is diagnosed as at risk or already ill.

These narratives then form the wider environment in which the anecdotes are deployed. Anecdotes are thus given the task of materialising these obesity statistics, transforming abstract numbers into a phenomenon that can be recognised and acted upon at an individual level. In other words, they are mobilised to capture what it means to be obese. This can be seen explicitly in a longer article on obesity in an Austrian tabloid under the headline 'Austrians get ever fatter' (*Neue Kronen-Zeitung* 2006/04/22). After having explained that more than 800,000 Austrians are overweight, that 80,000 can be classified as morbidly obese, and that 'Austria occupies the 6th place in an international ranking on obesity', the article continues by arguing that behind these 'sobering numbers are fates that people with normal weights cannot imagine', which then leads to one of the many anecdotes about a person experiencing her life with obesity.

In many of the anecdotes analysed, 'being obese' is reported through reference to the weight of the main protagonist, and, where possible, constructing a 'before and after' story, showing where people began and reporting on success (or failure) through reference to numbers. The importance of these anecdotes for the self-understanding of the main protagonists is then to be found in statements such as 'being overweight has been preoccupying me all my life' (*Neue Kronen-Zeitung* 2009/05/24), or 'for an eternity my friend has been nagging me about losing weight' (*Neue Kronen-Zeitung* 2009/05/17). This and other references support the idea of the existence of ideal body norms and standards against which individuals are being measured and should measure themselves. Any such project of standardising human bodies then makes 'conformity to these standards become part and parcel of the socialization process' (Busch 2011: 297).

The most prominent non-human actor in the obesity assemblage behind this conformity are the scales, which are omnipresent as a measurement device that 'speaks truth to people about their bodies'. This is already visible in one Austrian phrase that describes being overweight: 'to bring too many kilos onto the scales' (the literal translation of 'zu viele Kilos auf die Waage bringen'). My corpus of anecdotes contains frequent references to 'the needle on the scales', which would, in a quasi-objective, 'unbribable', or 'inexonerable' (*Kurier* 2005/01/15) manner, show success, stagnation, or failure. Consider the following short passage:

> After three weeks came the frustration. I had stuck to all my resolutions, only the scales would at no price react. For a whole week, every morning it showed the same weight. Merciless. (*Oberösterreichische Nachrichten* 2005/03/12)

Sometimes weighing scales come in combination with mirrors or with other visualising techniques that perform the obese body. In the same article, we find a description of how the mirror and scales together triggered the decision to lose weight:

It was only a short moment after my morning shower. The unfortunate position of the mirror over the bathtub revealed a view onto my body which horrified me, despite the fact that I should actually know it well. It was apparently the right moment. In particular, the three-digit figure on my scales already haunted me. (*Oberösterreichische Nachrichten* 2005/03/12)

This combination of perception in the mirror and reference to body weight, or, to put it differently, the combination of physical appearance and health status as expressed by an 'objective' measure, has a long history. Jutel (2005: 115) has argued that 'strong cultural beliefs about the significance of appearance provide a foundation for the preoccupation with calorie-counting, body sculpting, exercise and diets'. Appearance was believed to 'mirror the "true" inner self', while food was assumed to 'convey moral value to the person who eats it, a value that may be witnessed in physical appearance' (ibid.: 115).

Other smaller narrative elements similarly describe this performance of obesity as a process of (not) fitting: 'skirts and trousers are tight or would not even close anymore' (*Neue Kronen-Zeitung* 2006/01/28) would be a typical descriptor of not conforming to the norm. '[G]asp[ing] even when he had to do minor efforts' (*Kurier* 2005/04/13) was a further material proof of the problems related to obesity. Dieting women would be quoted saying that 'her best moment: the day when she could bend far enough down to lace her shoes' (*Der Standard* 2015/06/20), or that it was a moment of success to be able 'to cross one's legs again' (*Kurier* 2005/01/03).

Finally, we also encounter stories about moments when obese bodies would no longer fit into the mundane material world and thus cut people from living their lives. Readers are offered the following anecdote:

At one point in time I no longer wanted to meet friends in the coffee house, as I was afraid that I would not fit into the chairs,' explained Mrs Jandrisevits. 'I finally realized that I couldn't continue like that. With a height of 1.62 m at that time I already weighed 120 kg. (*Neue KronenZeitung* 2006/04/22)

This anecdote manages to perform two kinds of work. On the one hand, it underlines that we live in a world that has been constructed along a specific set of norms and standards, which are defined by an idealised and culturally specific body (Busch 2011). As a consequence, overweight bodies are classified as simply not fitting into the physical world around us – it is the connection between the standard world and the non-standard body which matters in this obesity assemblage. It is the body that has to adapt to the norm in order to participate in ordinary lives. On the other hand, the story turns obesity into a potentially shareable experience, something that is experienced rather than being abstractly defined through numbers. This is then linked to the emotions that this non-fit with the physical world created: fear and avoidance. Later in the article the anecdote's protagonist would explain how she transformed her experience into a capacity to act.

7.5.2 BODY WORK PRACTICES

A second key component of obesity, as assembled in anecdotes, comprises practices and (implicit) instructions concerning how to work on obese bodies, and in particular how to lose excess weight. Here again we encounter both components of the assemblage, but above all are made aware of how they are connected in specific ways in order to trigger action. This ranges from discussion of which approaches of weight loss worked to sketches of how they did so. Often this is supported again by numbers that document the drama of successes or failures. Weight-loss narratives, or at least narratives showing the efforts to lose weight, form a central part of the corpus, appearing in about 75% of the anecdotes.

Consider the following elements, taken from a weight-loss anecdote that presents serving plate size as a simple device to make food easily measurable and thus control weight: 'With this diet, Jennifer Aniston (40) does not need to count calories – but pay attention to the diameter of her plate. The diet prescribes that the plate is only allowed to be 18 cm for breakfast, 23 cm for lunch and dinner. These plates can only be filled with those foods that are permitted (low fat meat, fish, fresh vegetables and whole-grain products)' (*Oberösterreichische Nachrichten* 2009/03/24). Typically, such stories involve a celebrity, start by being critical towards the practice of calorie-counting, contain some form of 'easy device' for measuring food intake, and give a prescription of what is to be regarded as 'good' food.

Writing, taking notes, and self-tracking constitute a second group of technologies often referred to in anecdotes. Again, these have the aim of materialising behaviours seen as causing obesity. There are frequent narratives of moments of enlightenment that came from keeping track and producing data, and of how this self-objectification became a key bio-pedagogical moment. 'The taking of notes actually got me to eat less and with care' (*Kurier* 2005/01/20), explained one protagonist who had successfully lost weight. Another reported having 'noted down every bite' he took and stressed that 'this did help a lot' (*Kurier* 2005/04/13). Such stories describe how bookkeeping exercises would successfully restrain the main protagonists from taking 'another beer' or going to the fridge. Another version of this note taking is found in two men's narratives of changing their diet in combination with increased exercise. They stressed how they made space for their body work in their diaries: 'Just as for business meetings, I marked all my training hours into my diary' (*Kurier* 2005/05/13). This captures the special value attributed to sport: caring for the body was now on an equal level to work meetings.

Rules distinguishing 'good food' from 'bad food' was a third group of body work techniques that aimed at redefining how much and what we eat.

One protagonist expressed her hope that, after following specific prescriptions for a while, she 'would finally have the right feeling, how much I am allowed to eat per day' (*Kurier* 2011/07/01). This desire describes the importance of regaining 'the [right] feeling' for eating, a feeling that is often depicted, in the articles surrounding anecdotes, as something that those living in contemporary societies have lost. At the same time, we often encounter a connection between knowing the right things and acting in the right way: 'In the first place it is important to know what I do to my body through eating specific things. Only then I can construct my everyday life around this knowledge' (*Kurier* 2015/12/16). Such food-related prescriptions are then often accompanied by narratives about former bad habits, as well as by stories about culturally rooted, problematic behaviours such as eating all the food on your plate, even if you are not hungry, or finishing up what children have left. These are staged as values from the past that need to be abandoned in the name of a healthy body and a good life.

Finally, a large number of the anecdotes address the importance of raising and keeping track of physical activity. 'The power of movement' was the subheading of one article, a phrase that nicely captures the tone of most of the movement-related anecdotes. Take the following story about an overweight and diabetic man: 'Therefore, Renee Fugger, who had as a diabetic been injecting insulin for the last 10 years, took the "movement pill" exactly as prescribed. This highly overweight man managed to lose 20 kg by biking over a period of one and a half years. He could stop taking insulin. "I felt I was reborn", reported Fugger' (*Profil* 2007/08/13). These stories of transformational moments based on increased mobility are a frequently used element of obesity anecdotes. Many of them share tips for how to increase mobility and integrate it into everyday life. Embracing physical activity is described as liberating, as being transformative, or as making a new person.

7.5.3 VALUING IN PRACTICE: EMOTIONS, CHALLENGES AND RESPONSIBILITY

Obesity anecdotes are important spaces for the co-production of materiality and morality. They allow us to see how the various components of the obesity assemblage are connected, and how appreciations and feelings are expressed in making these connections. As easily recognisable stories, anecdotes serve as a resource for, and 'public proof' of, the validity of widespread societal value judgements concerning obesity. Unpicking health communication-related anecdotes therefore involves examining how different actors justify specific ways of living and of relating to their bodies, as well as the normative judgements against which these evaluations happen and the emotions that are entangled in this. This is of particular importance as the majority of these anecdotes suggest behavioural solutions, and thus place the individual in the limelight. If one makes the right choices and is disciplined, the outcome – a body closer to societal and biomedical norms – is taken for granted. While the wider newspaper articles in this corpus do refer to more structural factors, such as technological production of food or a lack of time to eat 'properly', the anecdotes quickly move the problem of body weight to the individual, sidelining more collective solutions (Penkler et al. 2015; Saguy et al. 2010).

Across most of the anecdotes we find the story of people who are ready 'to fundamentally turn [their] lives upside down' (*Neue Kronen-Zeitung* 2005/03/18), to abandon their previous lives and engage in totally different ones. This is captured in the transformation from being a passive person to an active one, from an addicted to a disciplined citizen, and from denying a problem to acknowledging it and getting support (be that at the level of dieting and physical activity or through surgical intervention). Transformations of this kind often lead to praising the work people did in overcoming hurdles towards 'a better body shape', which is equated with a better life. A high-level gastronomic expert, for example, is lauded for changing his eating habits, the reward being 'that he brings 40 kilos less onto the scales. Respect!' (*Kurier* 2005/09/23). These are stories of strong will even in difficult situations, and of the readiness to devote considerable efforts to reach the goal, attributes which together make a caring and responsible citizen. After narrating the challenges of weight reduction, one storyteller continued, 'But my will would not break. Fortunately' (*Oberösterreichische Nachrichten* 12/3/2005). The moment that the goal is reached holds great promise: 'As her body weight changed, so did her personality. "I again have faith in myself, have so much more self-confidence, can accept myself as I am"' (*Kurier* 2005/01/03).

However, next to such transformation narratives, we find some accounts of unsurmountable challenges and moments of despair and strong emotion. In particular, younger people with high body weight are seen as suffering and being shamed for their body weight: 14-year-old Alina told of how, in her school's yard, pupils would shout 'The panzer is rolling in' when she entered the court (*NEWS* 2006/34). Other young people talked of being called 'fatty', of having the nickname 'Mozartkugel' (Mozartkugel is a typically Austrian brand of brightly wrapped spherical chocolates, so the term alludes to both chocolate consumption and having a round body; *NEWS* 2007/01/25), or of having to live through other kinds of humiliations. In adults' stories we similarly find diverse kinds of discriminatory experiences or narratives of stigma that reference fat shaming, open discrimination, oppression, and humiliation, but also depression and self-hate. However, while these emotional elements add dramatic features to the narrative, the way out is always seen as the responsibility of the person in question. They are the ones that can and have to change in order to escape such situations. 'The worst thing', one person explained, 'is that people think that we fat people lack a strong will' (*Neue Kronen-Zeitung* 2007/06/03). Indeed, this narrative of lack of control repeatedly appears. Consider the following story:

One month ago, nearly every night my cravings for sweets got me out of bed. Between two and three in the morning it started: cake, tart, chocolate. When I could not find any sweets at home, I even drove to the next gas station to ensure replenishment. Most of the time, I prophylactically put candies and chocolate on the bedside table. (*NEWS* 2007/04)

Such dramatic moments support the vision that, at this moment in their life, obese people are out of control, completely refusing to take – or incapable of taking – responsibility for their own bodies. However, it is important to underline that many of these anecdotes are told in the past tense ('one month ago', in the story above), suggesting that the protagonists have made their way out of this dramatic situation. In most cases, anecdotes then showed people exercising self-critique, suggesting that 'fat people gorge too much food' (*Kurier* 2005/01/15) or describing themselves as addicted and permanently eating beyond reason. Letting the protagonist express these views allows for the inclusion of strong value judgements which would have been impossible for the journalist writing the article, say, to voice.

In such anecdotes dieting then becomes a key element used to acknowledge people's readiness to invest in improving their body. Even when unsuccessful in weight-loss attempts – perhaps because 'she could not change her incorrect eating behavior' (*NEWS* 2007/01/25) as one anecdote reported – the protagonists are not accused of being out of control, as they were demonstrating the will to continue dieting. Instead, they are pitied for not being able to lose weight despite their repeated attempts.

What these anecdotal elements all have in common – even though they never make such statements explicit – is that they all, in one way or another, support the first of what Susan Greenhalgh (2015: 30) has called the 'biomyths' of obesity: 'Weight is under individual control; virtually everyone can lose weight and keep it off through diet and exercise. Weight-loss treatments work; if they don't, it's due to lack of willpower on the part of the dieter.'

7.6 CONCLUSION

The starting point of this chapter was the need to study anecdotes, and their role in sense- and evidence-making, in science and health communication. In the context of media articles about obesity, anecdotes are generally embedded in wider reports that diagnose a dramatic rise in average body weight – a rise that not only endangers individual health, but constitutes a financial burden on public healthcare systems and the economy more generally. In short, obesity threatens a nation's future (Penkler et al. 2015). In this context, it is not surprising that virtually all of the anecdotes analysed here have a strong anticipatory component, connecting past, presents, and futures, and calling for new ways of governing bodies and lives. The moments of personal reminiscence encapsulated in anecdotes invite the reader to learn about obesity as a trajectory (Felt et al. 2014) on which they are situated, and where this trajectory will lead them. Obesity-related anecdotes are thus strong agents in an anticipatory governance of bodies, projecting the need to develop different bodies that have a better fit with normative imaginaries. All of the functions of anecdotes described above – their materialisation of standards, depiction of technologies of surveillance and of body work, and reinforcement of particular values – ensure that the obesity assemblages made within anecdotes tacitly govern bodies in specific, individualised ways.

What else can we learn from this analysis of the role of anecdotes in health communication in print media?

First, the study of anecdotes as spaces for assembling specific versions of obesity is one promising avenue for interrogating widespread cultural ideas of 'the obesity problem'. Using the notion of assemblage focused our attention not only on specific components, but also on how they were connected in specific ways. I have explored how elements were associated in new ways, drawing on wider registers of localising ways of knowing, interpreting, and acting upon elements as diverse as human bodies, healthcare, and material worlds. Anecdotes become spaces where knowledge of situated conditions, in particular social conditions – often tied to feelings like stress, being overwhelmed or out of control, but also of disciplining – can be legitimately expressed, conditions that are generally much less visible when there is expert talk on public health issues such as obesity. However, we should note that, while anecdotes participate in the making of a phenomenon, they are recognisable because of tacitly assumed connections between body weight and health. Anecdotes no longer need to refer to statistics, probabilities, costs, and medical facts. These are always already there, and are the invisible and thus unaccountable foundations for these anecdotes. This, then, opens up the question of the power of those who write media anecdotes, and who choose certain anecdotes over others, select specific choreographies, and give voice to some protagonists while silencing others.

Second, anecdotes perform in authoritative ways what it means to live with obesity, and to be obese. The narrative reiterations of specific tropes, albeit performed through seemingly different stories, work to impose a way of understanding the world, but also, more crucially, a way of being in that world. We have encountered narrative elements in anecdotes telling of how obese bodies experience the limitations of the material world around them, how they do not seem to fit, but also how obesity is materialised and realised through measuring and accounting tools. We have seen 'first-hand accounts' of the little devices which in one and the same move support the materialisation of the obese body or even the obese person, while also being staged as a tool to fight the personal war on obesity. It is also in these moments that pain, blame, and other profound feelings enter the scene. They are part of the 'in-between' of obesity assemblages, making the elements hold together while simultaneously being the outcome of assembling obesity in specific ways.

Third, we should reflect on the political power – the biopower – of such anecdotes. Mol (2002) reminds us that ontologies – in our case, the way we understand what obesity is – are never 'given in the order of things', but instead 'are brought into being, sustained, or allowed to wither away in common, day-to-day, sociomaterial practices' (ibid.: 6). Anecdotes are trying to capture specific versions of such mundane practices and thus to bring into being specific versions of obesity. My analysis of anecdotes, then, has shown the multiple ways in which problems are framed and thus 'bodies are shaped, and lives are pushed and pulled into one shape or another' (ibid.: viii). Anecdotes should therefore be understood as a political space, highlighting some versions of obesity, supporting some kinds of biopolitics and not others, while distributing responsibilities in specific ways and deploying their own classificatory and discriminatory practices. In that sense, we should see them as part of a wider ontological politics at work (ibid.). Anecdotes contribute to shaping one specific reality and not others. This means that attention has to be devoted to those realities that can(not) be or that are simply (not) performed when a specific set of dominant narratives has been established (Law, 2011).

Anecdotes are thus not just 'little stories', slices of personal life, illustrations that better connect readers to particular media stories. They are political spaces of bio-pedagogy that go well beyond the seemingly naïve way in which anecdotes are handled as mere illustrations of situated realities. They perform anecdotal evidence, making anecdotes have both epistemic and political dimensions; they deploy specific kinds of experiential knowledge claims which 'invite' action while very often still tacitly performing the dominant biomedical narrative of obesity as a societal problem. The call for action is an extended one, reaching both oneself and all the others whose bodies do not seem to fit. And, as explained earlier, the frequency of anecdotes is much higher in newspapers reaching out to less educated publics – which strongly supports both the biopedagogy as well as the biopower argument.

Evidence is present in two forms within anecdotes: through the dominant (bio)medical understandings of obesity that are tacitly performed, and through the epistemic claims that anecdotes present, in the form of assertions of the existence of a particular situation in the life of a 'real person'. As such the analysis has been primarily concerned with what Gabriel (2003: 31) calls 'facts-as-experience' rather than 'facts-as-information'. The anecdote can thus, in a rather unquestioned manner, propagate explicit health political claims that call for intervention, support, and conformity of citizens to these new imaginations of good food, good life, and good health.

Taking these observations together, we can see that anecdotes hold a particular power to perform evidence, and are anything but innocent stories about our lives. In media narratives on obesity, anecdotes are powerful educational sites, tacitly translating a still embattled collective diagnosis of an obesity epidemic, the purportedly clear relation between body weight and health, and the connection between body weight and a collective moral decline into stories of individual failures, struggles, and limitations. Anecdotes manage to enact normative beliefs about our bodies, health, and the way in which we inhabit the world through first-person accounts. But because anecdotes are not making explicit truth claims, but pretend to recount situated snippets of peoples' struggle with or handling of obesity-related challenges, they seem to be able to escape scrutiny, and with this the question of responsibility. In a medialised world, media messages are packaged into familiar and predictable forms that have proven successful in attracting the target audience's attention. This is particularly true for health communication (Dahlstrom 2014). But news stories are not simply out there ready to be selected. Reality becomes news, while news makes realities through the construction of complex assemblages which seem to fit the respective goal of those publishing the accounts, be it economic, educational, or normative. It thus seems essential not simply to see reporting on obesity as an interesting case where we gain insights into the ways in which food, work, and lifestyle undergo transformations. Instead, we need to ask the question of what responsible communication should look like at a time when storytelling, along with the production and diffusion of anecdotes, is seen as a strategic tool for improving health communication and health literacy, while also making individuals responsible for their bodies.

ACKNOWLEDGEMENTS

This work has been financially supported by the Vienna Science and Technology Fund in the framework of a project 'From Lab to Intervention and Back: Doing and Undoing Diversity in Obesity Research, Treatment and Prevention' (principal investigator: Ulrike Felt; project collaborators: Kay Felder, Michael Penkler, Bernhard Winkler). The sample used in this chapter was also part of the basis for a broader media analysis (Penkler et al. 2015). For this chapter, my thanks go to Bernhard Winkler, who has supported me in preparing the corpus of anecdotes taken from the body of articles in Austrian newspapers. He has written his Master's thesis specifically focusing on the moral work anecdotes do (Winkler 2018). I also thank the reviewer for valuable comments.

REFERENCES

Atanasova, Dimitrinka, Nelya Koteyko, and Barrie Gunter. 2012. 'Obesity in the News: Directions for Future Research'. *Obesity Reviews* 13 (6): 554–559. doi: 10.1111/j.1467-789X.2012.00985.x.

Boero, Nathalie. 2007. 'All the News that's Fat to Print: The American "Obesity Opidemic" and the Media'. *Qualitative Sociology* 30: 41–60.

Busch, Lawrence. 2011. *Standards: Recipes for Reality*. Cambridge, MA: The MIT Press.

Campos, Paul. 2004. *The Obesity Myth: Why America's Obsession with Weight is Hazardous to Your Health*. New York: Gotham Books.

Czarniawska, Barbara. 2004. *Narratives in Social Science Research*. London: Sage.

Dahlstrom, Michael F. 2014. 'Using Narratives and Storytelling to Communicate Science with Nonexpert Audiences'. *Proceedings of the National Academy of Sciences* 111, Suppl. 4: 13614–13620. doi: 10.1073/pnas.1320645111.

Deleuze, Gilles, and Claire Parnet. 2007. *Dialogues II: Revised edition*. New York: Columbia University Press.

Ely, Margot, Ruth Vinz, Maryann Downing, and Margret Anzul (eds.). 1997. *On Writing Qualitative Research: Living by Words*. London: Falmer.

Felt, Ulrike, Kay Felder, Theresa Ohler, and Michael Penkler. 2014. 'Timescapes of Obesity: Coming to Terms with a Complex Socio-Medical Phenomenon'. *Health (London)* 18 (6): 646–664. doi: 10.1177/1363459314530736.

Felt, Ulrike, Simone Schumann, and Claudia Schwarz. 2015. '(Re)assembling Natures, Cultures, and (Nano)technologies in Public Engagement'. *Science as Culture* 24 (4): 458–483. doi: 10.1080/09505431.2015.1055720.

Gabriel, Yiannis. 2000. *Storytelling in Organizations: Facts, Fictions, Fantasies*. Oxford: Oxford University Press.

Gard, Michael, and Jan Wright. 2005. *The Obesity Epidemic: Science, Morality and Ideology*. Abingdon and New York: Routledge.

Garde-Hansen, Joanne. 2011. *Media and Memory*. Edinburgh: Edinburgh University Press.

Greenhalgh, Susan. 2015. *Fat-Talk Nation: The Human Costs of America's War on Fat*. Ithaca, NY: Cornell University Press.

Inthorn, Sanna, and Tammy Boyce. 2010. '"It's Disgusting How Much Salt You Eat!" Television Discourses of Obesity, Health and Morality'. *International Journal of Cultural Studies* 13 (1): 83–100.

Jasanoff, Sheila. 2004. *States of Knowledge: The Co-Production of Science and Social Order*. Abingdon and New York: Routledge.

Jutel, Annemarie. 2005. 'Weighing Health: The Moral Burden of Obesity'. *Social Semiotics* 15 (2): 113–125.

Kiefer, Ingrid. 2006. *Österreichischer Adipositasbericht 2006. Grundlage für zukünftige Handlungsfelder: Kinder, Jugendliche, Erwachsene*. Vienna: Verein Altern mit Zukunft.

Latour, Bruno. 2005. *Reassembling the Social: An Introduction to Actor-Network-Theory*. Oxford: Oxford University Press.

Law, John. 2011. 'Collateral Realities'. In Fernando Dominguez Rubio and Patrick Baert (eds.), *The Politics of Knowledge*, pp. 156–178. Abingdon: Routledge.

Law, John, and Evelyn Ruppert. 2013. 'The Social Life of Methods: Devices'. *Journal of Cultural Economy* 6 (3): 229–240. doi: 10.1080/17530350.2013.812042.

Livingstone, Sonia, and Peter Lunt. 2014. 'Mediatization: An Emerging Paradigm for Media and Communication Studies'. In Knut Lundby (ed.), *Mediatization of Communication*, pp. 703–724. Berlin: de Gruyter.

Michael, Mike. 2012. 'Anecdote'. In Celia Lury and Nina Wakeford (eds.), *Inventive Methods: The Happening of the Social*, pp. 25–35. Abingdon: Routledge.

Mol, Annemarie. 2002. *The Body Multiple: Ontology in Medical Practice*. Durham, NC: Duke University Press.

Oliver, J. Eric. 2006. *Fat Politics: The Real Story behind America's Obesity Epidemic*. New York: Oxford University Press.

Penkler, Michael, Kay Felder, and Ulrike Felt. 2015. 'Diagnostic Narratives: Creating Visions of Austrian Society in Print Media Accounts of Obesity'. *Science Communication* 37 (3): 314–339.

Petersen, Imme, Harald Heinrichs, and Hans Peter Peters. 2010. 'Mass-Mediated Expertise as Informal Policy Advice'. *Science, Technology & Human Values* 35 (6): 865–887. doi: 10.1177/0162243909357914.

Raisborough, Jayne. 2016. *Fat Bodies, Health and the Media*. London: Palgrave Macmillan.

Rödder, Simone, Martina Franzen, and Peter Weingart (eds.). 2012. *The Sciences' Media Connection – Communication to the Public and its Repercussions. Yearbook of the Sociology of the Sciences*. Dordrecht: Springer.

Sætnan, Ann Rudinow, Heidi Mork Lomell, and Svein Hammer (eds.). 2011. *The Mutual Construction of Statistics and Society*. New York: Routledge.

Saguy, Abigail C., and Kjerstin Gruys. 2010. 'Morality and Health: News Media Constructions of Overweight and Eating Disorders'. *Social Problems* 57 (2): 231–250.

Saguy, Abigail C., Kjerstin Gruys, and Shanna Gong. 2010. 'Social Problem Construction and National Context: News Reporting on "Overweight" and "Obesity" in the U.S. and France'. *Social Problems* 57 (4): 586–610.

Shugart, Helene. 2013. 'Weight of Tradition: Culture as a Rationale for Obesity in Contemporary U.S. News Coverage'. *Obesity Reviews* 14: 736–744.

Van Manen, Max. 1989. 'By the Light of Anecdote'. *Phenomenology + Pedagogy* 7: 232–253.

Winkler, Bernhard. 2018. 'The Moral Work of Obesity Anecdotes'. MA thesis, Department of Science and Technology Studies, University of Vienna.

Wright, Jan, and Valerie Harwood (eds.). 2009. *Biopolitics and the "Obesity Epidemic": Governing Bodies*. New York and Abingdon: Routledge.

Reflections and Connections

In the following chapter, Erika Szymanski mobilises and develops ideas of relationality and practice – in her case, writing as practice. She is concerned with the work that science communication texts do in assembling (new) science and technology in specific ways, arguing that instances of communication – such as, in her case study, the representation of synthetic yeast in news media – do not 'translate' but instead *construct or enact science*. Facts, as we saw in Chapter 3, are made not only in labs but also in public.

In her case study, one key finding is that synthetic yeast – which certainly has the potential to be represented as a new and strange kind of science-made creature, one that calls forth the same negative emotions that genetically modified (GM) organisms have in the past – is instead thoroughly domesticated in media accounts. Its nature is consistently related to the mundane and familiar baker's or brewer's yeast. By placing this new technology as a straightforward development of existing micro-organisms rather than contextualising it through contentious debates on GM, these science communication accounts enact it as unthreatening and even rather fun, in its potential to make better beer.

Szymanski also opens up a set of reflections concerning the nature of good science communication and the *responsibilities* of communicators. If responsible science communication is not simply about 'accuracy' – a notion she deconstructs given that knowledge is always made in new ways within communication – then how should it be practised and assessed? As we noted, values are central to public communication. Szymanski suggests that one way of acknowledging this is to ask: How should science be made in public? What frames, reference points, and voices are relevant to it? Science communication, she argues, makes 'choices about what ... science becomes in audience's worlds'. As such, communicators need to take seriously how they make those choices, and be transparent about the fact that they exist.

8

CONSTRUCTING SCIENCE IN PUBLIC: FRAMING SYNTHETIC YEAST IN NEWS MEDIA

ERIKA SZYMANSKI

8.1 INTRODUCTION

Science communication to non-specialist audiences is often described as disseminating pre-existing scientific knowledge, and is assessed for how well those 'popularisations' cohere with scientific knowledge, that is, for their accuracy and completeness in comparison to a perceived scientific truth (Hansen 2016). In this chapter, I argue that conceiving of scientific popularisation as knowledge dissemination or translation understates its value and mistakes its action. Via material-semiotic lenses from science and technology studies (STS), science communication to non-specialist audiences can be more usefully seen not as translating but as *constructing* scientific objects in the worlds of non-specialist communities. Seeing science communication through this lens makes it clear that science communication involves making value-laden choices and taking considerable responsibility. Moreover, science communication has great opportunities to connect scientific concepts to other forms of knowledge, and likewise needs to take those additional epistemologies and social modes into account.

Seeing science *communication* as science *construction* eliminates identifying a single, authoritative version of scientific knowledge as the benchmark for accuracy and completeness. Such a perspectival shift also emphasises just how important science communication is – it is responsible for bringing scientific objects into being for its audiences, making knowledge, rather than (merely) communicating already-settled facts. An STS-informed approach enables asking many questions about what science communication *does* rather than focusing on few and limited questions about how accurately knowledge is communicated – knowledge which is easily assumed as correct, universal, and worth communicating. Here, I use news stories about a land-mark synthetic biology project – *Saccharomyces cerevisiae* 2.0 – to exemplify how studying popular science communication as popular science construction enables asking not how well science is being communicated to the public, but what kind of science is being made in public.

Saccharomyces cerevisiae 2.0, or the 'synthetic yeast' project, is an early testing ground for how whole-genome engineering will be rhetorically constructed for public use. The project aims to comprehensively re-design and synthesise the genome of a microbial species also known as baker's or brewer's yeast. As such, the project is simultaneously headline news and relatable to familiar features of everyday life. Unlike most model research organisms, yeast is sold on grocery store shelves, and even if news consumers have never personally used yeast to make bread, beer, or wine, they very likely know that yeast is involved in these common foods. Popular news stories about synthetic yeast are therefore in a position to locate where 'synthetic yeast' sits with respect to the 'yeast' readers are familiar with from the kitchen, the bakery, and the pub. Thus, news stories involve constructive choices. Do they make the 'yeast' of the synthetic yeast project and the 'yeast' of bread, beer, and wine the same 'yeast'?

Relating 'yeast' in synthetic biology labs and 'yeast' elsewhere involves polit-ically laden choices with ramifications far beyond non-specialists' acceptance of synthetic biology technology. The novelty of the synthetic yeast project largely rests on the extraordinary extent to which yeast is re-engineered, involving historically contentious genetic modification (GM) technologies. The perceived safety of the project largely rests on the harmlessness of the organism. And its relevance involves the breadth of potential applications enabled by yeast's widespread roles not only in food and industry, but also as a model organism for basic and applied biomedical research. Material-semiotic perspectives from STS make it possible to ask: How is synthetic yeast con-structed as something novel, or as something familiar? How are its potential uses mapped in terms of what readers already know about yeast? And how do constructions of synthetic yeast in public constrain or enable what synthetic biology products can do? The pertinent questions thus become not whether the identity of synthetic yeast is accurately represented by science writers, but how synthetic yeast-in-public is enacted, what it is made to be, and how it relates to the rest of what readers know and experience.

Contemporary STS scholarship in the material-semiotic tradition investi-gates the nature of 'things' as practices. Rather than imagining that humans discover, study, use, or modify stable and pre-existing objects, this perspective understands what we see as stable objects as 'assemblages' (Foucault 1969; Mol 2002) – the product of conceptual work necessary to make sense of myriad specific practices separated in time and space as 'the same thing'. Synthetic yeast in the lab can thus be investigated in terms of scientific practices invoking synthetic yeast as a unified thing across multiple spaces of practice. But synthetic yeast is not only practised through the computer algorithms, Petri dishes, and DNA sequence diagrams of synthetic biology labs. Synthetic yeast is brought into being in worlds outside the lab through the discursive practices (Foucault 1969) of the popular media, the only spaces of practice in which people who are not synthetic biologists can meet it. Consequently, the discursive practices of popular news construct what synthetic yeast becomes for these audiences.

8.2 TEXTS AS REALITY-MAKING PRACTICES

Science communication is often described as translating science into language that lay readers can understand. 'Translation' indicates that scientific knowledge is information best represented in scientific language, but which can and should be made intelligible to people illiterate in scientific language by replacing one set of words with another set of words. In contrast, discursive enactment indicates that different knowledges are constructed through different languages and can never be abstracted from the language through which they are made. Shifting from translation to enactment ties together two theoretical strands extending from Foucault's archaeological approach to knowledge. The first, material semiotics in the tradition of Mol (2002) and Law (Law & Lien 2012), advocates for the utility of seeing worlds as multiply enacted in practice and then variably assembled into unities. The second, critical discourse theory, sees texts as spaces where social relations are played out (Fairclough 1992). Bringing them together involves understanding texts as reality-making practices.

8.3 MATERIAL SEMIOTICS: THINGS ASSEMBLED IN PRACTICE

Material semiotics redefines metaphysical questions as empirical questions about observable practices, asking not what things fundamentally are but how they are made. For science communication, material semiotic perspectives redefine questions about how *accurately* science is represented as questions about how science is *practised* in popular communication – one subset of many practices through which scientific knowledge is enacted. Practices separated by time or space are not necessarily assumed to deal with 'the same thing'. Things, instead, can be seen as temporarily stable assemblages – as the product of conceptual work applied to understand a particular set of practices as being coherent such that they 'hold together for long enough to act in relation to something else' (Law 2008: 632).

Many assembled practices hold together for so long and acquire so many additional relations that they are difficult to think otherwise. Science communication, however, is often in a position to shape how scientific concepts are assembled in relation to other things. Material-semiotic perspectives indicate that popular science communication has important, value-laden consequences for how new scientific phenomena become part of the worlds lay readers inhabit.

8.4 DISCOURSE THEORY: LANGUAGE AS PRACTICE

Discourse theory observes that communication consists of utterances – discursive practices – that reciprocally reflect and construct the worlds of our lived experiences, aggregating to systematically pattern the worlds that language-users inhabit. Discursive objects – ways of using words, which contribute to assemblages, which become stable enough to be treated as things – can thus take different shapes in different discourse communities. In turn, discursive objects are information-handling tools that continue to construct the nature of the discursive object as an assemblage of discourse practices. Discursive objects are therefore always under construction, changing as they continue to be assembled, as a function of choices about which discursive instances to treat as talking about 'the same thing'.

This understanding of how things are made through discourse can be productively joined with material-semiotic understandings of how things are made through practices by seeing texts as practices. Texts are practised through acts of reading, performances between the text and a reader in a social context constraining which kinds of readings are possible (Austin 1962; Fish 1982). Context is itself reciprocally and iteratively constructed through ongoing readings, simultaneously enacting the futures with which STS research is often concerned (Michael 2017). Acts of making meaning between text and reader not only make meaning but also make context, aggregating in groups of textual performances that differ not merely in vocabulary or ways of phrasing things, but in the worlds they create (Law & Singleton 2014).

8.5 DISCURSIVE ENACTMENT AS AN ALTERNATIVE TO TRANSLATION

Scientific knowledge can never simply be translated from scientific discourse into popular discourse, because scientific and popular discourses practise and pattern the world in systematically different ways for the discourse communities created through sharing those utterances (Bakhtin 1981). Translation implies that science writing, whether for scientific or lay audiences, describes scientific knowledge existing outside, in advance, and independent of how science is written. To ask how clearly or accurately popularisations represent science, a researcher must either assume that scientific knowledge is fixed and remains constant as it moves across audiences, or that it has one appropriate, inevitable, or correct public representation. These are poor assumptions, as rhetoric of science research examining scientific knowledge across diverse texts indicate. Scientific knowledge is primarily constructed in and through language, because language constitutes most science-making practices that can be widely shared, assessed, and perpetuated (Bazerman 2000; Myers 1990).

Translation also implies agreement within a scientific community and correspondence between that agreement and the 'real' nature of science. Synthetic biology offers particularly good examples illustrating how those premises cannot be taken for granted. Science communication studies that begin by assuming that science is a unified, trustworthy body of knowledge tend to argue that good communication will promote public acceptance of synthetic biology, in contrast to the mass public mistrust around genetically modified (GM) products. When those studies conceptualise popular science as translating science, they also have to begin with assumptions about the real or most accurate relationship between synthetic biology and GM – a relationship that is far from codified within the synthetic biology community itself. For example, when Kronberger and co-authors (2009, 2012) studied citizen reactions to mock synthetic biology (SB) news stories, the researchers needed to assume that synthetic biology and GM are not necessarily related, but that describing synthetic biology in terms of GM might be 'good or bad news for SB', with 'good news' defined in terms of increasing public acceptance. Similarly, Ancilloti and co-authors' (2017: 239) study of synthetic biology in Nordic news asked 'whether articles were clear enough to enable the public to understand what SB is and to distinguish it from other biotechnologies', classifying news items as 'clear, not clear, misleading, and missing'.

Scientists, however, are neither clear about nor in agreement over what synthetic biology is, nor its relationship to GM or other biotechnologies ('What's in a name?' 2009). Most describe synthetic biology on a continuum with genetic engineering. Some call the name a fresh marketing slogan for ongoing engineering work; others relate it to greater systematisation versus genetic engineering. Meanwhile, social scientists have observed a relative absence of features distinctive to synthetic biology alone (O'Malley et al., 2008). The European Commission Scientific Committees, in line with other policy groups, have concluded that scientific criteria are 'unable to unambiguously differentiate synthetic biology from GM' (Epstein & Vermeire 2016: 601; see also Douglas & Stemerding 2014). Science communication researchers, in other words, continue to ignore what STS researcher Brian Wynne (2008: 21) calls the 'elephant in the room – what is the "science" which we are supposing people experience and sense?'

In the absence of consensus, asking whether scientific popularisations are effective or clear requires that science communication researchers themselves define authoritative knowledge against which popularisations can be evaluated. In contrast, refocusing on practice avoids comparing discursive representations to scientific things as they 'really are' – and therefore also avoids the problem of science communication researchers having to decide what scientific things 'really are' – because discursive representations are understood to construct things in themselves rather than representing things that already exist. Therefore, this method allows for asking how texts practise their objects rather than questioning whether texts accurately represent an assumed external fixed reality.

In sum, then, (scientific) things such as synthetic yeast take shape in practice. Writing is a practice. Written texts shape discursive objects-as-assemblages and relationships amongst them. Features of those texts matter to how such things and relationships take shape. Writing shapes things and relationships, offering choices about what discursive objects-as-assemblages become, what they can do, and where they can go. As science communication/STS scholars, we can examine *how* science-born creatures such as synthetic yeast take shape in writing and what values are embedded in those choices.

Below, I explore one example of how a scientific phenomenon is made in public, asking how synthetic yeast is constructed in relation to the yeast with which non-scientist readers may already be familiar.

8.6 METHODS

8.6.1 CORPUS CONSTRUCTION

Investigating how synthetic yeast is practised in public means identifying which public spaces are interesting. This presents a problem: which instances of science communication – and thus which audiences – should be considered together to comprise a 'public'? *The Economist* and the *Daily Mail* address very different audiences, but both address non-specialists whose only exposure to synthetic biology research is likely to be the news they read. Moreover, a curious lay reader browsing the internet may encounter articles from a wide range of sources. Consequently, I included in my corpus all written, general-audience news items focusing specifically on the *Saccharomyces cerevisiae* 2.0 project. However, I excluded articles from trade publications relating to wine, baking, and beer, as their audiences have specific professional interests in yeast and are thus likely to construct 'yeast' in categorically different ways and through different sets of practices compared with non-specialist readers. The corpus was limited to English-language text media for pragmatic reasons.

Synthetic yeast can be an interesting news item because yeast makes so many connections to everyday experience, but that same quality also makes comprehensively gathering public-facing articles difficult. Synthetic yeast finds many different non-scientist audiences, from readers of British tabloids who may be interested in scientific novelty, to followers of the quality press culturally invested in educating themselves about current scientific advances, to lay technology enthusiasts browsing the internet and workers in business and finance primed to see synthetic biology as disruptive technology for medicine and manufacturing. Systematically capturing *all* popular articles relating to synthetic yeast is difficult because no single database encompasses such varied sources. Furthermore, not all articles use the term '*Saccharomyces cerevisiae* 2.0', and the keywords 'synthetic yeast' dredge up a high proportion of unrelated articles. What is lost by not defining a narrower range of more systematically defined news articles is gained in capturing how synthetic yeast occurs across the diverse publications a 'general reader' might encounter. It should be noted, however, that available search methods (i.e., databases more likely to index newspapers from Europe and North America than from Africa, Asia, or South America) bias the results towards locating that reader in the United Kingdom or the United States.

I searched ProQuest Business, indexing international innovation news, for all mentions of 'yeast' and 'synthetic biology' across blogs, podcasts, websites, magazines, newspapers, and other sources (but excluding patents, law briefs, and other legal and financial documents), returning 182 results. I repeated the search in LexisLibrary, indexing UK national and regional newspapers, returning 27 results. Because neither database captures online popular science sites, I searched Google for 'synthetic yeast', manually excluding articles from yeast-related trade publications. After filtering off-target results and removing duplications (often the same press release repeated in different publications), the resulting corpus contained 66 individual items – essentially all public-facing English-language news articles about the synthetic yeast project. Given that the project as yet only exists in the public imagination in the news, not in consumer applications or other outcomes, the corpus is also essentially comprehensive of written contributions to how synthetic yeast is assembled in public.

Articles in the corpus primarily relate to two significant events. In March 2014, a *Nature* paper announced the completion of the first fully synthetic chromosome (Annaluru et al. 2014). In March 2017, as I began to compile the corpus for this study, a special issue of the journal *Science* announced five newly completed chromosomes. Both attracted significant media attention. A few items also date from 2013, when individual labs initially publicised their commitment to the project.

8.6.2 ANALYSIS

Popular science stories are rich with intertextual features contributing to how science takes shape in general discourse. To focus on how synthetic yeast is located with respect to more familiar yeasts, I closely read each article for (1) how the 'yeast' in 'synthetic yeast' was identified, (2) how titles and introductions as framing devices instruct readers in where to conceptually locate the story (Cook et al., 2013; Dahl 2015), and (3) which applications synthetic yeast was forecast to produce. I developed initial codes under the headings 'titles', 'introductions', 'images', 'applications', and 'identifying the yeast', grouped and refined those codes into thematic clusters, and re-read articles against the rationalised code book. I augmented this qualitative analysis with a word frequency table calculated across the entire corpus using NVivo.

8.7 RESULTS

8.7.1 IDENTIFYING THE YEAST

The most obvious means of positioning synthetic yeast with respect to other yeasts comes in how authors identify the organism. Most do not assume that *Saccharomyces cerevisiae* is familiar to their readers: only 29 of 66 used the scientific binomial, and every article also identifies the species in some other way. A few identify 'yeast' only as 'yeast', relying on the familiarity of *S. cerevisiae* to avoid confusion with the 1,500 or so other single-celled fungal species. Many use the colloquialisms 'brewer's yeast' (21 articles) or 'baker's yeast' (15 articles) without further explanation. An additional group descriptively identifies 'yeast' as the yeast used in beer, bread, and wine, giving readers more context without prioritising either brewers' or bakers' potential nominal ownership.

Beyond the creature's name, articles also identify yeast in terms of its valuable human relationships, either with human *society* or with human cells. *Futurism* (Caughill 2017) calls yeast a 'friend', Nova (Eck 2014) 'the most important micro-organism to human civilization', and *Wired* (Molteni 2017) 'civilization-supporting fermenters'. *The Financial Times* (Cookson 2017), exemplifying a strategy used by several others, explicitly connects traditional food production with newer scientific uses for yeast: 'used for thousands of years in baking, brewing and winemaking, yeast has more recently become the workhorse for modern biotechnology'.

Synthetic yeast is also portrayed as a eukaryote related to human cells, as in the *Daily Mail*'s explanation that 'baker's yeast is similar to human cells but simpler and easier to study' (Allen 2017) or *The Economist*'s 2017 article emphasising the great divide between prokaryotes and eukaryotes with bacteria on one side and yeast and humans together on the other. Synthetic yeast is therefore a step towards 'genome synthesis of more complex organisms, including humans', a point made both by *The Financial Times* (Cookson 2017) and *Gizmodo*'s tech blog *io9* (Dvorsky 2014). Yeast is introduced as an ecosystem actor independent from its relationships with humans only twice, on the activist website *Friends of the Earth* (2014), highlighting yeast's roles in plant health, and in a *Popular Mechanics* (Herkewitz 2014) piece calling yeast 'one of nature's great decomposers', before elaborating on its roles in food production.

Individually, these articles make different choices about which 'yeast' to emphasise, but each reflects choices about how to connect this unfamiliar, high-tech synthetic biology project to everyday experience. Each also reflects choices about what this new incarnation of yeast is 'good for'. Consequently, these articles assemble the identity of synthetic yeast in two ways. Individually, they identify that the yeast of the synthetic yeast project is 'the same yeast' as yeast in readers' familiar worlds. Collectively, they construct the identity of synthetic yeast by constituting the set of discourse practices through which 'synthetic yeast' manifests in public.

8.7.2 TITLES, INTRODUCTIONS, AND IMAGES

Titles, introductory sentences, and the images located at the top of most articles function as framing devices, tacitly instructing readers in how to read what follows (Entman 1993). In this corpus, those frames emphasise either what scientists achieve in making synthetic yeast or what synthetic yeast might achieve in the future. Titles and introductions focused on scientific accomplishments identify synthetic yeast as the object of scientific activity – creating, building, producing, developing, or rewriting – as in the *BBC News* headline 'Scientists [are] building the world's first synthetic yeast' (Hogenboom 2013). Some focus on scientific progress, as when 'Scientists create "designer yeast" in major step toward synthetic life' in a *Washington Post* headline (Kaplan 2017); others emphasise the making element of this process, as in an *NBC News* (2014) headline 'Gene gurus create synthetic yeast chromosome from scratch'. Titles and introductions focused on potential applications of synthetic yeast instead emphasise improved scientific understanding or producing pharmaceuticals and biofuels. *Scientific American* (Maxmen 2017), for example, points to scientific applications with 'Synthetic yeast chromosomes help probe mysteries of evolution', and *The Muslim News* (Buaras 2014) leads with 'Scientists create synthetic yeast chromosome that could revolutionise medicine'.

These two frames portray yeast differently, the first as passive objects of scientific activity, the second as active 'saviors' (McLeod et al., 2017) or co-workers in human exploration. Both cohere with identifying synthetic yeast as 'the same' yeast long used in the service of human needs. A notable subset of titles and first lines makes the connection more explicitly, however, by identifying synthetic yeast as a tool for making better beer. 'Boffins create synthetic yeast for beer', according to *The Sun* (Bannon 2013). 'Synthetic yeast may make beer cheaper', according to *The Daily Telegraph* (Gray 2013). Tech website *Muse* Collective (Herrera 2014) asserts that craft brewers need synthetic yeast because 'American tastes in beer are changing'. While bread and wine inevitably appear somewhere in lists detailing why yeast is important, beer is unique among fermented comestibles in framing full articles.

Headline images generally reinforce these titles by positioning synthetic yeast as a scientific wonder or source of potential applications, depicting scientists in the laboratory, laboratory equipment, microscopic images of yeast cells, DNA and DNA editing, or fermented foods. Among fermented foods, beer is almost exclusively depicted (excepting one small stock photo of bread and one cheerful image of wine drinkers), sometimes with foamy lager splashing enthusiastically across pages. The only two outliers reflected regional interests: the *ShanghaiDaily.com* (2017) included a photograph of the five Chinese scientists leading laboratories contributing to the project; *Mint* (2012), an Indian newspaper, showed a traditionally dressed man carrying a basket of coal on his head, suggesting the potential of synthetic yeast to reduce fossil fuel use. Although scientists appear in several of these images – the Chinese group, a headshot of the central project leader, young lab workers in white coats, or gloved hands holding Petri dishes – the only other humans are the coal-carrying man and the wine drinkers, with the focus otherwise on the yeast cell or DNA's familiar double-helix.

Images, like titles and introductions, largely reinforce familiar appeals to value science on the twin bases of wonder and speculative world improvement, making yeast part of a fantastic but far away world (Fahnestock 1998). Together, they help readers know where to locate the 'yeast' in question – in scientific laboratories, or maybe in the pub.

8.7.3 SYNTHETIC YEAST APPLICATIONS

Descriptions of synthetic yeast's anticipated applications, often in articles' conclusions, reinforce initial instructions to readers about where in the world to locate synthetic yeast. Excepting a group of very short (<100 word) newspaper blurbs and two longer articles from tech publications discussing technical intricacies only, every article appeals to synthetic yeast's importance on the basis of anticipated applications: medicine, biofuels, and food discussed in aggregate; scientific progress; designer humans; or beer. A majority simply list general and uncontroversial social priorities: medicine, biofuels, food, and sometimes generic industrial applications:

> 'Food and energy of various kinds' and 'solutions to global problems, including energy shortages and pollution' (*ShanghaiDaily.com* 2017)

> 'Vaccines, medicines and more sustainable biofuels' (Brown 2017)

> '...unmet needs in medicine and industry' (Hots 2017)

Some identify synthetic yeast as a stepping stone towards genomes 'honed for specific roles' (*The Guardian* 2017; see also *The Washington Post* 2017; NPR's

Policy-ish 2017). Nine take the additional step of connecting synthetic yeast to the potential for future designer human genomes specifically. Two and a half years before the nascent Genome Project-Write's intention to synthesise a full human genome made front-page news (Pollack 2016), tech site *Gizmodo's* blog *io9* forecast that:

> We'll be able to use this sort of biotech to do such things as increase human immune function, slow down the effects of aging or even boost our memory and intelligence. They could provide new forms of immunization, protecting against specific diseases like AIDS or certain cancers. And we could also be endowed with new capacities altogether, including the ability to see ultraviolet light, or navigation in the dark by a system of sonar similar to that employed by bats. (Dvorsky 2014)

Synthetic yeast, here, is not the 'humble' (*Christian Science Monitor, Scientific American, Gizmodo, The Independent, USA Today*) yeast of bread and beer, but an agent of highly advanced human development.

Word frequencies across the corpus reinforce that picture. 'Human' appears 208 times, making it the 12th most frequent word of three letters or more, after 'biology' and 'Boeke' (the surname of the project's leader) but before 'cells' and 'genetic'. As terms for identifying 'yeast', 'baker's', 'brewer's', and 'cerevisiae' appear with relatively equal frequency (35, 33, and 29 times, respectively). GM technology is mentioned in only three articles: as part of a timeline of British accomplishments in genetics, in a warning that the beer industry will only be able to harness synthetic yeast if it is not intimidated by public concerns about GM (Herkewitz 2017), and in a statement that 'the breakthrough will reignite the debate over GM food' (Allen 2017). 'Beer' appears 107 times, the 36th most frequent word of three letters or longer and much more common than either 'bread' (41 appearances) or 'wine' (36 appearances).

8.8 DISCUSSION

While popular news articles assemble synthetic yeast with the yeasts of baking and brewing, most take that familiar creature and make clear that this yeast is also an advanced scientific tool, making synthetic yeast a simultaneous inhabitant of domestic and high-tech worlds. This snapshot leads to at least three observations about how synthetic yeast may act and travel in public. First, 'yeast' is not natural but already a human tool, and so is not subject to a typical objection that genetic engineering threatens important ontological lines between nature and artefact (reviewed in Preston 2013). Synthetic yeast is not a synthetic sea turtle or a synthetic giant sequoia. The distinction is not only about micro-organisms versus charismatic megafauna or megaflora, but about organisms defined in relation to humanity rather than appreciated chiefly for their beauty, environmental contributions, or existential value. 'Yeast' is 'domesticated', a 'workhorse', and 'civilisation-supporting', a technology serving human purposes. Consequently, while yeast may be alive, it is also – and more significantly in these popular articles – a tool. We are invited to think more about the wonderful uses of living tools, and less about engineering living creatures. Moreover, yeast is similar to human cells in ways that make yeast useful to medicine, providing a potentially compelling reason why humans *should* engineer it for life-saving purposes.

Second, synthetic yeast is not genetically modified yeast. The near-total absence of 'GM' in this corpus coheres with previous analyses of synthetic biology in Nordic (Ancillotti et al., 2017), Swiss (Schmid-Petri et al., 2014), and German-language (Gschmeidler & Seiringer 2012) news; all find that synthetic biology is largely not aligned with GM and that benefits are emphasised over potential risks or ethical concerns. How products of synthetic biology like synthetic yeast become defined in relation to GM will be important not just for how GM debates are or are not carried over, but also for how products' identities develop and interact with existing institutions. Another incidental finding worth following in greater detail is the equation of synthetic yeast with 'artificial life' or 'synthetic life'. Attempting to make sense of 'artificial' or 'synthetic' life adds an additional layer to ongoing debates about precisely what we mean by 'life' among scholars concerned with theories of biology. What these terms mean in popular discourse is a different matter, and an empirical rather than a purely theoretical question. How whole-genome engineering is seen to connect with ideas about new life will be increasingly important as scientific interest in synthesising a complete human genome increasingly enters public conversation.

Third, this now high-tech yeast remains much more closely tied to beer than to any of its other traditional roots. Nearly 15% of articles were framed entirely in terms of beer. None was similarly framed in terms of bread, wine, or any other fermented product. In contrast to artisan baking and artisan or 'authentic' wine-making – both defined through a return to 'natural' or 'wild' yeasts and traditional processes – craft brewing is characterised by tales of wacky and sometimes wildly untraditional innovation (e.g., Acitelli 2013). Tech lovers and beer enthusiasts are overlapping demographics, a common anecdotal observation which can be substantiated by searching online archives of the science and technology magazine *Popular Mechanics*. The search term 'wine' returns 12 results, including one about stain removal, one about removing labels from bottles, three about home woodworking projects, one that's actually about beer... in short, only *one* about wine. 'Bread' returns nine results, including a story about a smaller-than-a-bread-basket cell tower and five stories about toasters. Searching for 'beer' returns 144 results, most indeed about brewing or drinking beer. The expectations of tech-savvy, innovative, small-batch production that put the 'craft' in craft brewing appear to make ample space for engineering and, perhaps, for engineered synthetic yeast to move from bench to bar.

While synthetic yeast's safety is emphasised through its twin links to the safety of yeast and to the outstanding accomplishment of scientists, its novelty is being compartmentalised to places where novelty is likely to be expected and accepted: in cutting-edge science pursuing uncontroversial and widely valued improvements to human and environmental health, and in beer. Synthetic yeast in public is being normalised as another scientific breakthrough for improving the future, with its ethical importance linked to its potential heralding of human genome synthesis rather than the involvement of the yeast itself. These frames can be expected to inform popular understandings and shape future public conversations about synthetic yeast and about synthetic biology more broadly. Along these lines, it will be worth observing the degree to which this most charismatic of micro-organisms becomes a keyword in public talk about whole-organism engineering and, if so, how 'yeast' shapes conversations about making cells into tools, chassis, and factories.

8.9 CONCLUSIONS

In this chapter, I have aimed to do two things. First, I outlined a rationale for seeing popular science communication as public science construction, enacting what new science becomes for non-specialist audiences rather than communicating with more or less accuracy about a fixed scientific object. Second, I used that lens to examine popular English-language news articles about the synthetic yeast project, asking what kind of yeast they make 'synthetic yeast' and thus where they locate synthetic yeast with respect to familiar elements of readers' worlds.

News articles construct synthetic yeast as a discursive object in the world outside the lab by locating it among existing features of that landscape. In this sense, synthetic yeast is an easy science story because even if 'synthetic' can be difficult to explain, 'yeast' is a feature of common experience. Most articles locate familiar baker's or brewer's yeast in an equally familiar narrative of scientific breakthroughs holding numerous, if poorly defined, benefits for human and environmental health. A distinct minority locates synthetic yeast in the brewing world, where craft fanatics are willing to try new things in search of new flavours and everyday drinkers might welcome technology for producing a stronger or cheaper pint. Both positions evade potential common objections to GM and place synthetic yeast in a familiar trajectory of scientific advances benefiting humanity. Importantly, asking how synthetic yeast is constructed makes no assumptions about relationships between whole-genome synthetic biology and GM. Such judgements invariably reflect the position and values of authors given the lack of scientific consensus on the nature of synthetic biology, while focusing attention on a notion of 'accuracy' that is defined in terms of an unexplored normative agenda.

Investigating science communication as construction entails, at least initially, asking what science communication is currently doing rather than evaluating whether or not it is doing it well. It does not, however, avoid evaluating science communication at all. Evaluating science communication as translation means asking: how accurately and completely do popularisations convey scientific knowledge? Evaluating science communication as enactment instead encourages asking: how do popularisations construct scientific objects and, in so doing, shape public conversation about how science acts in shared social spaces?

Certainly, good popular science communication should be consistent with disciplinary science communication in such a way that the 'things' constructed through public and specialist discourses cohere. Such coherence not only permits non-specialists to learn from specialists in any particular field, but also facilitates conversation about things understood to be held in common across specialist and non-specialist communities. In addition, however, good popular science communication should *also* make space for such cross-community conversations and other forms of public discussion by making connections between new science stories and what lay readers already know – that is, by making science *relevant* (Huang & Soergel 2013).

The nature of those connections is neither a foregone conclusion nor merely a question of accuracy insofar as these new scientific objects do not already exist in public discourse but are being newly brought into being through popular discursive practices. How those connections and objects are made is inescapably value-laden. Ultimately, therefore, the primary advantage of studying popular science communication as popular science construction comes in highlighting where science communication involves making value-laden decisions. Making these communication decisions visible also makes it possible to see them as contingent and fluid rhetorical problems with multiple potential solutions that may be better or worse depending on the interests and goals of those involved. Seeing them in such terms makes it possible to ask what goods or priorities or values science communication serves, rather than working through the values of any particular scientific community without recognising them as values at all.

Consequently, the assessment criteria for evaluating science communication must be a product of explicit decision making. The alternative – deriving assessment criteria from ideals of scientific accuracy – makes one of two assumptions: either that those criteria are value-neutral, or that the values of a singular scientific knowledge-making community are the best values which should be accepted by everyone. Neither assumption can be valid if science is acknowledged as being only one among multiple valid ways of knowing, and if scientific knowledge is acknowledged as always contingent (see Chapters 2 and 3 in this volume). Neither assumption can be valid in contemporary societies where a plurality of views is acknowledged and accepted, and if scientific ways of knowing are themselves acknowledged as being multiple.

Practically speaking, science communicators should consider that they are never simply communicating about new science or translating scientific knowledge, but making choices about what that science becomes in audience's worlds. Science communication is not simply about truth. It involves choices about how to locate scientific objects-as-popular-discursive-constructions, closer or further from ordinary domestic life and familiar industries, safely enclosed in a lab or mixed up in social and economic activities with all their potential dangers and promised benefits. These choices contribute to building the future in which synthetic biologists, readers, yeast, and the rest of us will reside as we collectively undertake the ongoing process of deciding what relationships new scientific technologies make with the outside world. Making such choices visible is important to understanding – and in so doing, creating opportunities to alter – that world-making project.

Finally, joining science communication and STS around rhetorical construction also speaks to the methods we use to construct the boundaries among these (inter)disciplinary communities. In science communication scholarship, texts are often *vehicles* for content, and the content is often extracted for analysis against some benchmark defining 'effective' science communication. In much of STS, science communication texts are themselves parts of heterogeneous material-social actor-networks (Law 1992); while written texts are frequently implicated in STS concerns, internal features of the texts themselves are rarely a focal point. In contrast, examining how internal elements of science communication texts enact scientific knowledge bridges science communication and STS interests about how science is shared with lay audiences and about how scientific knowledge is made. This conjunction again gives rise to opportunities to intervene through the intratextual features of science communication texts. It also disturbs the typical hierarchy between scientists who discover facts and science communicators who must merely convey those facts accurately, thereby distributing responsibility for making knowledge that does desirable things – in whatever ways 'desirable' is constituted – more widely.

ACKNOWLEDGEMENTS

This work was conducted with support from the Biological and Biotechnological Sciences Research Council (BB/M005690/1, ERASynBio-IESY) and the European Research Council (ERC 616510-ENLIFE). I gratefully acknowledge the research foundations and ongoing assistance of the 'Engineering Life' team, led by Jane Calvert and including Dominic Berry, Emma Frow, Pablo Schyfter, Deborah Scott, and Robert Smith. I also thank the editors and other contributors to this volume for their constructive critiques on earlier drafts of this chapter.

REFERENCES

Acitelli, Tom. 2013. *The Audacity of Hops*. Chicago, IL: Chicago Review Press.

Allen, Victoria. 2017. 'Scientists Create Synthetic Life after Building Yeast DNA'. *The Daily Mail*, 9 March. http://www.dailymail.co.uk/sciencetech/article-4298238/Scientists-create-synthetic-life-building-yeast-DNA.html.

Ancillotti, Mirko, Niklas Holmberg, Mikael Lindfelt, and Stefan Eriksson. 2017. 'Uncritical and Unbalanced Coverage of Synthetic Biology in the Nordic Press'. *Public Understanding of Science* 26 (2): 235–250. doi:10.1177/0963662515609834.

Annaluru, Narayana, Héloïse Muller, Leslie A. Mitchell, Sivaprakash Ramalingam, Giovanni Stracquadanio, Sarah M. Richardson, Jessica S. Dymond, et al. 2014. 'Total Synthesis of a Functional Designer Eukaryotic Chromosome'. *Science (New York, N.Y.)* 344 (6179): 55–58. https://doi.org/10.1126/science.1249252.

Austin, J. L. 1962. *How to do Things with Words: The William James Lectures Delivered at Harvard University in 1955*. Oxford: Clarendon Press.

Bakhtin, M. M. 1981. *The Dialogic Imagination: Four Essays*. Edited by Michael Holquist. Translated by Caryl Emerson and Michael Holquist. Austin, TX: University of Texas Press.

Bannon, Aoife. 2013. 'Brew Genius! Boffins Create Synthetic Yeast for Beer'. *The Sun* (England), 12 July.

Bazerman, Charles. 2000. *Shaping Written Knowledge: The Genre and Activity of the Experimental Article in Science*. WAC Clearinghouse Landmark Publications in Writing Studies. WAC Clearinghouse. http://wac.colostate.edu/books/bazerman_shaping/.

Brown, Kristen V. 2017. 'Scientists Just Took a Major Step Toward Creating Synthetic Life'. *Gizmodo*, 9 March. http://gizmodo.com/scientists-just-took-a-major-step-toward-the-first-comp-1793106676.

Buaras, Elham Assad. 2014. 'Scientists Create Synthetic Yeast Chromosome that Could Revolutionise Medicine'. *The Muslim News*, 25 April.

Caughill, Patrick. 2017. 'Scientists are Close to Creating a Fully Synthetic Genome'. *Futurism*, 12 March. https://futurism.com/scientists-are-close-to-creating-a-fully-synthetic-genome/.

Cook, Brian R., Mike Kesby, Ioan Fasey, and Chris Spray. 2013. 'The Persistence of "Normal" Catchment Management Despite the Participatory Turn: Exploring the Power Effects of Competing Frames of Reference'. *Social Studies of Science* 43 (5): 754–779. doi:10.1177/0306312713478670.

Cookson, Clive. 2017. 'Synthetic Yeast Project Brings Lab-Created Life a Step Closer'. *Financial Times*, 9 March. https://www.ft.com/content/3fa90392-04b7-11e7-aa5b-6bb07f5c8e12.

Dahl, Trine. 2015. 'Contested Science in the Media Linguistic Traces of News Writers' Framing Activity'. *Written Communication* 32 (1): 39–65. doi:10.1177/0741088314557623.

Douglas, Conor M. W., and Dirk Stemerding. 2014. 'Challenges for the European Governance of Synthetic Biology for Human Health'. *Life Sciences, Society and Policy* 10 (December): 6. doi:10.1186/s40504-014-0006-7.

Dvorsky, George. 2014. 'Biologists Have Built an Artificial Chromosome from Scratch.' *io9*, 28 March. http://io9.gizmodo.com/biologists-have-built-an-artificial-chromosome-from-scr-1553800146.

Eck, Alison. 2014. 'College Students Create Groundbreaking Synthetic Yeast Chromosome'. *NOVA Next*, 28 March. http://www.pbs.org/wgbh/nova/next/tech/undergrads/.

Entman, Robert M. 1993. 'Framing: Toward Clarification of a Fractured Paradigm'. *Journal of Communication* 43 (4): 51–58. doi:10.1111/j.1460-2466.1993.tb01304.x.

Epstein, Michelle M., and Theo Vermeire. 2016. 'Scientific Opinion on Risk Assessment of Synthetic Biology'. *Trends in Biotechnology* 34 (8): 601–603. doi:10.1016/j.tibtech.2016.04.013.

Fahnestock, J. 1998. 'Accommodating Science: The Rhetorical Life of Science Facts'. *Written Communication* 15 (3): 330–350.

Fairclough, Norman. 1992. *Discourse and Social Change*. London: Polity Press.

Fish, Stanley. 1982. *Is There a Text in This Class? The Authority of Interpretive Communities*. Cambridge, MA: Harvard University Press.

Foucault, Michael. 1969. *The Archaeology of Knowledge and the Discourse on Language*. Translated by A. M. Sheridan. New York: Vintage.

Friends of the Earth. 2014. 'Emerging Tech Project'. *Friends of the Earth*, 27 June.

Gray, Richard. 2013. 'Synthetic Yeast May Make Beer Cheaper'. *The Daily Telegraph* (London), 11 July.

Gschmeidler, Brigitte, and Alexandra Seiringer. 2012. '"Knight in Shining Armour" or "Frankenstein's Creation"? The Coverage of Synthetic Biology in German-Language Media'. *Public Understanding of Science* 21 (2): 163–173.

Herkewitz, William. 2014. 'Scientists Create Synthetic Yeast Chromosome (and Unlock the Future of Beer)'. *Popular Mechanics*, 27 March. https://www.popularmechanics.com/science/health/a10289/scientists-create-synthetic-yeasts-and-open-the-door-to-the-future-of-beer-16637455/

Herrera, Anne. 2014. 'Future of Beer – Synthetic Yeast'. *Muse* Collective, 4 May. http://musecollective.com/future-of-beer-scientists-create-synthetic-yeast/.

Hogenboom, Melissa. 2013. 'Scientists Building the World's First Synthetic Yeast'. *BBC News*, 11 July. http://www.bbc.co.uk/news/science-environment-23244768.

Hots, Robert Lee. 2017. 'Scientists Make Progress Toward Engineering Synthetic Yeast'. *The Wall Street Journal*, March 10.

Huang, Xiaoli, and Dagobert Soergel. 2013. 'Relevance: An Improved Framework for Explicating the Notion'. *Journal of the American Society for Information Science and Technology* 64 (1): 18–35. doi:10.1002/asi.22811.

Kaplan, Sarah. 2017. 'Scientists Create "Designer Yeast" in Major Step toward Synthetic Life'. *The Washington Post*, 9 March. https://www.washingtonpost.com/news/speaking-of-science/wp/2017/03/09/scientists-create-designer-yeast-in-major-step-toward-synthetic-life/?utm_term=.7ddc0a3ae798.

Kronberger, Nicole, Peter Holts, and Wolfgang Wagner. 2012. 'Consequences of Media Information Uptake and Deliberation: Focus Groups' Symbolic Coping with Synthetic Biology'. *Public Understanding of Science* 21 (2): 174–187. doi:10.1177/0963662511400331.

Kronberger, Nicole, Peter Holts, Wolfgang Kerbe, Ewald Strasser, and Wolfgang Wagner. 2009. 'Communicating Synthetic Biology: From the Lab via the Media to the Broader Public'. *Systems and Synthetic Biology* 3 (1–4): 19–26. doi:10.1007/s11693-009-9031-x.

Law, John. 1992. 'Notes on the Theory of the Actor-Network: Ordering, Strategy, and Heterogeneity'. *Systems Practice* 5 (4): 379–393.

Law, John. 2008. 'On Sociology and STS'. *The Sociological Review* 56 (4): 623–649. doi:10.1111/j.1467-954X.2008.00808.x.

Law, John, and Marianne Elisabeth Lien. 2012. 'Slippery: Field Notes in Empirical Ontology'. *Social Studies of Science* 43 (3): 363–378.

Law, John, and Vicky Singleton. 2014. 'ANT, Multiplicity and Policy'. *Critical Policy Studies* 8 (4): 379–396.

Maxmen, Amy. 2017. 'Synthetic Yeast Chromosomes Help Probe Mysteries of Evolution Scientific American – Google Search'. *Scientific American*, 10 March. https://www.google.co.uk/search?q=Synthetic+yeast+chromosomes+help+probe+mysteries+of+evolution+scientific+american&oq=Synthetic+yeast+chromosomes+help+probe+mysteries+of+evolution+scientific+american&aqs=chrome..69i57.3255j0j4&sourceid=chrome&ie=UTF-8.

McLeod, Carmen, Brigitte Nerlich, and Alison Mohr. 2017. 'Working with Bacteria and Putting Bacteria to Work: The Biopolitics of Synthetic Biology for Energy in the United Kingdom'. *Energy Research & Social Science* 30: 35–42.

Michael, Mike. 2017. 'Enacting Big Futures, Little Futures: Toward an Ecology of Futures'. *The Sociological Review* 65 (3): 509–524.

Mint 2012. 'India Joins Project on Creating Artificial Life'. *Mint*, New Delhi, 28 November. http://search.proquest.com.esproxy.is.ed.ac.uk/businesspremium/docview/1217685507/abstract/B9C4B7AA50BD44ADPQ/5.

Mol, Annemarie. 2002. *The Body Multilple: Ontology in Medical Practice*. Durham, NC: Duke University Press.

Molteni, Megan. 2017. 'A New Lab-Built Fungus Eats Sugar and Burps Out Drugs'. *WIRED*, March. https://www.wired.com/2017/03/synthetic-yeast-genome/.

Myers, Greg. 1990. *Writing Biology: Texts in the Social Construction of Scientific Knowledge*. Madison, WI: University of Wisconsin Press.

NBC News. 2014. 'Gene Gurus Create Synthetic Yeast Chromosome from Scratch'. *NBC News*, 27 March. http://www.nbcnews.com/science/science-news/gene-gurus-create-synthetic-yeast-chromosome-scratch-n63316.

O'Malley, Maureen, Alexander Powell, Jonathan F. Davies, and Jane Calvert. 2008. 'Knowledge-Making Distinctions in Synthetic Biology'. *BioEssays* 30 (1): 57–65. doi:10.1002/bies.20664.

Preston, Beth. 2013. 'Synthetic Biology as Red Herring'. *Studies in History and Philosophy of Science Part C: Studies in History and Philosophy of Biological and Biomedical Sciences* 44 (4, Part B): 649–659. doi:10.1016/j.shpsc.2013.05.012.

Schmid-Petri, Hannah, Stefanie Knocks, Patricia Sager, and Silke Adam. 2014. 'La Biologie Synthétique dans la Société: Une Nouvelle Technologie dans le Débat Public'. *Berne: TA-SWISS*. https://www.ta-swiss.ch/?redirect=getfile.php&cmd%5Bgetfile%5D%5Buid%5D=2779.

ShanghaiDaily.com. 2017. 'Chinese Scientists Create 4 Synthetic Yeast Chromosomes'. *ShanghaiDaily.com*, 10 March. http://www.shanghaidaily.com/nation/Chinese-scientists-create-4-synthetic-yeast-chromosomes/shdaily.shtml.

The Economist. 2017. 'A Big Step towards an Artificial Yeast Genome'. *The Economist*, 11 March. https://www.economist.com/news/science-and-technology/21718479-success-would-usher-true-genetic-engineering-big-step-towards-artificial.

The Guardian. 2017. 'Synthetic Genome Nearly Complete, Paving Way for Bespoke Organisms' (Ian Sample). *The Guardian*, 9 March. https://www.theguardian.com/science/2017/mar/09/synthetic-yeast-genome-nearly-complete-paving-way-for-bespoke-organisms.

UK Synthetic Biology Roadmap Coordination Group. 2012. *A Synthetic Biology Roadmap for the UK*. Swindon: Technology Strategy Board. bt1209-1071.

"What's in a Name?" 2009. *Nature Biotechnology* 27 (12): 1071–1073. https://doi.org/10.1038/nbt1209-1071.

Wynne, Brian. 2008. 'Elephants in the Rooms Where Publics Encounter "Science"? A Response to Darrin Durant, "Accounting for Expertise: Wynne and the Autonomy of the Lay Public"'. *Public Understanding of Science* 17 (1): 21–33.

Reflections and Connections

Emotion is an integral part of both science and science communication. In this chapter, Oliver Marsh unpicks the role of emotions in one particular online space, the hugely successful Facebook page 'I Fucking Love Science' (IFLScience). He shows that interactions based around this site are not only about expressing enthusiasm for science, but also about articulating a (shared) identity as a 'science lover'.

Such identities are, however, not always unproblematic to perform. Marsh also argues that discussions about and within IFLScience feature *boundary-work*. Within such discussion, some emotions and behaviours are framed as appropriate to the identity of science lover, while others are policed as inappropriate and unscientific. Loving science is thus performed in specific ways, and behaviours that are not in line with these – such as only 'liking' the spectacular, rather than the dull or difficult, aspects of research, or expressing criticism towards a scientific consensus – are criticised or reprimanded.

The chapter further highlights that exchanges around science take place through a broad variety of utterances, which in this context mainly consist of very brief comments expressing support, anger, or ridicule, or are expressed through (written or visual) jokes. This allows the creation of a distinction between an in-group and an out-group, thus *constructing specific publics* and their relation to science.

We thus see the *co-production* of (a version of) science with a particular community. It is significant that this takes place within a specific online space, with a particular *atmosphere* that structures norms of behaviour and emotion. As Marsh suggests, some of this atmosphere derives from the conventions of online interactions.

9

SCIENCE, EMOTION, AND IDENTITY ONLINE: CONSTRUCTING SCIENCE AND SELVES ON 'I FUCKING LOVE SCIENCE'

OLIVER MARSH

9.1 INTRODUCTION

Science and emotion can be uneasy bedfellows. Thinking of science – or science communication – as a single, universal concept can lead to disagreements on a proper role for emotion. If science is an objective process, then emotion must be kept out in order to minimise bias (Merton 1942). But scientists know that emotion is an integral part of their daily lives, a factor which directs career trajectories and drives research projects (Gilbert & Mulkay 1984). Meanwhile communicators must work out how to incorporate *appropriate* emotions in their work to motivate engagement, without overstepping a line and encouraging 'unscientific' types or levels of emotion (Davies & Horst 2016).

Under an STS framework, which frames 'science' in more context-dependent terms, these issues become less problematic. Science and associated emotions are constructed differently in different contexts, and there need be no universal standards of 'appropriate' emotion. But instead, a series of other questions arise. Do emotions shape the ways in which science is performed; and, in turn, what different emotional responses might these performances generate? When actors speak of 'appropriate' emotional responses, is this related to their view of 'legitimate' science – and how (if at all) are these views policed? Can examining the co-production of science and emotion deepen our understanding of key ordering instruments within STS, from identity to patterns of discourse?

This chapter examines a case study of online science communication, which has provoked extensive discussion around emotions that are 'appropriate' in relation to science: the Facebook page 'I Fucking Love Science' (IFLScience). At the time of data collection (2014–2016) page communicates science-related content, in an irreverent style, to approximately 25 million followers – around ten times the numbers for the Facebook pages of *New Scientist* and *Scientific American*, and twice as many as the page for *Fox News*. As suggested by the page's name, strong emotional attachment to science is an important part of its brand identity. Commentators writing about the page have focused on emotion, often to criticise the page's approach to science communication. Comment threads on the page feature a variety of emotions, from joy at scientific content to anger at the behaviour of 'unscientific' people. I examine these discussions through discourse analysis, drawing on studies of how people portray themselves and others online. I explore how emotions are explicitly referenced in discourse, as well as how emotion features implicitly within discourse – and how both of these shape, and are shaped by, different performances of science.

9.2 EMOTION IN STS AND ONLINE

Since the Enlightenment, emotion has frequently been portrayed as a pollutant to the rationality associated with science (Daston & Galison 2007). The Mertonian account of scientific method proposed 'organised scepticism' as a defence against emotional bias (Merton 1942). However, STS scholars have shown that emotional behaviours – from friendship networks (Shapin 2008) to personal pride (Latour & Woolgar 1979) – play essential roles in constructing the practices of contemporary science. In both historical and contemporary accounts, science and emotions are co-produced. Daston and Park (1998) reveal how conceptions of 'wonder' have historically shifted along with changing practices in the study of nature. Through interview data, Gilbert and Mulkay (1984) show contemporary scientists moving between different versions of scientific life: one in which science is an abstract process and emotion an unwelcome intruder, and another where humour, passion, and excitement are integral parts of science as a human practice.

As noted in Chapter 3, STS scholars of science communication must be sensitive to the 'atmospheres' within which communication takes place; how elements of the environment produce emotional, subjective experiences. This is a relatively new project within STS work on science communication. Sarah Davies notes that much work on science communication 'tends to take a normative perspective by outlining what should have happened in any particular process' (2014: 91). She argues, quoting Matthew Harvey (2009: 146), that this misses how engagement with science can involve 'sites of intense emotion, argument, tension, and humor' (Davies 2014: 94). Irreverent responses to science communication, such as pulling faces at CCTV cameras or writing graffiti, are often dismissed by science communicators as not 'serious' engagement. However, from the participants' perspective they can serve important roles, building social bonds and creating emotional experiences (Horst & Michael 2011).

In this chapter I bring together an STS-informed approach and work from internet studies. Online settings have provided data of great scale, variety, and detail for investigating atmospheres. At a basic level, whether someone participates online at all depends on emotional factors, particularly feelings of comfort (or discomfort) within digital settings (Nonnecke et al. 2006). Early adopters of online networks re-created offline forms of community and friendship, and showed how text-based communications can convey kindness, hostility, or other forms of emotional subtext (Baym 2000). Tailored social media newsfeeds mean information we receive online is shaped by our emotional responses to certain content, as well as the responses of our friends (Jenkins 2006; Tufekci 2015). Online, who is talking and what they see are shaped by emotional experiences.

A key theme in the study described here, which bridged STS and internet studies, was the use of emotion to construct personal and group identity. As discussed in Chapter 2, examining how science communication constructs identities – whether 'scientific' and 'unscientific', 'expert' and 'non-expert', or 'communicator' and 'audience' – is an important ordering instrument for STS. Online, the construction of identity is shaped by hopes (or fears) of being perceived in a certain way, and desires to 'fit in' or mark oneself as 'different' (Marwick & boyd 2010). In the absence of many offline factors, such as body language or shared location, online groups build communal identity through developing shared values, jokes, and norms. For instance, communities that involve sharing deeply personal experiences may develop an 'ethic of friendliness', an emotional atmosphere in which participants experience welcome and support from others in the group (Baym 2000). For groups in which the atmosphere is suffused with competitive discussion, norms may involve combative language, mockery, and negative identity labels for those deemed inferior (Bennett 2013). I draw on these two sets of work, STS and internet studies, to investigate a case study of science communication. I do so to show how emotional behaviours interact with expressions of identity during performances of science.

9.3 CASE STUDY: I FUCKING LOVE SCIENCE[1]

The Facebook page 'I Fucking Love Science' (IFLScience) was created in March 2012 by Elise Andrew, a biology undergraduate, to share fun science-related content with her Facebook friends (although there is dispute over whether Andrew was the sole founder; see Senapathy & D'Entremont 2015). Unexpectedly, the page gained a thousand likes in its first day, and a million in six months (Hudson 2012). At the time this research was carried out (2014–2016), the page had around 25 million likes. Over the three months that I collected data, IFLScience made more than 1,000 posts, each of which received on average 45,000 likes and 24,000 shares. Many science communicators would be very envious of these numbers.

The page mixes posts about recent science news, engaging images, jokes, and motivational slogans. Originally it featured material from across the internet, but by 2013 Andrew and collaborators were producing their own blog posts on a dedicated IFLScience website. IFLScience generates revenue through merchandise, adverts on the website, and producing branded content (IFLScience 2014). Nowadays the main roles of Facebook for IFLScience are (1) growing an audience and (2) spreading website content. IFLScience was incorporated as a company in 2015, with an office in London's fashionable Covent Garden. Since then it has maintained a team of around 15–20 employees, mostly staff writers. At the close of the 2017 financial year, it had £34,000 in net assets (down from £182,000 the year before).[2]

According to IFLScience's numbers, in 2016 the website received 50 million unique monthly visitors: 50% were from the US, 67% were aged between 18 and 34, and 45% did not have a degree (IFLScience 2016). The interests of this audience are reflected in the page's content, which does not require high levels of scientific education and invokes cultural references likely to resonate with a youthful US-based audience. There is little visible evidence of Facebook being used to develop a two-way relationship between the page and its audience, and staff members rarely take part in comments threads. Overall the page provides a traditional one-way broadcast of popularised science, a science blog with an extraordinarily large audience.

9.4 METHODS

I examined references to, and uses of, emotion in discussions *about* and *within* IFLScience. Discussions about IFLScience include blog posts, newspaper articles, interviews with key players, the 'about' pages of IFLScience, and media

---

[1]Data for this chapter is drawn from a broader three-year study of emotion across four online participatory websites, in which participants discuss 'science' in a non-professional capacity (Marsh 2018).

[2]Numbers from https://beta.companieshouse.gov.uk/company/09435049/filing-history, accessed 13/10/18.

packs produced by IFLScience. By discussions within IFLScience, I mean comments threads below posts on the IFLScience Facebook page.

To gather discussions about IFLScience, I used multiple search tools, including search functions on social media platforms, academic journals, and popular science communication websites, to collect articles that mentioned IFLScience. I also followed references to people, outlets, and articles in the already-collected data to gather more data. This process was carried out multiple times across 2014–2016. During this period, I found no academic literature about IFLScience, but numerous blog posts and articles in mainstream outlets.

For discussions within IFLScience, I collected posts and associated comments threads made on IFLScience in three month-long periods: March 2015, August 2015, and January 2016. Separate months minimised the risk of discussions being dominated by any single topical event. Data was collected using a program I wrote in the open-source language Python. As well as the text of posts and comments, I also collected associated data such as number of 'likes' and word counts for each post/comment. It must be noted that comments only give a partial window into the behaviour of audiences; many people will read content without commenting. Nonetheless, comments threads reveal how IFLScience's content provides resources for various forms of online interpersonal interactions.

Collection produced over 25 million words of posts and comments. This was too much to read manually. I therefore constructed two samples:

1. A cluster sample, formed by dividing comments threads into three strata based on total number of words (small, medium, and large), and selecting a random sample of five threads from each stratum. Large threads were not analysed in full, but only until theoretical saturation (the point at which data stopped yielding new insights) was reached (Charmaz 2000).
2. A purposive sample of threads and comments that discussed 'science' as a broad concept, as opposed to discipline-specific knowledge. This meant: six comments threads that explicitly mentioned 'science' in the post title, or mentioned practices often contrasted to 'science', such as religion and perceived pseudosciences (Gieryn 1999); and individual comments (below any posts) that explicitly mentioned 'science', including stemmed words such as 'scientist' or 'pseudoscience'. Comments totalled 1.6 million words, so were randomly ordered and analysed until theoretical saturation was reached.

These samples gave a broad overview of participation in general, while also locating data relevant to the aims of the project (studying how participants engaged with science).

I analysed the discussions about and within IFLScience through discourse analysis. Broadly conceived, discourse analysis is 'studying discourse as texts and talk in social practices', examining how social contexts both shape and are shaped by discourse (Potter 1997: 146). I took a practice-based approach to discourse analysis, which involves examining how people use language to construct interpretations of the world, and to potentially shape the world (Bazeley 2009, Antaki et al. 2003). I applied this to the study of emotion in three ways. First, examining language used *about* emotion. This was informed by studies of how emotion is often contrasted with 'objectivity' and 'rationality', concepts frequently associated with science (Daston & Galison 2007). Second, focusing on *explicit* emotional language. These included expressions of feelings, such as 'I like this', as well as emphatic language, such as 'that is horrible'. I drew on studies of text-based discourse (particularly online) that examine how language alters the ways text is read and responded to (Herring 2004). Third, following studies of online communities, I examined how language was used to *implicitly* convey or create emotional experiences. Key examples included phatic communication[3] to build interpersonal bonds, praise/hostility to display like/dislike, and humour to entertain others (Baym 2000).

Using data from Facebook raises ethical questions. It can be argued that Facebook data is 'already public'; if people are concerned about privacy, they can change their account settings. However, people – both researchers and participants – may not be aware of Facebook's privacy regulations (Lewis et al. 2008). Much social media includes data that people cannot easily control, such as photos they appear in, or data accessed through friends' profiles (Zimmer 2010). However, the traditional gold standard of social science – informed consent – is hard to apply when studying millions of individuals, and can bias recruitment towards people who are more confident online (Nonnecke et al. 2006). Strict requirements for informed consent also risk hampering academic research into social media, by comparison with private companies (Savage & Burrows 2007). In response to these competing concerns, I did not seek informed consent from participants in IFLScience (although I did contact the IFLScience moderators, through multiple channels, but received no response). Nevertheless, I do not report any personally identifiable information during the research, and I paraphrase rather than quote specific comments. This further supported the rigour of my arguments, as it forced me to report recurring themes rather than pick the 'best' quotations.

9.5 DISCUSSIONS ABOUT IFLSCIENCE: 'REAL' AND 'NOT-REAL' LOVE OF SCIENCE

In this section I examine how IFLScience and its users are portrayed in discussions about IFLScience. I then move on to analysing how these accounts

---

[3]Forms of communication, such as pleasantries or small-talk, 'in which ties of union are created by a mere exchange of words. ... They fulfil a social function and that is their principal aim', Malinowski 1923: 316.

co-produce science and emotion. I begin with the page's description of itself, in the 'About' section:

> We're here for the science - the funny side of science. Quotes, jokes, memes and anything your admin finds awesome and strange.
>
> If you take yourself seriously, you're on the wrong page.
>
> We're dedicated to bringing the amazing world of science straight to your news-feed in an amusing and accessible way. (IFLScience 2015)

We see that terms like 'awesome' and 'amazing' feature prominently. The text also foregrounds references to humour – the rejection of people who 'take [themselves] seriously' is given a line of its own. Similarly, the page's mission, as stated in the IFLScience Media Kit (a pack for potential advertisers), includes using 'visuals that excite and stimulate curiosity', and content that 'entertains and delights', language that emphasises emotional responses (IFLScience 2016). All this bolsters the impression given by the page's name – 'I fucking love science' – which irreverently conveys strong emotional attachment to science. Andrew and supporters of the page see this impression as important for attracting followers who might not usually engage with science (Anderson 2014; Metcalf 2014). A profile in *Columbia Journalism Review* described IFLScience as a 'digital-age evangelist' for science, which 'bring[s] millions of science geeks out of the closet – and maybe create[s] a few new ones' (Fitts 2014). In an interview for *Wired* magazine, Andrew presented IFLScience as a 'gateway drug to science' (Kelly 2014). The language used – references to evangelism and gateway drugs – draws connections between the emotional experience offered by IFLScience and its ability to 'convert' people to science.

Some commentators, both supportive and critical, see IFLScience's mission to excite emotion as surpassing – sometimes even conflicting with – its ability to convey information. In the 'About' section, only one word ('accessible') points to the page's role as a communicator of information. Even IFLScience's supporters rarely reference its quality as a place to learn about science. This is a contrast to other online science communication sites. For example, commentary about the popular YouTube channel ASAPScience refers to their 'simple yet informative explanations' (Bondar 2012) and 'fun yet heady topics' (Forbes 2017). Hashem Al-Ghaili, another successful Facebook-based science communicator, has been described as 'able to summarize and present complex data in an excellent manner' (Plackett 2016). Similar comments are rarely, if ever, made about IFLScience. Criticisms of IFLScience often refer to the page's content with language that suggests an *over-emphasis* of emotion, such as 'sensationalised' or 'overdramatised' (Metcalf 2014), or a 'fervor to promote ... popsci' which 'actually misinform[s] people' (Maddox 2012). Andrew herself has stated that 'I'm not trying to teach people about science ... I'm trying to give people that moment where they say, O.K., this is interesting, and I WANT to learn more', acknowledging that IFLScience's role as an emotional hook may surpass its role as a communicator of scientific information (*TIME*, 2016).

The idea that emotion can attract people to learn about science is a familiar one, as are arguments that emotion can conflict with accuracy in science communication (Koppman et al. 2014; McCrory 2013). An STS perspective directs attention to a deeper matter: how the use of emotion to criticise IFLScience is tied to specific performances of 'science'. Blogger Joe Veix has referred to IFLScience's content as 'the opposite of the slow, contemplative, solitary, frustrating practice of actual science' (Veix 2014). Science writers Kavin Senapathy and Yvette d'Entremont describe IFLScience's posts as 'sensationalized headlines that hardly resemble the scientific work from which they preen clickbait', contrasting with the scientific method as 'a frustrating, often boring process' (Senapathy & D'Entremont 2015). These accounts do not straightforwardly contrast emotion with 'rational' science (cf. Merton 1942). Rather, they co-produce images of 'real' science and 'legitimate' emotional relations to science. In critics' portrayals, 'real' science is a process, not simply results; 'real' love of science therefore requires boredom and dedication to the process, not just excitement at results.

The most forthright portrayal of IFLScience as 'wrongly' performing science (and love thereof) comes from the blogger Maddox, in his post 'you're not a nerd, geeks aren't sexy, and you don't fucking love science' (Maddox 2012). Maddox compares the number of likes received by IFLScience posts which he classifies as 'actual science' and 'not science' (Figure 9.1). He also cites the proportion of images in IFLScience's content, usually of aesthetically pleasing natural phenomena, as evidence that 'what you actually "love" is photography, not science'. As with aforementioned critics, Maddox presents a 'legitimate' form of emotional engagement with science: 'losing yourself in what you do, often at the expense of friends, family and hygiene [and] obsessive dedication to a craft'. By describing this emotional experience, Maddox also constructs an image of science as a lengthy, demanding process. In contrast, Maddox describes the 'love' shown by IFLScience's followers as a 'passing interest' by people who have not 'paid their dues' to the scientific life. Such emotional engagement, Maddox suggests, both supports and is supported by IFLScience's portrayal of 'science' as images/results, which one can enjoy without following the full process. Hence, the co-production of specific emotional relations to science and particular images of science.

STS scholars refer to the construction of contrasts between 'real' and 'not-real' science as boundary-work (Gieryn 1999). Boundary-work is closely linked to identity; certain people have more likelihood of being described as 'scientific', and can use different tactics for prescribing what counts as 'science' (Jasanoff 1987). It is productive to examine portrayals of IFLScience through the framing of identity. Many commentators have described IFLScience followers as 'fans' (Thomas 2015) or 'like groupies' (Fitts 2014). As noted by scholars of fandom, such descriptions can have negative connotations, suggesting abnormal and unintelligent emotional attachments (Jensen 1992). Such connotations are suggested in commentary on IFLScience. Ben Thomas has referred to 'science fandom' as 'misguided' and 'uncritical hyping of science content' (Thomas 2015). Maddox claims that:

> Any time I see people on Facebook simultaneously liking 'iCarly, One Direction' and 'The Pauly D Project' while also ~~liking~~ fucking loving science, it raises some red flags. (Maddox 2012)

Here Maddox presents the idea of 'fucking loving science' as incompatible with being fans of a teen-idol band (One Direction) or an MTV reality show (The Pauly D Project), forms of entertainment often dismissed as 'low-brow' or not intellectual. Through this contrast, Maddox performs a recognisable image of science as accessible only to the intellectually superior (Shapin 1992). Such an image of science reinforces Maddox's argument that 'loving' science requires engagement with the technical content of science (recall his labelling of ion chromatography in Figure 9.1 as 'actual science'). Here we see co-production of science, and the identity of people who are 'allowed' to love science.

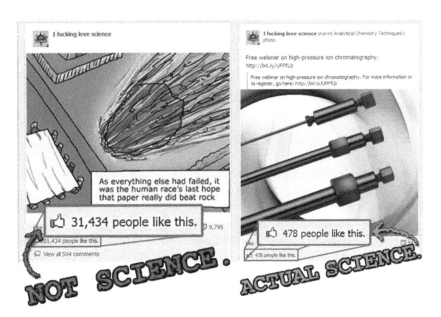

Figure 9.1 Comparisons of likes received on 'not science' and 'actual science' content (Maddox 2012)

Critics of IFLScience frequently tie the page's 'illegitimate' portrayal of science to a specific emotional factor. They argue that followers of IFLScience are motivated to share the content as a way of displaying a superior social identity (Hogg & Abrams 1988). The posts allow 'the person sharing it to associate themselves with intellectual rigor, without putting in the effort to understand anything' (Veix 2014) or are 'pre-packaged cultural tokens that can be shared and reshared without any investment in analysis ... to reinforce one's *aesthetic* self-identification as a "science lover"' (Thomas 2015, emphasis in original). These arguments refer to a common feature of social media behaviour: that people share content in order to construct a desirable public identity (Marwick & boyd 2010). They also draw on cultural ideas that science is an intellectually demanding activity, inaccessible to many people (Shapin 1992). Critics thereby reinforce their co-production of 'real' science and 'real' love of science, and 'illegitimate' science and love thereof, by drawing on recognisable cultural stereotypes and identity labels.

In concluding, we should note that commentators use emotion to portray their own relationship with science, whether explicitly or implicitly. Multiple commentators claim that they too love science, to ally themselves with IFLScience's underlying purpose of science communication (Hudson 2012) and/or to underscore their disappointment at IFLScience's inaccuracies (Metcalf 2014; Senapathy & D'Entremont 2015). Some critics express explicit anger towards IFLScience. Joe Veix implores IFLScience's audience 'if you truly fucking love science, stop fucking looking at stupid fucking memes, and go fucking love reading a fucking book' (Veix 2014). Maddox claims that IFLScience's style of communication 'pisses me off' and makes him feel 'a sharp pang in my head'. His piece concludes in a similar tone: 'go commit cultural fraud someplace else, and take your phony "I fucking love science" group with you' (Maddox 2012). By displaying these emotional states, they construct their self-identity as 'real' lovers of science, with the associated intellectual capabilities needed to assess 'real' science – in contrast to the 'cultural fraud' of IFLScience's audiences.

All the above shows a more complex picture than a simple science–emotion dichotomy (cf. Merton 1942). The key question is not 'is it appropriate to show love for science', or even 'is it appropriate to show *this kind of emotion* towards *this version of science*'. The question instead is 'is it appropriate for *this type of person* to show *this kind of emotion* towards *this version of science*?'. I shall contextualise these findings further within a co-productionist framework in my conclusion. For now, I also note that emotion is both a *referent* and a *tool* in constructing images of science and scientifically minded people; that is, commentators explicitly refer to emotions in building up their images, and also implicitly draw on emotional subtexts to emphasise their own and others' attachments to science. STS research has shown how speakers mobilise a variety of resources – including professional status (Jasanoff 1987), institutional structures (Collins & Pinch 1979), and types of media (Mellor 2003) – to construct an image of science which presents the speaker as 'scientific' and opponents as 'unscientific'. My findings show how *emotions* are a similar resource for such boundary-work in contemporary science communication. This use of emotion to identify oneself as a 'real' science lover, and to distinguish oneself from others, was a key theme in discussions within IFLScience comments threads. It is to these data that I now turn.

9.6 DISCUSSION WITHIN COMMENTS THREADS: 'SCIENCE LOVER' AS SOCIAL IDENTITY

In comments threads, as in the commentaries discussed in the previous section, references to emotion were more prominent than in-depth discussions of information. The average IFLScience post in my dataset received over 2,500 comments; on average, comments were only 8.5 words long. For comparison, average comment length in other case studies in my broader project varied from 30 words to over 300 words. The low average word count was largely due to three common types of comment: first, brief emotional responses such as 'wow' or 'that's cool'; second, tagging a friend – sometimes, but not always, including a short message such as 'you might like this' (tagging involves typing a friend's name which automatically sends them a link to the post); third, jokes – often in the form of 'meme' images with no accompanying text within the comment, which substantially reduced the average comment length. While these three types do not exhaustively describe all IFLScience comments, they did make up a substantial proportion. I shall describe each in greater detail, before analysing how they were used as resources in co-producing science, emotion, and identities.

The first type of comment, brief emotional responses, took a range of forms. Posts that featured visually striking material, such as designs for new technology or astronomical images, often received comments such as 'wow' or 'beautiful'. New discoveries were frequently described as 'exciting' or 'amazing'. Perceived 'unscientific' views in wider society – such as climate change denial, scepticism of vaccination, and religious beliefs – induced anger or sadness. Some comments used objective, de-personalised language: 'that is cool', 'how sad', or similar. Others involved subjective language and self-reference, such as 'I find this amazing'. These brief comments did not generally elicit replies from other participants, but *en masse* exhibited periodic repetition, which gave a sense of shared response (cf. Papacharissi 2014).

Tagging, the second key type of comment, appeared in around 30% of the collected comments. In some cases, tags were used to alert friends to content that might interest them; the tagged friend sometimes responded 'interesting' or 'thanks for pointing this out', or similar brief acknowledgements. In other cases, people tagged friends in a way that used the post as a prompt for discussions about some shared facet of their lives. There were multiple examples of people tagging their partner to discuss buying a flying car (*Who Wants a Flying Car*) or comparing a cartoon of Pluto looking sad as the New Horizons spacecraft flies past to 'that feeling when you don't reply to my texts' (*How Pluto Felt This Week*). Some tags even turned into people arranging social plans.

Such behaviour reflects the most common primary motivation cited for using Facebook: to keep in touch with friends (Wilson et al. 2012).

Finally, the third important type of comment was those featuring humour. These often took the form of 'memes': images that gain cultural recognition through being shared across a range of online contexts. Examples are given in Figure 9.2.

Figure 9.2   Examples of memes from IFLScience comments

The meme on the left depicts two characters from the 1970s American sit-com *Sanford and Son*, designed to look as if the characters are remarking on previous comments in the thread. This meme is extremely flexible; it could be used in a comments thread for an entirely different page, with no modification required. The meme on the right uses a similar format – stock image plus short caption – but is more specifically related to science, satirising arguments of climate change sceptics. It is possible that it was created specifically for commenting on IFLScience, or some other pro-science social media page; having appeared on one such page, it may then circulate into others. There were also many examples of jokes that did not use images, but drew on shared cultural knowledge in a similar manner to memes. For example, multiple commenters responded to the post *How Much Did It Cost to Send a Spacecraft to Pluto* with the answer 'about tree fiddy', a catchphrase from the TV series *South Park*. A post about the detection of gravitational waves featured numerous comments 'mistaking' the gravitational wave detector LIGO for the popular toy LEGO. Humorous comments often received more likes than non-humorous comments. However, they rarely turned into extended multi-participant jokes, in the manner noted by Baym (2000). Instead, like brief emotional responses, many commenters periodically repeated similar jokes in the same thread.

These types of comments were used in various ways by commenters to perform the identity of a 'science lover'. I noted that brief emotional expressions frequently used self-referential language – for example, 'I find this fascinating' or 'this angers me'. Such language was used by commenters to portray themselves as emotionally invested in science. Commenters frequently expressed their personal love for science, and/or the work of famous science communicators such as Neil DeGrasse Tyson or Brian Cox. (Recall that IFLScience audiences do not generally have high levels of scientific qualifications, so are more likely to encounter these figures than less well-known researchers.) Many comments below the post *In Science We Trust* (Figure 9.3) took forms such as 'yes I do!' or 'can I get this on a T-shirt?'. More negatively, some commenters also expressed anger at the visual layout of the phrase 'in science we trust' (see Figure 9.3), particularly the use of the Greek letter sigma to stand in for 'E'. Again, the language used was often explicitly self-referential, with phrases such as 'it really annoys me that...' portraying the commenter as someone annoyed by the 'incorrect' use of mathematical symbols. Such self-presentations were not universal. Some commenters mocked those comments for taking the post too seriously, disputing the 'correct' emotional response to the content. However, such disputes were relatively rare, and more commonly the products from IFLScience's performance of science – the images, news stories, and other content – were used as a resource for commenters to perform the identity of a 'science lover'.

Figure 9.3 Facebook post 'In Science We Trust'

I noted above that negative emotions, such as sadness and anger, were often expressed about people who misunderstood and/or disputed mainstream scientific consensus. Many IFLScience posts criticised perceived pseudosciences (e.g., *How to Argue with Anti-Vaxxers Using Science*, or *Large Study Concludes Homeopathy Does Not Effectively Treat Any Health Condition*) and these often received higher-than-average lengths of comments (Marsh 2016). Many comments took a similar form to these posts, expressing dislike or ridicule for unscientific views in society. For example, the post *In Science We Trust* prompted numerous comments that criticised religion, alternative medicine, and other 'unscientific' practices, often referring to believers' intelligence or mental health. Labels such as 'anti-vaxxer' or 'climate sceptic' were used to describe followers of specific pseudoscientific beliefs, while phrases such as 'woo' referred to more generally anti-science people. Stereotypes of Bible readers or tinfoil hat wearers were also used to connote opposition to science. (Tinfoil hats are associated with extreme conspiracy theorists, who attempt to protect their brains from mind-control rays.) All these built up a portrayal of an 'imagined other' – a familiar behaviour in online and offline groups (Anderson 2006; Gearon 2001).

Within IFLScience comments, this 'other' was co-produced with another familiar image of science: as a body of consensus knowledge, opposed to 'unscientific' or 'pseudoscientific' practices existing outside mainstream professional science. There were comments within IFLScience which disputed mainstream scientific consensus. For example, posts about vaccinations often received comments arguing that vaccines 'are not as safe as people think', while threads about the *New Horizons* flyby of Pluto featured claims about faked NASA missions (although it is also possible that such comments were 'trolling' – deliberate attempts to antagonise people by expressing unwelcome views). Such comments attracted numerous responses – an unusual feature in IFLScience threads, which rarely featured dialogue. These sometimes led to debates between the opposed views; in many other cases, replies were simply insults or jokes from multiple participants. Such attacks on 'unscientific' views often received relatively high numbers of likes. As numbers of likes are displayed on comments, this visibly showed contrasts in popularity between different views.

In online groups, such mass humour and/or hostility towards 'others' acts to enforce both *what* the group believes and *how* the group should behave; it also provides emotional benefits for those who align with in-group behaviour (Bennett 2013). In the above case, comments enforced the following norms: (1) people were expected to follow mainstream scientific consensus, and (2) hostility and scorn were accepted, even encouraged, as ways to deal with 'unscientific' comments. An emotional atmosphere of humour and ridicule therefore drew on, and supported, a community's performance of 'science' as inviolable consensus knowledge. This also demonstrates how IFLScience commenters could move, as a group, away from the aforementioned performances of science as a collection of wondrous objects and towards performing science as consensus mainstream knowledge. Again, we see co-production of science, emotion, and identity.

These findings reflect my previous analysis of supporters and critics of IFLScience in section 9.5: performing 'science' and 'not-science' was used to satisfy emotional needs such as displaying a desired social identity and/or creating a sense of community. The particular form of these behaviours on IFLScience reflected familiar findings from STS, that contrasts between 'scientific' and 'unscientific' are created in order to claim intellectual and epistemic authority (Gieryn 1999; Shapin 1992). Such associations with 'science' provided participants with resources to align themselves with the social identity of superior 'scientific' people; in doing so, they built an in-group within which they shared humour, anger at 'unscientificity' in society, and self-portrayals as science lovers.

9.7 CONCLUSION

The case study of IFLScience provided extensive examples of negotiations around science, emotion, and identity. The online data allowed for close analysis of how these three concepts were co-produced with discourse. Content from the IFLScience page largely performed 'science' as a collection of objects and ideas, which respondents met by performing the identity of an excited or awe-struck 'science lover'. Critics used references to obsession and boredom to build a contrasting picture of 'real science' as a process, which could only be loved by the intellectually dedicated. In IFLScience comments, we saw how anger and ridicule were used to build an in-group and an out-group, which enforced an image of science as a body of consensus knowledge at war with ignorance and pseudoscience. These findings encourage us not simply to ask 'is it appropriate to show love for science', or even 'is it appropriate to show *this kind of emotion* towards *this version of science*'. The key question instead is 'is it appropriate for *this type of person* to show *this kind of emotion* towards *this version of science*?'. All three elements are constructed in tandem with one another.

Some features of the above findings may reflect specific features of the online setting; in particular, concerns around self-presentation and high levels of aggression (Marwick & boyd 2010; Santana 2014). However, my broader arguments reflect findings from other STS works, particularly of historical case studies, which have shown how science and emotion have been co-produced across a macro scale (Daston & Park 1998; Shapin 2008). By focusing on a specific case study of online communication, including unfolding 'events' of participation in comments threads, I have contributed a more fine-grained understanding of how emotion, science, and identity are co-produced in contemporary science communication.

This study contributes to an emerging project within STS: a deeper understanding of science communication as emotional event (Horst & Michael 2011). STS work on science communication has largely focused on instrumental concerns that underlie the construction of contemporary science; for example, professional autonomy, the elevation of accredited expertise, and institutional structures (Davies 2014). I have examined how factors that are less clearly instrumental, such as shared humour, in-group bonding, or finding an identity within an informal community, shape interactions through which demarcation of science from non-science is carried out. It is worth remembering that this took place in the absence of professional scientists or science communicators. There is more to be explored about how such concerns are also at play in interactions among professionals, or between professionals and non-professionals. I have also illustrated how emotional atmospheres and images of science shift *within* events. For example, the appearance of 'pseudoscientific' comments within IFLScience threads created a hostile emotional atmosphere; this was tied to a move from performing science as a collection of wondrous objects to science as consensus mainstream knowledge. Studying other interactions with such a framing would reveal how such shifts take place within more extended dialogues, and how they interact with other institutional and interpersonal contexts.

To conclude with the key point for science communicators: it is not the case that there is a singular, universal science, which people engage with from various emotional standpoints. Rather science *becomes* a certain thing because of the emotions evoked to portray it, and to oppose others' portrayals. Science communicators have long been aware that emotion is an integral part of engaging certain audiences with science. Creating certain emotional connections and atmospheres can make the difference between participants feeling inspired to seek further engagement or deciding that 'science is not for me'. But emotional atmospheres also shape what science *is* within a discussion. The 'science' in a heated argument about climate change can be fundamentally different from the 'science' in an excited discussion about the frontiers of space flight. And, of course, participants may not agree (whether explicitly or implicitly) about what science is – a feature that can further exacerbate emotional tensions. This fluidity may be a challenge for science communicators. It is also an opportunity to open up wider ranges of emotional engagement, by being playful with different constructions of science.

ACKNOWLEDGEMENTS

The project on which this chapter was based owes a considerable debt to Karen Bultitude, Simon Lock, and Tiago Mata. For their input into the chapter, the author would also like to thank Karoliina Pulkkinen, Trudi Martin, Edward Thomas Bankes, and Leo Doulton.

REFERENCES

Specific Facebook posts cited in the text are listed below. I provide month accessed rather than full date, as data was downloaded by the programme over the course of several days.

How Much Did It Cost to Send a Spacecraft to Pluto, www.facebook.com/ IFeakingLoveScience/posts/1163249173696092, August 2015.
How Pluto Felt This Week, www.facebook.com/IFeakingLoveScience/ posts/116044119397690, July 2015.

How to Argue with Anti-Vaxxers, Using Science, www.facebook.com/
IFeakingLoveScience/posts/, August 2015.
IFLScience in Science We Trust, www.facebook.com/IFeakingLoveScience/
posts/1060950617259282, March 2015.
Large Study Concludes Homeopathy Does Not Effectively Treat Any Health Condition, www.
facebook.com/IFeakingLoveScience/posts/1060263840661293, March 2015.
Who Wants a Flying Car?, www.facebook.com/IFeakingLoveScience/
posts/1064837200203957, March 2015.

Anderson, Benedict. 2006. *Imagined Communities: Reflections on the Origin and Spread of Nationalism* (3rd edition). Abingdon and New York: Verso.
Anderson, P. F. 2014. 'Case Study: I F***ing Love Science & Rare Diseases'. *Emerging Technologies Librarian*. https://etechlib.wordpress.com/2014/09/19/case-study-i-fing-love-science-rare-diseases/, accessed 19 August 2017.
Antaki, Charles, Michael Billig, Derek Edwards, and Jonathan Potter. 2003. 'Discourse Analysis Means Doing Analysis: A Critique of Six Analytic Shortcomings'. *Discourse Analysis Online* 1 (1).
Baym, Nancy K. 2000. *Tune In, Log On: Soaps, Fandom, and Online Community*. Thousand Oaks, CA: Sage.
Bazeley, Pat. 2009. 'Analysing Qualitative Data: More Than "Identifying Themes"'. *The Malaysian Journal of Qualitative Research* 2 (2): 6–22.
Bennett, Lucy. 2013. 'Discourses of Order and Rationality: Drooling R. E. M. Fans as "matter out of place"'. *Continuum: Journal of Media & Cultural Studies* 27 (2): 37–41.
Bondar, Carin. 2012. 'ASAP Science: Fun, Informative and Extremely Successful'. *Scientific American*, December.
Charmaz, Kathy. 2000. 'Grounded Theory: Objectivist and Constructivist Methods'. In Norman K. Denzin and Yvonna S. Lincoln (eds.), *SAGE Handbook of Qualitative Research*, pp. 509–535. Thousand Oaks, CA: Sage.
Collins, Harry M., and Trevor Pinch. 1979. 'The Construction of the Paranormal: Nothing Unscientific is Happening'. In Roy Wallis (ed.), *On the Margins of Science: The Social Construction of Rejected Knowledge*, pp. 237–270. Keele: University of Keele.
Daston, Lorraine, and Peter Galison. 2007. *Objectivity*. New York: Zone Books.
Daston, Lorraine, and Katharine Park. 1998. *Wonders and the Order of Nature, 1150–1750*. New York: Zone Books.
Davies, Sarah R. 2014. 'Knowing and Loving: Public Engagement beyond Discourse'. *Science and Technology Studies* 27 (3): 90–110.
Davies, Sarah R., and Maja Horst. 2016. *Science Communication: Culture, Identity and Citizenship*. London: Palgrave Macmillan.
Fitts, Alexis Sobel. 2014. 'Do You Know Elise Andrew?' *Columbia Journalism Review*, http://archives.cjr.org/cover_story/elise_andrew.php, accessed 19 August 2017.
Forbes. 2017. 'AsapSCIENCE.' *Forbes*, https://www.forbes.com/profile/asapscience/ accessed 13 October 2018.
Gearon, Liam. 2001. 'The Imagined Other: Postcolonial Theory and Religious Education'. *British Journal of Religious Education* 23 (2): 98–106.
Gieryn, Thomas F. 1999. *Cultural Boundaries of Science: Credibility on the Line*. Chicago, IL: University of Chicago Press.
Gilbert, Nigel G., and Michael Mulkay. 1984. *Opening Pandora's Box: A Sociological Analysis of Scientists' Discourse*. (Contemporary Sociology, Vol. 14). Cambridge: Cambridge University Press.

Harvey, Matthew. 2009. 'Drama, Talk, and Emotion Omitted Aspects of Public Participation'. *Science, Technology & Human Values* 34 (2): 139–161.

Herring, Susan C. 2004. 'Computer-Mediated Discourse Analysis: An Approach to Researching Online Behavior'. In Sasha Barab, Rob Kling, and James H. Gray (eds.), *Designing for Virtual Communities*, pp. 338–376. Cambridge: Cambridge University Press.

Hogg, Michael A., and Dominic Abrams. 1988. *Social Identifications: A Social Psychology of Intergroup Relations and Group Processes*. Abingdon: Routledge.

Horst, Maja, and Mike Michael. 2011. 'On the Shoulders of Idiots: Re-Thinking Science Communication as "Event"'. *Science as Culture* 20 (3): 283–306.

Hudson, Rich. 2012. 'Interview with Elise Andrew'. *The Chemical Blog*, http://www.thechemicalblog.co.uk/interview-with-elise-andrew/, acccessed 7 August 2014.

IFLScience. 2014. 'IFLScience Media Kit 2014'. IFLScience.org. 2014.

IFLScience. 2015. '"About" Page'. 2015.

IFLScience. 2016. 'IFLScience Media Kit 2016'. 2016.

Jasanoff, Sheila. 1987. 'Contested Boundaries in Policy-Relevant Science'. *Social Studies of Science* 17 (2): 195–230.

Jenkins, Henry. 2006. *Convergence Culture: Where Old and New Media Collide*. New York: New York University Press.

Jensen, Joli. 1992. 'Fandom as Pathology: The Consequences of Characterization'. In Lisa A. Lewis (ed.), *The Adoring Audience: Fan Culture and Popular Media*, pp. 9–26. New York: Routledge.

Kelly, Tiffany. 2014. 'Nature Can Be Cute, But It Still Wants to Kill You'. *Wired*, July.

Koppman, Sharon, Cindy L. Cain, and Erin Leahey. 2014. 'The Joy of Science: Disciplinary Diversity in Emotional Accounts'. *Science, Technology & Human Values* 40 (1): 30–70.

Latour, Bruno, and Steve Woolgar. 1979. *Laboratory Life: The Construction of Scientific Facts*. Beverly Hills, CA: Sage.

Lewis, Kevin, Jason Kaufman, Marco Gonzalez, Andreas Wimmer, and Nicholas Christakis. 2008. 'Tastes, Ties, and Time: A New Social Network Dataset Using Facebook.com'. *Social Networks* 30 (4): 330–342.

Maddox. 2012. 'You're Not a Nerd, Geeks Aren't Sexy and You Don't "Fucking Love" Science', http://thebestpageintheuniverse.net/c.cgi?u=youre_not_a_nerd, accessed 13 May 2014.

Malinowski, Bronislaw. 1923. 'Supplement 1: The Problem of Meaning in Primitive Languages'. In Charles K. Ogden and Ian A. Richards (eds.), *The Meaning of Meaning*, pp. 296–336. Abingdon: Routledge & Kegan Paul.

Marsh, Oliver. 2016. ' "People Seem to Really Enjoy the Mix of Humour and Intelligence": Science Humour in Online Settings'. *Journal of Science Communication* 15 (2): 1–9.

Marsh, Oliver. 2018. '"Nah, Musing is Fine. You Don't Have to be 'Doing Science'"': Emotional and Descriptive Meaning-Making in Online Non-Professional Discussions about Science'. University College London.

Marwick, Alice, and danah boyd. 2010. 'I Tweet Honestly, I Tweet Passionately: Twitter Users, Context Collapse, and the Imagined Audience'. *New Media & Society* 13 (1): 114–133.

McCrory, Paul. 2013. 'In Defence of the Classroom Science Demonstration'. *School Science Review* 95 (350): 81–88.

Mellor, Felicity. 2003. 'Between Fact and Fiction: Demarcating Science from Non-Science in Popular Physics Books'. *Social Studies of Science* 33 (4): 509–538.

Merton, Robert K. 1942. *The Sociology of Science: Theoretical and Empirical Investigations*. Chicago, IL: University of Chicago Press.

Metcalf, Victoria. 2014. 'Sensationalising Science: Sometimes Behind the Sizzle is Just Fizzle'. *SciBlogs*, https://sciblogs.co.nz/ice-doctor/2014/07/25/sensationalising-science-sometimes-behind-the-sizzle-is-just-fizzle/ accessed 13 October 2018.

Nonnecke, Blair, Dorine Andrews, and Jenny Preece. 2006. 'Non-Public and Public Online Community Participation: Needs, Attitudes and Behavior'. *Electronic Commerce Research* 6 (1): 7–20.

Papacharissi, Zizi. 2014. *Affective Publics: Sentiment, Technology, and Politics*. New York: Oxford University Press.

Plackett, Benjamin. 2016. 'A Yemeni Youth Becomes a Science Superstar on Facebook'. *Al-Fanar Media*, https://www.al-fanarmedia.org/2016/03/a-yemeni-youth-becomes-a-science-superstar-on-facebook/, accessed 13 October 2018.

Potter, Jonathan. 1997. 'Discourse Analysis as a Way of Analysing Naturally Occurring Talk.' In David Silverman (ed.) *Qualitative Research: Theory, Method and Practice*, pp. 144–160. London: Sage.

Santana, Arthur D. 2014. 'Virtuous or Vitriolic: The Effect of Anonymity on Civility in Online Newspaper Reader Comment Boards'. *Journalism Practice* 8 (1): 18–33.

Savage, Mike, and Roger Burrows. 2007. 'The Coming Crisis of Empirical Sociology'. *Sociology* 41(5): 885–99.

Senapathy, Kavin, and Yvette D'Entremont. 2015. 'Pop Sci to Pop Sigh: I Fucking Love Science Ex-Admins Speak Out'. *Skepchick*, http://skepchick.org/2015/08/i-fucking-love-science-ex-admins-speak-out/, accessed 19 August 2017.

Shapin, Steven. 1992. 'Why the Public Ought to Understand Science-in-the-Making'. *Public Understanding of Science* 1: 27–30.

Shapin, Steven. 2008. *The Scientific Life: A Moral History of a Late Modern Vocation*. Chicago, IL: University of Chicago Press.

Thomas, Ben. 2015. 'A Disease of Scienceyness'. *Mix Tape*, https://medium.com/@writingben/a?disease?of?scienceyness?7b5571a34953, accessed 18 August 2017.

TIME. 2016. 'The 30 Most Influential People on the Internet', *TIME Magazine*, https://time.com/4258291/30-most-influential-people-on-the-internet-2016/ , accessed 13 October 2018.

Tufekci, Zeynep. 2015. 'Facebook Said Its Algorithms Do Help Form Echo Chambers, and the Tech Press Missed It'. *New Perspectives Quarterly* 32 (3): 9–12.

Veix, Joe. 2014. 'For Those Who Hate "I F*cking Love Science"'. *Deathandtaxes Magazine*. April.

Wilson, Robert E., Samuel D. Gosling, and Lindsay T. Graham. 2012. 'A Review of Facebook Research in the Social Sciences'. *Perspectives on Psychological Science* 7 (3): 203–220.

Zimmer, Michael. 2010. '"But the Data Is Already Public": On the Ethics of Research in Facebook.' *Ethics and Information Technology* 12(4): 313–325.

Reflections and Connections

This chapter – written by Erela Teharlev Ben-Shachar and Nadav Davidovitch – takes as its focus nutritional communication. Its approach is longitudinal and context-specific. By examining the history of nutrition communication in Israel from the 1940s to the 1980s, Teharlev Ben-Shachar and Davidovitch are able to show how knowledge about food is *co-produced* with specific versions of wider society and, in particular, of nationhood.

One key thing that is made through this nutritional advice is *citizenship*, specifically that of women (generally framed as the ones concerned with taking care of food). The role of women in Israeli society does not stay static across the period that Teharlev Ben-Shachar and Davidovitch study. While in their earlier material women behave as good citizens by learning to cook with native produce, thus supporting Israeli farmers and showing themselves to be committed to the nation and its land, by the 1970s citizenship is about taking individual responsibility for one's body. Teharlev Ben-Shachar and Davidovitch thus demonstrate how seemingly innocuous advice about nutrition and food is *value-laden*, implying particular models of society and how one should live in it.

They also nicely show how such nutritional communication becomes *a space where expertise is claimed, contested, and negotiated*. Not all women readily accepted the advice of 'experts' about how they should cook, but instead relied on their own knowledges and experiences. At other moments, more experiential knowledge came to the fore in nutrition communication. Overall, then, the chapter demonstrates not only how public facts are made in conjunction with particular forms of living, but how these assemblages change over time.

10

CO-PRODUCING KNOWLEDGE AND NATION-STATES: NUTRITION COMMUNICATION AND THE MAKING OF CITIZENS

ERELA TEHARLEV BEN-SHACHAR AND NADAV DAVIDOVITCH

10.1 INTRODUCTION

A woman living in Palestine (Israel) in the 1940s looking for a nutrition guide in Hebrew would probably encounter a booklet, one of the very few that were published at the time, titled *Do You Spend Your Money Wisely?* (Bromberg 1942). The booklet framed nutritional knowledge as key to helping women (in Hebrew pronouns are gendered, so the book is explicitly addressed to women) to save and plan their budget while feeding their families. The author's dual role – she was both regarded as a nutritional expert and as a representative of a women's Zionist organisation, Hadassah – underscores the connection between nutrition and nationhood. At that time, food was perceived as a tool to advance the building of the Israeli nation, as stated explicitly in the introduction of a nutritional survey published in that period. According to the author, a biochemist, the survey and related nutritional research were meant to 'articulate a national nutritional policy that would create a harmony between local produce and the requirements of the climate' (Kliegler, in Guggenheim et al. 1991: 147).

Three decades later, in the 1970s, a woman looking for a Hebrew nutrition guide would find a totally different kind of publication. A typical example would be *The Winners are the Losers* (Gal & Sofer 1976), a book providing a choice of diets for losing weight and authored by two women who together succeeded in losing a total of 60 kilos. Nutritional knowledge – in this case in the form of the experiential knowledge of two women – was presented as a means to help individual women shape their bodies.

This chapter offers a longitudinal engagement with this shift in the representation of dietary practices that took place in nutritional guides across half a century. We will use this engagement to show how nutritional knowledge and dietary recommendations have evolved in tandem with changes in society and the nation-state. Studying the communication spaces of nutritional guides is an excellent way to unpack how knowledge orders related to nutrition are co-produced with social orders (Jasanoff 2004) and, specifically, with assumptions about how the bodies of good citizens should be fed. We therefore understand dietary guides as a space in which knowledge about nutrition is communicated, and as providing insights into the way in which nutritional knowledge shapes and is being shaped by the interests and values of those in power.

10.2 CONCEPTUAL FRAMEWORK

Our central concern is with how different dietary regimes have been intertwined with the history of and transformations in Israeli society. The chapter looks at the different dietary guides that were published in Israel between the 1940s and 1980s, treating these as a source of information about the co-production of nutritional knowledge and wider society. Investigating the history of nutritional guides in Israel leads us to encounter different experts, publics, authorities, knowledges, and material elements operating across different spaces. It takes us from a vegetable garden in which representatives of Zionist organisations taught homemakers which vegetables are edible, to the pages of women's magazines and recipe columns that gave instructions on how to cook with milk and egg powders, and to healthy-eating columns in which certified dietitians presented nutritional value tables and advice aimed at guiding laypeople to eat healthier. We will look at how these nutritional communication 'events' each involve a unique assemblage of objects, subjects, representations, and assumptions (Law 2017: 47; see also Chapter 2 in this volume).

Looking at different historical moments allows us to investigate a range of communication events, and to understand the role that nutrition played in society at each point in time. It also situates the always context-specific interactions between nutritional knowledge and diverse stakeholders, drawing our attention to the (un)intended governance effects of nutritional communication.

This longitudinal approach to knowledge communication will thus allow us to see how, at different moments in time, the relations between knowledges and social orders have had to be reconfigured in order to relate food and nutrition to the idea of nation building.

Our central framework is thus Jasanoff's notion of co-production (2004), which underlines that social and moral orders are always entangled with knowledge orders. Our analysis focuses on the formation of discourses, identities, and the state in and through different forms of nutritional guidance. We therefore pay attention to the places, networks, and people that are involved in interactions between knowledge and society (Law 2017: 31), and understand nutritional guides as specific spaces in which knowledge is produced, publics are created, and normative ideas about a healthy or good life are performed. They are, most fundamentally, spaces where we can observe what Hacking (1986) has called 'making up people' and, simultaneously, the making of a nation.

Based on this, in the analysis that follows we focus on three important aspects of the communication events we sample. First, using Law's concept of 'knowing spaces' (Law 2017), we will examine the ways that the different spaces in which communication events took place shaped knowledge about nutrition and societal ideals. The analysis will take us to vegetable plots, recipe books, and finally to women's magazines. We will investigate how these different spaces in which communication took place opened up or closed down different kinds of questions, thus framing nutritional knowledge and, through it, citizens and the nation-state, in particular ways.

Second, following Felt (1999), we will also discuss the way that nutritional knowledge and the specific audience addressed mutually constitute each other. We will track the audiences that different guides imagined and addressed, from homemakers through to policy makers, experts, and laypeople. This will make it possible to show how nutritional guidance performs specific kinds of publics, as well as the normative visions and expectations related to them. We will also pay attention to the negotiation that takes place when audiences – whether homemakers, dieters, or laypeople generally – resist the ideas inscribed in nutritional guides (Felt & Fochler 2010).

Finally, we will use this material to identify the different actors who are staged as experts, from representatives of Zionist organisations to women who succeeded in losing weight and university-certified dietitians. We will analyse nutritional guides to show how such experts were presented, how their authority was established or negotiated in the communication process, how different sources of credibility could be used during different periods, and how the performance of expertise intervenes in the making of knowledge and social orders (Hilgartner, 2000).

The rest of the chapter runs as follows. We begin with an overview of the political and social agendas framing nutrition in the newly formed Israeli state, summarising key moments in the history of nutrition and diet in Israel.

This will establish the historical context in which the different communication events that we study were situated. After presenting our methodological approach, we engage with three distinct time periods and with examples of communication about diet within each of these. The last section discusses the implications of the research, and reflects on the way longitudinal research of nutrition guides in the context of their time may help shed light on the way communication events produce not only scientific knowledge and publics, but also nations.

10.3 THE HISTORY OF DIET AND NUTRITION IN ISRAEL

Ideas about nutrition and what is 'healthy' food are not neutral, but connected to political and social ideologies. Sociologists have described the varying ways that hierarchies of good and bad food, the social class of audiences that recommendations are directed to, and the goals that healthy eating is supposed to achieve are constructed (Beardsworth & Keil 1997; Germov & Williams 2009; Lupton 1996: 6–37).

Israeli history is a particularly interesting case of such interrelations between society and nutrition because, since the pre-state years, there has been extensive interest in nutrition and diet. This section presents a short history of the main ways in which ideas about 'nutrition' have simultaneously shaped and been shaped by nationality or social order within Israel, in order to contextualise the analysis that follows. We base this account on scholarship of how food was used to create a nation (Raviv 2002), the ways in which cookbooks produced homeowners as members of the community (Tene 2002), how austerity policy made women rebel, triggering the first buds of individualism (Rozin 2008: 11), the history of eating from the Kibbutz Cafeteria to the Chinese and Indian restaurants era (Almog 1998), and the history of nutrition in general (Endvelet 2002).

In the pre-state era, diet was intended to support agriculture, making newcomers native-like and assisting in immigration efforts, as well as establishing a unified or collective way to eat. Dietary planning and its public communication were primarily conducted by volunteer-based Zionist women's organisations, such as WIZO (Women's International Zionist Organization) and Hadassah. Agriculture was at that time one of the main projects of the Zionist movement. Farming symbolised attachment to and ownership of the land, as well as supporting the transformation of the exiled Jew, perceived as frail, sick, fearful, and submissive, into a new Jew – a strong, corporeal one fit to be a worker and a fighter (Weiss 2004: 88).

Food consumption was thus supposed to support Jewish farmers. The correct diet included fruits and vegetables that grew relatively easily in Israel, such as aubergines and courgettes. Eating such produce was not only about supporting farmers, but served as proof of having turned into a local and a native, rather than seeking to preserve diasporic homelands in the kitchen. Eating local produce was also connected to proving that there was enough food in Palestine for more immigrants. At this time, the British, who then ruled the country, limited the number of Jews who were allowed to immigrate. They defined this 'quota' according to what they perceived as the number of immigrants the country could feed. Thus, nutritional science, and the diets that resulted from it, sought to demonstrate the capacity of the country to healthily nourish many people, trying to prove that the British were wrong in their calculations. The nature of a 'good diet' was therefore planned to achieve many goals, most of them having to do with the Zionist project. The nutritional science of the time sought to demonstrate that health would not be harmed, even when people followed a diet in line with national goals.

The relationship between nation and nutrition changed after the establishment of the State of Israel. In this period, the new Israeli government ushered in an austerity policy, in which the State dictated what and how much people could eat. This rationing policy (the *Tzena*) forced people to eat according to national goals, with the government's main goal being to enable hundreds of thousands of Jewish people across the world to immigrate to Israel (Rozin 2006: 58). This period is remembered as one of hunger, as well as of unappealing foods like milk powder, egg powder, and frozen fish fillets. Nutritional experts developed and communicated knowledge in order to feed as many people as possible while still maintaining health.

The 1970s were a time of change in Israel. Many historians describe it as a decade in which the narrative of a consolidated, ascetic, unified, national society was gradually replaced by a narrative that emphasised individualism, self-fulfilment, hedonism, consumerism, and self-achievement (Ram 2005: 48). Nutrition was similarly framed in new ways in this era. It was no longer thought of as a way to create a nation, express a connection to the land, or make it possible to balance the demographic situation. Rather, it began to be viewed as a way to express individualism and subjectivity (Tene 2002: 92).

Nutritional information thus started to travel into different kinds of spaces. It was not only found in cookbooks and recipes, or in writing about food grown on the land or personal economics. Readers could choose whether they preferred guides that would help them express their taste, curiosity, and adventurous nature by cooking and eating, or whether they preferred to see diet as a way to improve their health or shape their bodies. All kinds of new books were concerned with diet and nutrition. On the one hand, there were cookbooks that offered a variety of culinary options from different cultures (Moroccan, Yemenite, Chinese, Italian, and more) and which allowed people to express their individuality by experimenting with different tastes and flavours. On the other hand, there were increasing numbers of manuals and nutrition columns that taught people how to use food to maximise their health and to eat to minimise risk of diseases, as well as how to lose weight.

The new diet and nutrition columns and guides were different from their forerunners in the 1930s to 1950s. These newer texts focused on the components of foods, and on how they were digested and absorbed inside the body. Food was often looked on as a synthesis of vitamins, minerals, proteins, and calories rather than as vegetables or fruits. Accordingly, references to the places or the people that grew these vegetables disappeared from the guides. The availability of the food and its price were no longer considered relevant to nutrition guidance. Rather, emphasis was put on the correlation between eating and getting sick, or between eating and getting fat. The relationship between eating and health or sickness was presented more often and in more definitive terms. In addition, scientific expertise took on a new role. The way that biochemical components of different foods brought about disease or health was often backed up by scientific research, and researchers were referred to much more frequently in these new guides. The growing discipline of epidemiology emphasised individual risk factors, including food ingredients such as fat, sugar, and salt. Food was increasingly depicted either as medicine (garlic, lettuce, honey, broccoli) or as poison (salt, sugar, or saturated fats). Broader social, personal, and political goals, such as supporting the nation, agriculture, or saving money, were no longer mentioned.

10.4 METHODOLOGICAL APPROACH

The preceding history sketched out some of the ways in which nutrition and dietary advice are intertwined with Israel's history. The rest of this chapter fleshes this out through focused analysis of three particular moments, or specific spaces of public communication, within this history. We focus on three periods between the 1940s and 1980s that represent the different models of governance articulated in different dietary regimes. The first is the 1940s – that is, a moment within the pre-state era (*Yishuv*). At this time Israel did not have state institutions in place. Recruiting people to nation building was based on volunteerism, and society as a whole was nationalistic and collectivist. This was a point at which nutrition was one more tool within the collective effort to establish the state.

The second period is the end of the 1940s and beginning of the 1950s. These were the first years of statehood and nation building, and massive immigration and economic strain meant that the government decided to impose an austerity policy (the *Tzena*) which limited access to some foods (Rozin 2006). During this austerity period citizens were not able to choose and select their food for themselves, and thus information about nutrition took on a new significance. The last period we will discuss is the end of the 1970s, a point at which the Labour party lost the election to a right-wing party (the *Likud*). This change of regime happened simultaneously with wider changes in society, and with moves towards greater individualism, commercialism, and capitalism

(Aharoni 1998; Ram 2005: 48). During that period nutritional information was perceived as knowledge that would help individuals to maximise their health or improve the shape of their body (a development that has been similarly charted in other national contexts; e.g., Lupton 1996).

In order to investigate the communication of nutritional knowledge, we explored different texts within each period. In the 1940s, communication of nutrition was mainly conducted by the two leading women's Zionist organisations, WIZO and Hadassah. To gather information about these, we looked in archives for documents by and about their leading guides and experts. The documents we retrieved included reports about their guidance activities (mainly through exhibitions and demonstrations), the cookbooks they published, nutrition booklets, and the articles they published in the only women's magazine published since the 1930s, *Dvar Hapoelet* (a monthly supplement published by *DAVAR* – the paper of the Labour Federation).

For the next period, when commercial women's magazines began to be published in Palestine and Israel, we looked at all of the cookery and nutrition-based columns in the weekly magazine *La'Isha*, published over the period when the austerity policy had been declared, between 1947 and 1957. We also drew from the archives any information published by the nutritional department of the government at that time. After 1967, a second women's magazine began circulation. The research also followed this new publication, tracking the nutrition and diet-based columns that began blossoming in the second half of the 1970s, including weight-watching columns, scientific nutrition columns, and vegetarian and healthy-eating columns.

In our analysis of this material – the guidance from WIZO and Hadassah, the booklets, the columns, and the recipes – we systematically focused on the following elements. We registered the space in which the communication events took place, either physical spaces such as backyards, or cultural or symbolic spaces such as women's magazines. In the case of physical spaces, we checked where it was located, who populated it, and to whom this place was affiliated. In the case of non-physical spaces, we checked the publishing house (Was it one that belonged to some party or to the state or was it a commercial publishing house?), to whom it was addressed, who funded it, and what the readership was.

We then performed an analysis of authority in the materials we collected. In each sample we checked whether the experts had a formal education or whether they mobilised other sources of expertise (such as personal experience). In addition, we noted whether the guides represented institutions (such as Zionist organisations). We highlighted instances in which the experts described or tried to convince the readers of their authority, or sentences that revealed readers' doubts about the authority of the writers. Finally, we tracked places in the texts that referred to the audience being addressed. We differentiated these audiences according to a few parameters – their gender, education, the reason they wanted (according to the text) the information. Finally, we examined how audiences were (implicitly) defined, and asked who was included and excluded by this.

10.5 ANALYSIS: AN INGREDIENTS LIST FOR SHAPING SOCIETY

In order to explore how nutrition guides co-produce society and knowledge, we analysed three cases that represent archetypical instances of communication events within each of the different periods defined above. The pre-state years are represented by the case of the 'travelling instructors', in which Zionist women organisations taught pioneer homemakers how and what to eat in their vegetable gardens. The first years of statehood and the period of austerity are represented by two kinds of nutrition guides published at that time: recipes and constituent tables. The 1970s are represented here by two other kinds of texts, the weight-loss diet monthly column and healthy-eating guides, both of which were published in women's magazines.

10.5.1 NUTRITION GUIDES IN THE PRE-STATE: NATION BUILDING IN THE VEGETABLE GARDEN

Demonstrations, exhibitions, travelling instructors, textbooks, and cookbooks were all used as ways to communicate nutrition information during the *Yishuv*, or pre-state era, when diet was conceptualised as an eating strategy for promoting the national project. The travelling instructors, in particular, illustrate how nutritional recommendations were co-produced with Zionist goals and national society, through an assemblage that included the teaching/knowing space, the objects to be found in this space, people claiming to be experts in the field, and the public to whom the knowledge was addressed. But in order to understand how the travelling instructors' instructions co-produced national identity through nutritional knowledge, it is important to know something of the story of WIZO, the organisation that produced these communication events and that thus actively created this specific assemblage of place, authority, and publics.

WIZO was established for the purpose of empowering Zionist women pioneers. This was initially done by training women to be farmers (Greenberg & Herzog, 1978), a job that was considered very prestigious during this period and yet was customarily off-limits to women. WIZO began its activities in the 1920s by establishing farming schools for girls. Later on, during the economic depression of the mid-1920s, the organisation began teaching city women to grow vegetables in their backyards, both as a means of empowerment and as a solution to the food shortages of the time. This was done with the aid of travelling instructors who walked from house to house in Tel-Aviv, providing women with seeds and showing them how to plough, sow, and plant. Eventually these homemakers succeeded in producing high vegetable yields. However, they had very little knowledge of how to use their new produce, which many referred to still as 'weeds'. This in turn created the need for travelling WIZO instructors to provide additional instruction, both on the nutritional value of the vegetables and on how to cook them (Greenberg & Herzog 1978).

The backyard was the 'knowing space' (Law 2017) where information about nutrition shaped and was shaped by the specific public of homemakers and Zionist instructors. The backyard was not only the place where the unknown vegetables grew. It could also be looked on as a piece of the promised land – a space where the imaginary of the Jews as a people of the land (*this* land), working as farmers and feeding on local food, could spread and develop. Moreover, this communication event exemplifies how a spatial dimension is involved in the making of publics as well as of issues. There, in the back yard, nutrition was framed as the knowledge that helps people feed on local food. Nutritional information was constructed as the science that gives answers to questions, such as: Which of the produce that grows in our land can be eaten? What are the nutritional benefits of eating local food? And how can we prepare it, so it is healthy and tasty? In more general terms, this communication performed nutrition as a tool of nation building. The yard was not only a background, it was populated by different actors: some human, such as the Zionist organisation representative or the homemaker; others non-human, such as the strange and unknown vegetables, non-fertile sand, seeds, or ploughs. Questions that knowledge was shaped to answer in this space were: How should we eat what grows in this place? What is the nutritional value of the food that grows here? Other questions were closed down, such as: What are the healthiest foods? Or what foods suit different people? The case of the travelling instructors thus emphasises the importance of the physical space in which a communication event takes place for the reconfiguration of knowledge and society that occurs through it.

In tandem with the production and shaping of nutritional information, the audience was formed and particular kinds of authority staged. Information about the nutritional benefits of backyard produce was directed to homemakers. Addressing homemakers as the audience for nutritional guidance was thus closely related to how women's citizenship was imagined in this era: homemakers were those who, by feeding their families with local food, would help in the nation-building project. We can also observe the ways that authority is established and negotiated through this communication event, as well as how it is implicated in values and imaginaries of society. The fact that WIZO representatives (who were also graduates of nutritional schools) served both as experts in nutrition and as representatives of the collective effort in essence served to tie nutritional science and Zionist goals together. However, their credibility was not a given, but was negotiated throughout the communication event.

Accounts of the guidance provided by the instructors of the Zionist women organisations show that, at the beginning, homemakers were often reluctant to listen to the instructors. They didn't acknowledge WIZO's authority; or rather, they did not acknowledge their own ignorance in cooking and feeding their families. According to one instructor's memoirs, 'The audience ignored us. The homemaker's response to the instructor was usually "I know how to cook without learning"' (Katinsky 1938: 1). The dialogue that took place in these communication events illustrates how an audience can 'speak back' to science-based authority, and even protest against the presumption of their ignorance. Indeed, those homemakers who refused to be perceived as being in need of knowledge can be seen as protesting against how nutrition and society were co-produced in these nutritional lessons. Thus, in this context, the audience participated in the negotiation not only of authority, and of their own identity as 'pupils', but of the very narrative of eating as a part of nation building. They were resisting the definition of their identities as pioneers and Zionist homemakers.

This portrayal of homemakers' resistance to WIZO instructors is supported by another kind of nutritional communication event that took place during the same time. This was the first cook book to be published in Israel, in 1937. In it, the expert (another WIZO representative) argued explicitly that the intention of the recipes in the book was to transform the identity of the readers and to steer them away from the habits of exile that they brought with them from their previous homeland. The aim was to turn them into local cooks and members of the nation:

> 'What should I cook?' That is a question that housewives ask themselves all over the world. But this question bothers the Israeli housewife even more. As the difference in climate and conditions forces the woman who came from Europe to change her lifestyle and her way of cooking. And this change is harder than it seems. ... Time has come for us women to devote our energies to release our kitchen from the exile heritage that sticks to it, as long as it doesn't fit our land's conditions.... (Meyer 1937: 8)

The way this negotiation of authority was solved is a good place to end discussion of the co-production of society and nutritional knowledge that took place in these communication events. The Zionist organisation representatives took advantage of their affiliation to a well-funded organisation, and used the free distribution of seeds as a way to buy the right to pass on their knowledge (Rozov, in Greenberg & Herzog 1978: 67). This illustrates one more way in which state building and knowledge are mutually shaped – when the audience gets some distinct benefit from accepting the narratives and imaginaries inherent to the knowledge.

10.5.2 THE CO-PRODUCTION OF RECIPES, TABLES, AND CENTRALISED GOVERNMENT

The post-independence era shows communication of nutritional knowledge and society being made together in a slightly different way. The first years of statehood were a time of economic strain and massive immigration. As described above, the Israeli government responded by declaring an austerity policy that limited and controlled the amount and the kinds of food people could access. Analysis of nutritional communication during this austerity period reveals that different texts and narratives were presented to different parts of the public. This, we suggest, highlights the use of knowledge to shape docile citizens who obey the government's decision to control the public's diet.

One thing that stands out during this period is the sheer abundance of recipes. Recipes appeared in daily papers, weekend magazines, women's magazines, and pamphlets. These recipes taught women how to cook with the era's central ingredients: egg powder, milk powder, and dry bread. In the context of austerity, these texts participated in (per)forming the readers as docile citizens – those who don't go to the black market to find contraband produce, and who cooperate with the restrictions that the government enforces. For instance, one answer (in a newspaper column) to a reader's complaint about a recipe that used a lot of milk – four cups, more than government restrictions would allow – demonstrates how the editors of these columns and guides perceived their role. The editor saw his job in publishing recipes as enhancing or enabling readers' obedience: 'The recipes in our paper are written every week to suit the products delivered to the public and according to the foods that are available to us' (*Tevat Ha'Doar*, 13 October 1949).

The plethora of recipes in the mass media for cooking with food substitutes not only emphasises obedience to state policy, but is suggestive of the facts that are not being communicated – scientific facts about nutrition and health. The absence of nutritional information in most of the columns about food and eating *de facto* made these facts non-negotiable. This picture is complemented by the texts that did supply nutritional facts. The nutritional values of foods appeared in nutritional value tables that were published (starting in 1953, during the austerity period) by Yehiel Karl Guggenheim, the nutrition advisor for the Israeli Government at the time (Endvelt 2002: 1; Guggenheim 1955). These tables displayed the composition of foods according to eight different nutritional values. The fact that the information was presented in long lists, replete with numbers and technical concepts, made it clear that it was addressed only to professionals and experts. Simultaneously, these tables drew a boundary around facts about the nutritional value of the foods, excluding laypeople from the relevant 'knowing community' and shutting down questions about the validity of the government's rationing policy. This exclusion was made explicit in the introductions to the tables, which noted that they were addressed to dietitians in order to help them plan and evaluate diets (Guggenheim 1955: 4).

The manner in which the different guides segregated the public into lay-people and experts, defining the issues each of them should be concerned with (cooking versus understanding nutrition), reinforced a political situation in which a centralist government could dictate the diet of its citizens. This notion that knowledge about food's composition is irrelevant to the public was later articulated by Professor Ezra Zohar, a physician and writer of a self-help nutrition book published in the 1970s:

> what about the food composition tables that are published by ministries of health all over the world including those of the UN? These tables report the minimal recommended amount of proteins, minerals, vitamins and more ingredients, even calories. ... The importance of these tables is mainly from a national point of view, to be used by government offices, importation computation and so on. There is no need to take them into consideration for personal use or home cooking. (Zohar 1971: 179)

To summarise, while communicating information about food and nutrition in 1950s publications, recipe columns and nutritional value tables defined what knowledge is of interest to the public and what is not; which publics should have access to scientific information and which should be distanced from it; and what type of knowledge is negotiable and what is not. Thus, through recipes and nutritional value tables, nutritional knowledge and a centralised society (in which the government ruled many aspects of citizens' lives) were co-produced.

10.5.3 THE RISE OF INDIVIDUALITY AND CULTURE OF THE SELF IN MAGAZINE DIET COLUMNS

Amid the gradual transformation of nutrition from a science aimed at helping nation building into a science for helping individuals control their health and body, nutritional information travelled to a different site. It landed in between sewing guides, knitting instructions, cosmetic tips, and cleaning recommendations – in other words, between the covers of women's magazines.

Two different kinds of diet guide were published in women's magazine in the 1970s, each of them exemplifying a slightly different assemblage and making nutritional knowledge and society in different ways. First, however, it is important to understand the space in which both types of guide were situated. The ideology of women's magazines has long been discussed by feminist writers (Friedan 1974; White 1977; Winship 1983a). This ideology reveals itself through the typical characteristics of the genre: an abundance of tips and advice, presentation of the magazine as the reader's 'best friend', an inherent conception of women as in need of (self-)improvement, and a profusion of advertisements for products that are supposed to help them improve themselves. All of these elements are entangled in a culture of self-responsibility, de-politicisation, individualism, capitalism, and consumerism (Roy 2008; Winship 1983b).

Nutrition and diet guides published in this space framed nutrition as a type of knowledge that should be used by an individual in order to help her better her body and her life, rather than for the sake of social or national goals. In Israel, the first diet column to be published in a women's magazine was a monthly weight-loss column that appeared in 1972 in *At*, while six years later the second women's magazine, *La'Isha*, joined in with another column for dieters. In these columns (later published as books), new kinds of authority were presented. For example, the authority of the dieters themselves: 'The main reason for writing this book is that we have tried and we have succeeded. Every diet in this book was tested on our body' (Gal & Sofer 1976: 10).

By publishing a weekly column these women performed their expertise, using personal success in dieting as a source of authority. They made it possible to claim a new type of expertise as authoritative knowledge – that of personal experience. In addition, the weekly or monthly columns (and the books that were based on them) presented a never-ending variety of diets (with a new diet published every week), giving readers a choice and emphasising that every individual is unique and that their diet should be constructed accordingly: 'There isn't one diet that fits everyone – losing weight is an individual process' (Nir, 8.1975 111) and 'Only when you know what makes you fat and why, you can choose the diet that fits you. Fruit lovers, for example, would do right not to choose a protein diet, and someone that spends most of the day at home, would rather abstain from adopting a diet of two meals a day' (Gal & Sofer 1976: 16). In such ways the public of the columns, the readers, was imagined as being made of unique individuals. This stands in stark contrast to the collectivised members of 'the nation' addressed by nutrition guides in the pre-state period. Choice, personalisation, and customisation of diet therefore framed it as one more way to invent and express the self (Giddens 1991), at a time when individuality was viewed as primary. These columns framed the self as a key source of knowledge, and self-improvement and physique as the main goals of nutrition. Knowledge about losing weight was made along with an individualist society that emphasised freedom of choice, self-responsibility, and self-fulfilment.

A similar *Zeitgeist* is found in a different kind of diet column published in women's magazines, one that provided information about healthy nutrition. In these texts, a new kind of expert was introduced, the certified dietitian. This was a new breed of professionals, all of whom acquired their education in a school that was established in 1969 in the Faculty of Agriculture in the Hebrew University. Prior to the establishment of this department, nutritional science in Israel was taught in a 'College for Home Economics and Nutrition', which emphasised training home economics teachers and which focused on teaching them how to cook and to feed others. The new department emphasised biochemistry, links between nutrition and health, and scientific research. This new kind of nutritional expertise performed in these columns was thus that of a paramedical advisor who taught the public the biochemical construction of foods in order to help them eat healthily. Performing and presenting scientific knowledge as public knowledge that everyone should possess, an early column read: 'Before you decide what is the right food for an individual, you must understand what are the components of this food and what it turns into inside the body' (Markovitz 1979: 29).

The communication of 'facts' from nutritional science in a way that frames readers as responsible for their own nutrition – rather than this responsibility being deferred to cooks or kitchen managers – was a novelty. The texts themselves emphasise this: 'Learning how to eat is like learning how to drive. At first sight it seems very strange' (Markovitz 1979: 3). However, transforming laypeople into a public responsible for acquiring their own knowledge was also a process of negotiation within these guides. For example, 'Even if you are not a professional, you can know the ingredients that nourish your body. As you have free choice of the ingredients you select, you should aspire to consume the healthiest of them' (Markovitz 1979: 3). The choices and responsibilities one has regarding one's health are emphasised here. This was a new conception, co-produced with the emerging perception of citizens as individuals who are free to choose and who are responsible for their situation (rather than the former docile national citizens of the past). Making nutritional science a public fact, and addressing the public as a whole, rather than particular experts, as the relevant audience for this knowledge therefore helps co-produce a society that emphasises individualism, personal choice, and responsibility.

To summarise, the diet instruction columns that appeared in women's magazines in the 1970s staged knowledge of diet along with an individualistic, capitalistic society in which individuals were in charge of their own fates (and bodies), free to choose, and responsible for their situation.

10.6 CONCLUSION

This chapter has analysed dietary guides that were published at different moments in the history of Israel between the 1940s and 1980s. This longitudinal approach has enabled us to set nutritional guides into their historical context, from the nation-building era to the first years of statehood and the shift to an individualistic society, and has exposed the rich relationship between society and nutritional knowledge. This approach has demonstrated that diet guides are a space in which narratives and imaginations of nations are performed, where people are made, and where values are performed and tested, rather than simply being a means of the transmission of facts about nutrition.

The story of the transformations that have occurred in nutrition guides, and the way that nutrition communication is comprised of unique combinations of human and non-human actors within different spaces, illustrates the relationship between these 'events' and the social context in which they arise. We have seen, for example, how an assemblage of vegetables, seeds, Zionist representatives, and newly immigrated homemakers in backyards is interwoven with an imaginary of a society of solidarity and recruited to the project of nation building. This connection is emphasised by comparing it with a different assemblage which includes scientific researchers, the nutritional value of foods, and certified dietitians with a university degree; these components, assembled together within the space of women's magazines, provides advice (purportedly to improve womens' lives) that is inextricably entangled with a society that values individualism and egoism.

This study has also illustrated how nutritional guides addressed different publics in each period, and how they were involved in identifying pioneer homemakers, weight losers, or individuals responsible for their own health. Taking into consideration the historical moments in which each event took place helps us to see not only how scientific citizenship is shaped, but how it is exercised and tested in these communicative contexts. Thus, for example, the research showed how women immigrants were staged by nutritional guidance as 'natives' who would take part in nation building through cooking with local produce; and how, later, women were imagined as taking part in society through feeding their families with the scarce foods that the government supplied. Later again, their citizenship was performed in diet columns, as articulated through practices of weight watching and strictly controlled eating to fit a new culture of thinness. As we have seen, in healthy-eating columns, individual citizenship was constructed as taking responsibility for one's own health through informed choices about food and eating.

Following nutritional communication over time and into different spaces also helps us to see how knowledge and authority are staged in these settings. Thus, the nutritional expert who was also a Zionist women's organisation representative helped connect 'right' eating with nation-building goals, women who lost weight claimed credibility because of their personal experience (and in doing so co-produced a culture of self), and certified dietitians intertwined scientific knowledge with personal responsibility and choice. Tracking the history of diet guides and setting them in their historical background has thus helped us to see the way in which communicational nutrition events are involved not only in producing knowledge about nutrition, and making the publics that are its audience, but in co-producing imaginaries, narratives, nations, and citizens.

REFERENCES

Aharoni, Yair. 1998. 'The Changing Political Economy of Israel'. *Annals of the American Academy of Political and Social Science* 555 (1): 127–148.

Almog, Oz. 1998. 'From Vegetable Salad and LebAenia to Hamburger and Sushi: The Coca-Colonization of Israel'. *Place for Thought* (2): 7–19 (in Hebrew).

Beardsworth, Alan, and Keil Teresa. 1997. *Sociology on the Menu – an Invitation to the Study of Food and Society*. Abingdon and New York: Routledge.

Bromberg (Bavly), Sarah. 1942. *Do You Spend Your Money Wisely?* Jerusalem: Haddasah Health Center (in Hebrew).

Endvelt, Ronit. 2002. 'Policy and Development of Nutrition Services for the Infant and Child in Israel'. PhD dissertation, Ben-Gurion Univesity.

Felt, Ulrike. 1999. 'Why Should the Public "Understand" Science? A Historical Perspective on Aspects of the Public Understanding of Science'. In Meinolf Dierkes and Claudia Von Grote (eds.), *Between Understanding and Trust: The Public, Science and Technology*, pp. 7–38. Amsterdam: Harwood Academic Publishers.

Felt, Ulrike, and Maximilian Fochler. 2010. 'Machineries for Making Publics: Inscribing and De-Scribing Publics in Public Engagement'. *Minerva* 48 (3): 219–238.

Friedan, Betty. 1974. *The Feminine Mystique*. Ithaca, NY: Dell.

Gal, Naomi, and Esther Sofer. 1976. *The Winners are the Losers* [in Hebrew: *Ein Davar Haomed Bifnei Ha' Razon*]. Jerusalem: Idan.

Germov, John, and Lauren Williams. 2009. *A Sociology of Food and Nutrition*. Oxford: Oxford Univesity Press.

Giddens, Anthony. 1991. *The Consequences of Modernity*. Stanford, CA: Stanford University Press.

Greenberg, Ofra, and Hannah Herzog. 1978. *Women Volunteers Organization in a Society in Creation: The Contribution of WIZO to the Israeli Society*. Tel-Aviv: The Institute for Social Research of the Sociology and Anthropology Department.

Guggenheim, Yehiel, K. 1955. *Food Constituents' Tables*. Jerusalem: The Ministry of Education, The Nutrition Department.

Guggenheim, Yehiel, K., Habibi Eliahu Reshef Avraham. 1991. 'The First Days of Nutritional Research and Foods in Israel'. *Katedra* 59: 144–164 (in Hebrew).

Hacking, Ian. 1986. 'Making Up People'. In Thomas C. Heller, Morton Sosna and David E. Wellbery (eds.), *Reconstructing Individualism: Autonomy, Individuality, and the Self in Western Thought*, pp. 222–236. Stanford, CA: Stanford University Press.

Hilgartner, Stephen. 2000. *Science on Stage: Expert Advice as Public Drama*. Stanford, CA: Stanford University Press.

Jasanoff, Sheila. 2004. *States of Knowledge: The Co-Production of Science and Social Order*. Abingdon and New York: Routledge.

Katinsky, Zipora. 1938. 'Teaching in Kitchens in the Kibbutz'. *AZM*, F49/1341.

Law, John. 2017. 'STS as Method'. In Ulrike Felt, Rayvon Fouché, Clark A. Miller, and Laurel Smith-Doerr (eds.), *The Handbook of Science and Technology Studies*, pp. 31–57. Cambridge, MA: The MIT Press.

Lupton, Deborah. 1996. *Food, the Body and the Self*. London: Sage.

Markovitz, Issa. 1979. 'What is a Diet?' *La'Isha*, 13 August.

Meyer, Erna. 1937. *How to Cook in Palestine*. Tel-Aviv: WIZO Women's Organization.

Ram, Uri. 2005. *The Globalization of Israel: McWorld in Tel Aviv, Jihad in Jerusalem*. Tel Aviv: Resling (in Hebrew).

Raviv, Yael. 2002. 'Recipe for a Nation: Cuisine, Jewish Nationalism and the Israeli State'. PhD dissertation, New York University.

Roy, Stephany. 2008. '"Taking Charge of Your Health": Discourses of Responsibility in English-Canadian Women's Magazines'. *Sociology of Health & Illness* 30 (3): 463–477.

Rozin, Orit. 2006. 'Food, Identity and Nation Building in Israel's Formative Years'. *Israel Studies Forum* 21 (1): 52–80.

Rozin, Orit. 2008. *Duty and Love: Individualism and Collectivism in the 1950's in Israel*. Ramat Gan: Am-Oved.

Tene, Ofra. 2002. Thus You Shall Cook! Reading in Israeli Cookbooks. MA dissertation, Tel Aviv University (in Hebrew).

Tevat Ha'Doar (Inbox). 1949. *La'Isha*, 13 October.

Weiss, Meira. 2004. *The Chosen Body: The Politics of the Body in Israeli Society*. Stanford, CA: Stanford University Press.

White, Cinthia, L. 1977. *The Women's Periodical Press in Britain 1946–1976*. London: HMSO.

Winship, Janice. 1983a. *Inside Women's Magazines*. London and New York: Pandora Press.

Winship, Janice. 1983b. '"Options – for the Way You Want to Live Now", or a Magazine for Superwoman'. *Theory, Culture & Society* 1 (3): 44–65.

Zohar, Ezra. 1971. *The Man and His Food or: What is the Truth in the Stories You Heard about Food*. Haifa: Shekmona (in Hebrew).

Reflections and Connections

The following chapter differs from those that precede it in that, rather than primarily focusing on spaces, moments, or products of science communication, it turns the lens back onto scientists, and the ways in which they understand their public audiences. Within it, Nina Amelung, Rafaela Granja, and Helena Machado unpick how a particular epistemic community, or *thought collective*, develop shared imaginations of the nature of different publics, and how these imaginations co-produce the process of communication and, simultaneously, perform boundary-work.

Amelung et al. work with a highly specific epistemic community, that of forensic geneticists. Their chapter thus demonstrates that science communication is always specific and contingent. Topic matters. In this case, forensic genetics has particular *epistemic norms* due to the fact that its knowledge is produced for a specific context: the legal system and, in particular, the courtroom. These norms shape scientific practice, but they also affect how public communication is understood by these geneticists.

A key issue is what has become known as the 'CSI effect': widespread public awareness of forensic genetics technologies alongside (what forensic geneticists believe are) overly high expectations of what these technologies can deliver. The publics of forensic genetics – whether the public at large or the specific publics of the legal system – are therefore constructed as too 'enthusiastic'. The result is a complex set of negotiations by scientists as they talk about and practice communication. They must manage expectations, while maintaining boundaries around their discipline in order to protect their authority to interpret DNA evidence, while also distributing responsibility to their audiences in the legal system such that final decisions about justice – the binary decision of guilt or innocence – are made outside science. The result is a fascinating case where scientists maintain their authority through framing their own science – and their fellow scientists – as deficient in certain ways.

11

COMMUNICATING FORENSIC GENETICS: 'ENTHUSIASTIC' PUBLICS AND THE MANAGEMENT OF EXPECTATIONS

NINA AMELUNG, RAFAELA GRANJA AND HELENA MACHADO

11.1 INTRODUCTION

'One of the most important problems in forensic medicine', write forensic geneticists Angel Carracedo and Lourdes Prieto, 'is the so-called "CSI effect"' (Carracedo & Prieto 2018: 4). Their description of the threat posed by TV shows such as *Crime Scene Investigation* (CSI) to their discipline runs as follows: '[m]ost TV series present forensic evidence as infallible – one hundred percent reliable, with no margin for doubt – when reality is very different: the scientific validity of forensic tests is variable' (ibid.). When looking at the communication of forensic science, we therefore seem to be confronted with an interesting paradox. While researchers and policy makers tend to complain about public disinterest in science and see this as threatening its cultural authority, in the case of forensic science we encounter the exact opposite. It is the prominence of forensic science in popular culture which seems to have raised expectations to a degree which might actually have negative consequences for the use of this knowledge in the context of criminal investigations and in the judicial system.

Indeed, forensic genetics, as a specialisation of genetics and forensic science, is communicated and negotiated in particular settings. On the one hand, its identity is generally negotiated in and structured by the physical and social space of the forensic genetics laboratory, a space that is important in the chain of custody for producing DNA evidence that can be used for police criminal investigation and in the courtroom. On the other hand, the results of forensic genetic science are always eventually communicated in the courtroom, which becomes 'a theatre' (Felt and Davies, in Chapter 3, referring to Jasanoff) in which evidence needs to be demonstrated in a manner legible to the common sense of judges and jurors. In recent decades, public understandings of forensic genetics – publics including here also judges and police officers – have been understood as being strongly shaped by media representations in prominent TV series. As a consequence, forensic geneticists have had to reflect on the views of publics they encounter and to develop communication strategies to protect and defend their profession's identity, including the provision of guidance about 'good communication'.

In the present chapter we explore forensic geneticists' perceptions of how they carry out science communication to their specific publics in the criminal justice system. More particularly, we examine how forensic geneticists reconstruct their self-conception and relations to their publics when performing the presentation of DNA evidence in court. The research questions guiding our investigations are the following: What are the particularities of communicating forensic genetics? How do forensic geneticists cope with these particularities? And how do imaginaries of publics shape forensic geneticists' experiences of communication?

In what follows we will reflect on two strands of Science and Technology Studies (STS) debates that inform our study. After presenting our material and the methods we use, we present our analysis along three lines and draw concluding remarks.

11.2 SCIENCE COMMUNICATION AS BOUNDARY-WORK: PROTECTING SCIENCE'S IDENTITY AND DELEGATING RESPONSIBILITIES

Science communication scholars have highlighted that STS can offer relevant perspectives to understand how science and publics are co-produced in science communication practices (Davies & Horst 2016: 204). Indeed, there is a quite large body of literature pointing to the fact that publics are not simply out there waiting to be informed about science, but are actively made through the precise settings and the spaces in which science communication happens (Felt & Fochler 2010; Lezaun & Soneryd 2007). In this context it is also useful to consider the distinction introduced by Mike Michael (2009) between 'publics-in-particular' – namely specific, situated publics with identifiable stakes and interests – and 'publics-in-general', a rather undifferentiated vision of 'people out there'. Thus, we have to consider that the criminal justice system, and in particular the courtroom, are specific spaces (see Chapter 3) in which forensic geneticists communicate about DNA evidence. This gives form to specific kinds of publics, and shapes the roles that can be taken on, how these are distributed, and the kinds of knowledge that can and need to be communicated.

We also suggest reading our case in the light of the dominant sense-making narratives used by science communication scholars and practitioners today, such as the so-called 'deficit model' (Davies & Horst 2016: 37–39; Irwin 2014; McNeil 2013). The reference to the 'deficit model' usually serves as an established classification to describe certain ways of performing science communication (in particular one-way instead of two-way science communication; Davies & Horst 2016: 37–39). This model has been used instrumentally, in the sense that it serves as a justification to argue for increasing scientific literacy or for excluding lay publics from some types of decision making. The 'deficit model' is thereby a manifestation of broader imaginations of what scientific governance should look like (Irwin & Wynne 1996). In this chapter we will explore an additional, quite different, notion of the 'deficit model', applied not only to publics, but also to science/scientists. For our particular case, we will argue that the deficit model, as applied to science within forensic geneticists' discussions about science communication, serves as a gateway to renegotiate the responsibilities within forensic genetics and the use of forensic genetics' findings beyond its own communities.

Approaching science communication as relational and emergent also means paying attention to how imaginaries of publics prefigure science communication practices and to the role that communication plays in performing boundary-work (Gieryn 1983). Such boundary-work contributes on the one hand to maintaining the authority, credibility, and integrity of a specific scientific community (Jasanoff 1993, 2004), but on the other hand it also allows the performance of specific distributions of duties and responsibilities. As we will show, in this case, science is framed as being responsible for demonstrating the reliability and veracity of research results, while those who apply the results in the criminal justice system are presented as being responsible for the appropriate use of these results.

11.3 DNA DOESN'T SPEAK – PEOPLE DO: COMMUNICATING DNA EVIDENCE IN THE CRIMINAL JUSTICE SYSTEM

Particularly significant characteristics of forensic genetics derive from its specific epistemic culture (Cole 2013), which is distinct from other forensic science cultures as well as from science in general, and which impacts upon the particularities of communicating it. Forensic genetics differs from other forensic sciences by being celebrated as the 'gold standard' (Lynch 2003) among forensic sciences, suggesting a higher level of certainty and reliability due to its quantifiable estimations. Another important distinction comes from the type of work undertaken by forensic geneticists: these professionals tend to produce a specific type of scientific knowledge, designed to contribute to the investigation of a single criminal incident, and specifically to aid convictions or exonerations. Forensic genetic science's temporally limited nature within legal truth-finding processes thus comes from the specificity of knowledge claims and data produced (Cole 2013: 39).

Most relevant, in terms of impact on the particularities of communicating forensic genetics, is forensic geneticists' specific target audience, comprising police officers, prosecutors, judges, jurors – the so-called 'law-set' (Edmond 2001). The members of the criminal justice system that we will regard as forensic geneticists' publics-in-particular (Michael 2009) are specific and situated publics with identifiable stakes and interests in specific aspects of DNA evidence, which in turn helps them to fulfil their duties. By contrast, publics-in-general (Michael 2009) – or 'wider publics' as they are often referred to – are for most forensic geneticists an undifferentiated mass, who largely take their knowledge of forensic genetics from TV media.

One other particularity of communicating forensic genetics relates to how courts have emerged as democratising agents in disputes over the control and deployment of new DNA technologies, thereby advancing and sustaining a public dialogue about the *limits* of forensic genetics' expertise (Jasanoff 1995; Lynch & Jasanoff 1998). Following the work of Michael Lynch and Sheila Jasanoff on that topic, a growing body of literature has addressed how the field of forensic genetics evolved and has been constructed through a complex series of practices and procedures that functioned to close down initial controversies and to guarantee the credibility and reliability of forensic DNA evidence in criminal justice systems worldwide (Aronson 2007; Derksen 2003; Lazer 2004; Lynch et al. 2008).

Although foundational controversies involving DNA evidence have been resolved, standardisation and legal acceptance does not mean the end of controversies surrounding the uses and interpretation of DNA evidence in court. Within the forensic genetics community, negotiations about diverse issues involving the uses and interpretation of DNA evidence mean that there is a continual need to seek common agreements in order to stabilise the field. Among these issues is a lack of protocol for dealing with diverse forms of reporting DNA evidence to non-experts (such as those found in courtrooms; Howes et al. 2014), and the challenges of communicating probabilistic results and likelihood ratios in typical identification cases (Amorim et al. 2016). Finally, the interpretation of complex DNA profiles, such as partial or mixed profiles, is also portrayed as being notably prone to reporting inconsistencies due to subjective decisions about whether a result is probative or inconclusive (Gill et al. 2008).

STS literature on forensic genetics has also explored one other important dimension affecting the communication of DNA evidence in the criminal justice system: the so-called 'CSI effect', a concept employed by scholars, and increasingly also by practitioners and public media, to capture the assumption that members of the criminal justice system, and the public-in-general, confuse the idealised portrayal of DNA evidence on television with the actual capabilities of forensic genetics in the criminal justice system (Cole & Dioso-Villa 2009; Kruse 2010; Podlas 2009). The CSI effect, together with a lack of literacy on the probabilistic framework involved in the interpretation of DNA evidence, is considered by many forensic geneticists to be the major obstacle in their task of communicating the results of DNA analysis to members of the criminal justice system (Amorim 2012; Amorim et al. 2016). Although there is no consensus in social science studies about whether or not a CSI effect really does exist and what exactly it would consist of (see Ley et al. 2010), as we will show it is nevertheless an important element of forensic geneticists' narratives about the challenges of communicating forensic genetics analysis in courtrooms.

11.4 METHODS

This chapter draws on qualitative data derived from nine interviews conducted with forensic geneticists who work in forensic laboratories and/or university departments of forensic sciences based in different countries in Europe. Taking into consideration the diversity of the forensic genetics community (Cole 2013; Lynch et al. 2008), we adopted the following selection criteria to recruit participants in this study: they needed to hold a degree in disciplines directly connected to forensic genetics (Biology, Genetics and Medicine) and be the head of or employed by a forensic laboratory that provides DNA analysis for presentation as evidence in criminal cases. In line with Cole's proposal, our sample therefore aggregates *forensic genetic scientists* and *research scientists* (Cole 2013). Although the interview sample is small, for the purpose of pointing at the diverse argumentative repertoires that are the core interest of this chapter the diversity was large enough.

Recruitment was conducted by sending an invitation letter by email. Prior to the interviews, all the interviewees signed a written informed consent form and agreed to be audio-recorded. All the interviews were digitally recorded, transcribed verbatim, and anonymised. The script for the interviews covered the following themes: views and experiences of the expansion of criminal forensic DNA databases in different European jurisdictions, and of the transnational exchange of DNA data; opinions about the challenges of the uses of DNA technologies in the criminal justice system; perceptions on DNA technology development and innovation; and opinions about ethical issues and public engagement with forensic genetics.

In order to avoid narrow framings of 'science communication' and 'public', for analysis purposes we use terms such as 'public(s)' but also others which appear to be used synonymously, such as 'citizens', 'collectives', 'lay groups', 'communities', 'society', or 'people'. Relevant quotations pertaining to the communication of DNA evidence were coded and subjected to multiple readings to develop in-depth understandings of prevalent notions of forensic genetic science communication and the relations between forensic genetics and society. These quotations were systematically compared, contrasted, synthesised, and coded by theme and by thematic category following the principles of grounded theory (Charmaz 2006), and interpreted using a qualitative content analysis approach (Mayring 2004).

11.5 EMPIRICAL ANALYSIS

11.5.1 THE CSI EFFECT AND THE 'THREAT' OF ENTHUSIASTIC PUBLICS

The particularities of communicating forensic genetics are understood by forensic geneticists as being shaped by the CSI effect and media coverage of high-profile cases, which they perceive as responsible for publics' beliefs in the alleged 'superior role' of DNA evidence (Lynch et al. 2008). This CSI effect is framed as having two interrelated consequences on publics. On the one hand, it has helped to foster public interest in forensic genetics, and to make citizens aware of the existence and evolution of DNA technologies. On the other hand, it disseminates exaggerated understandings of the alleged power of DNA to solve criminal cases. One of our interviewees explains this juxtaposition of implications:

> The CSI effect has been significant, and the positive side of it is how young people have grown to be much more curious about the field. … That's the good thing. The downside to CSI [effect] is presenting the tests as infallible, [as if it] always works…. [CO1]

Forensic geneticists thus accuse the media of providing an incomplete picture of DNA technologies. By exaggerating the possibilities, the speed, and the certainty of outcomes of DNA technologies, media narratives do not provide an adequate description of inherent limitations of genetic evidence: 'There is this famous CSI thing. But they [the publics] are not really educated about the pitfalls and limitations [of DNA evidence]' [OO1]. Entertainment media narratives are represented as focusing on dramatic and emotionalised events in the portrayal of fictionalised representations of forensic science (Machado & Santos 2011), standing in direct contrast to the efforts of accurately communicating 'sound science' (Hansen 2016). The emphasis on uncertainties in forensic geneticists' explanation of DNA evidence is framed as incompatible with mainstream forms of communication. As such, as noted by the following interviewee, forensic geneticists struggle with media representations of DNA evidence, which are portrayed as being assured facts:

> [The main challenge of communicating science is] the information that people receive from television programs and the media and the sort of impression that science is about certainty: 'scientist says this and therefore it must be true' and, in fact, science is full of uncertainties. People do not understand that, they do not appreciate it. ... Uncertainties do not make good ... audience. [D09]

Consequently, forensic geneticists tend to portray their publics as overly 'enthusiastic' and as holding what they perceive to be unrealistic views about the possibilities of DNA technologies in criminal justice systems. However, these inflated perspectives on the potential contributions of DNA analysis to criminal investigation processes are not only present in forensic geneticists' views of lay publics, but also in framings of the *publics-in-particular* that are active members of the criminal justice system. Several of our interviewees outlined how police officers, prosecutors, and judges also attribute too much importance to DNA technologies when addressing criminal cases. In their opinion, DNA is generally considered to be 'a sort of priority type of evidence' [E01] which plays a decisive role in how criminal cases are presented in court:

> This public perception is that if you have the DNA, that's it! That's all you need! And if you don't have the DNA, we'll have prosecutors [saying] 'You can't make a case with this, with no DNA!' [laughs]. [E01]

Not being immune to representations that portray DNA as infallible, stakeholders directly involved in the criminal justice system are thus perceived as being strongly influenced by overly bright prospects fostered by the entertainment media: 'The CSI effect is a very common phenomenon, and therefore it shapes police officers' expectations about what is possible' [C04].

This poses several challenges to an adequate use of forensic genetic science in criminal investigations. Members of the criminal justice system are described as not being very well informed about the kind of information that can(not) be obtained from DNA technologies, and under what conditions such information can be retrieved. As a consequence, forensic geneticists often describe how they are confronted with frustration and disappointment on the part of members of the criminal justice system when they are unable to provide clear results – namely, a match or non-match – on the basis of a DNA profile:

> It is so popular the perception that it [DNA] is infallible and there is a fairly substantial lack of scientific education in most inspectors who work with DNA. ... They will have either questions or issues with the results. ... You get back a mixed result, or a negative result, and they say 'We sent you a DNA analysis, so where is

my result?' and we say 'Well, this is why we couldn't get a result', and they can't understand that. [E01]

The repercussions of overly positive expectations about the possibilities of DNA technologies are wide-ranging. A major concern, in the view of forensic geneticists, is that 'misrepresentations' might lead to miscarriages of justice, especially in cases where DNA technologies play a relevant role in deliberations in court. Forensic geneticists also voice their dissatisfaction with judges when the latter ignore the potential risks and the unintended consequences of overstating DNA evidence. One interviewee would put it as follows:

> Evidently, it [DNA evidence] is given much more importance by judges than it should. They must be aware that it's a clear mistake, they should be much more careful. … Do judges know that 30% of incorrect rulings are linked to wrong identification of testimonies? Do judges know the real value behind each specific piece of scientific forensic evidence? They don't. And they make a barbaric number of mistakes because of that. [C05]

By pointing to a lack of knowledge among members of the criminal justice system and to the need to tackle their 'misconceptions', forensic geneticists engage in a standard 'deficit model' narrative. At the same time, they underline that this is a serious issue that touches on the shared responsibilities of members of the criminal justice system. Such a lack of awareness has potentially serious consequences, such as a possible miscarriage of justice. According to this view, one of the key types of DNA-related errors therefore results from misunderstanding the 'real value' of DNA evidence in court settings, rather than from errors that occur in the process of DNA analysis in the lab. Such a position also performs important boundary-work focused on constructing distinctions between the tasks of different professional groups in making use of DNA analysis: carrying out an analysis in the lab is the responsibility of forensic geneticists, while its final interpretation is the responsibility of judges in courts (Machado & Granja 2018). According to forensic geneticists' views, the final (and therefore decisive) instance of interpretation of the evidence in order to reach a decision about guilt or innocence must be enacted by judges. As the following quotation illustrates, from such a perspective, forensic geneticists see their role as presenting and explaining DNA evidence, while also outlining the ambiguity involved in its interpretation:

> I think that sometimes the expectation of the court [is] that they are going to be provided with some unambiguous scientific evidence of fact that is just going to allow them to come to the right conclusion in terms of guilt or innocence. I think there is a general difference in the perspective of the scientist, who will say: 'Well, we found this profile and it is up to the court to decide what its significance is, particularly in regard to the guilt or innocence of the accused person'. [D11]

Forensic geneticists represent themselves as confronted by publics-in-particular that they feel have too strong expectations of DNA evidence, namely that it should provide a 'result' that forms a clear basis for deciding whether the accused is 'guilty' or 'innocent'. Members of the criminal justice system are regarded as having a specific 'deficit': one of being overly optimistic about the capacity of DNA analysis, which is seen as synonymous with their lack of scientific literacy for understanding the 'real value' and the probabilistic framework of DNA evidence. These forensic geneticists clearly subscribe to a 'deficit model', and with it to a particular vision of the publics-in-particular they encounter in the criminal justice system. This vision is instrumental in the sense that it reifies the boundary between the worlds of science and of non-science. On the one hand, their use of this 'deficit model' stabilises forensic genetics' authority over understanding DNA evidence; on the other hand, it constructs an enthusiastic, yet ignorant, public who have idealised views of DNA evidence, and thus who could potentially become a threat to the credibility of forensic genetics' epistemic authority (Marris 2015).

11.5.2 BOUNDARY-WORK ALONG 'DEFICITS': ESTABLISHING RISK COMMUNICATION TO DELEGATE RESPONSIBILITY

In order to cope with the particular challenges of communicating their work, forensic geneticists develop coping strategies within their epistemic community, strategies which attempt to counterbalance excessive expectations towards DNA technologies. Among these is the emergence of what can be called a 'proactive *ethos* of public responsibility' (Bliss 2012: 166–172; Machado & Granja, 2018). This means that they aim to perform (forensic genetic) science in a way that is committed to and engaged with its wider social implications and the ways that its results are taken up in different arenas. One of the dimensions of this ethos is active communication of the limitations associated with DNA analysis within the criminal justice system, therefore deconstructing dominant visions that associate forensic science with a 'truth machine' (Lynch et al. 2008) that is able to provide certainty with regard to results. The adoption of such an idiom of uncertainty, one that addresses and attempts to manage the risks and uncertainties underlying forensic science, seems to have become part of the epistemic culture of forensic geneticists, as illustrated by the following quotation:

> So, it is a question of trying to give as much genetic data as we can, but at the same time not offering a service that makes exaggerated claims about the accuracy or the precision of the tests from very small amounts of DNA. So, I think it is important that we are realistic about the limitations. [CO4]

Here we can detect a type of boundary-work that frames the identity of 'responsible' forensic genetics experts as characterised by a felt need to reflect on and clearly communicate the limitations of the evidence they can provide. Therefore, as a response to the high expectations present in the public arena, science communication is often preoccupied with caution concerning what forensic genetics *cannot* provide. Against the high expectations of its publics, the propagated approach for science communication here emphasises the responsibility for fully disclosing the limits and uncertainties, for example the deficits inherent to 'their science'. This is a new twist in applying a 'deficit model', this time to science (and scientists' responsibilities to cope with science's deficits).

A certain degree of formalisation and standardisation of such 'risk communication' has been established in protocols for using quantitative probabilistic value descriptions for reporting the results of DNA analysis when reaching out to members of the criminal justice system. Although being transparent about the limitations and risks of DNA results has become a routine part of reporting, it remains essential to make a distinction from 'messy' laboratory practices and to maintain the appearance of technical order (Lynch 2002) in producing evidence. The need to communicate that the uncertainties of DNA evidence are tamed and under control therefore also derives from the need to protect the epistemic community's credibility from becoming 'fodder for impeachment' (Cole 2013: 41) when exposed to potential fallibility. More recently, additional strategies for addressing such transparency-oriented approaches to risk communication have emerged. Some examples of this trend include providing concrete models for good practice for evaluative expert reporting and suggesting standards for evaluative reporting within professional networks, such as the European Network of Forensic Science Institutes (ENFSI) (Biedermann et al. 2017). According to several forensic geneticists, this type of risk communication is increasingly important as more sensitive methods of DNA analysis are being developed and, as a consequence, sensitivity to issues such as contamination has also risen (Gill et al. 2008). Some participants in our study therefore advocate the adoption of an even more careful strategy of interpretation and communication:

> Now we are getting weak profiles, partial profiles, from contact stains, there may be secondary transfer, and all of these other things, and this also has to be taken into consideration for the interpretation of the evidence. And the awareness of this situation is not very widespread. This is something that we need to promote and to make public, that there are limits of testing that … we are victims of our own success. … Because we have made it [DNA technologies] very sensitive, and now we have to live with the consequences. [O01]

Although some forensic geneticists might be committed to communicating the limitations and uncertainties of DNA analysis, judges and other members of the criminal justice system might not be willing to interpret, understand, engage with, or even accept such 'uncertain' premises. However, in the end, forensic geneticists partly delegate responsibility for managing the difficulties of interpreting DNA evidence to members of the criminal justice system. These types of tensions therefore illustrate the boundaries and tensions between the rationalities that guide the different epistemic cultures at work – those of science and the criminal justice system. This was addressed in the following quote:

> In order to be successful in this interplay, of course we have the right to try to explain [DNA evidence], but the other guys, judges and lawyers, also have the duty of trying to understand. And unfortunately, as the society is organized, they prefer not to. Because the judges, most of them ... prefer that the DNA speaks for itself, they do not realise that they are deciding. And they go mad when I resist their pressing on me to state a probability or something like that. Which is misunderstanding everything I am trying to do. [NO1]

In adopting risk communication strategies anchored to policies of transparency, forensic geneticists thus attempt to leave the 'black box' of forensic evidence deliberately open, leaving uncertainty and the limitations of DNA technologies visible (Amorim 2012). However, this creates friction in as much as the intent of the criminal justice system – especially in decision-making spaces such as the courts – is to search for factual certainty in order to ensure that justice is done in each individual case (Jasanoff 2006), while the science system is quite used to handling a reasonable degree of uncertainty and error.

Besides delegating responsibility for interpreting DNA evidence to members of the criminal justice system, forensic geneticists also enact other kinds of boundary-work by defining what makes a good scientist (Machado & Granja 2018) – that is, the one who communicates limitations – and delineating those who don't accept the same norms. Such individuals are framed as what Jasanoff (1993: 78) has called 'misfits, deviants, charlatans, or outsiders' to the enterprise of science. Several forensic geneticists demonstrate this pattern of othering 'bad behaviour', that is, attributing certain behaviours to colleagues who are seen as less committed to these norms of humility when it comes to the capacity of producing evidence with certainty. They are quite sceptical, doubting whether other colleagues stick to the ideal of communicating the limitations of DNA evidence:

> When I am testifying in court I always try also to make clear where the limits of this evidence are. ... But I am not quite sure about my other colleagues. ... So basically, my impression is that there may be cases ... where the DNA was overstated, already in the report; there was no quality check because there was nobody in the court asking questions. Everyone just accepted that as a given fact, there was no criticism. [OO1]

Our findings suggest that these coping strategies of risk communication, and particularly the emphasis on limitations of forensic genetics' capacity to deliver unquestionable evidence, is not yet mainstream among forensic geneticists. It is, however, perceived as a reasonable approach to render the all-too-easily black-boxed aspects of uncertainty accompanying statistical interpretation of DNA evidence more explicit and visible (Amorim 2012; Biedermann et al. 2017). One way of stabilising the field of forensic genetics against criticism and keeping its authority is thus presented as the use of its own understanding of DNA evidence, with all its limitations made explicit, while delegating responsibility for binary decisions to other members of the criminal justice system.

11.5.3 COMMUNICATING AND MOBILISING A FORENSIC GENETICS' UNDERSTANDING OF DNA EVIDENCE

While the previously described coping strategies of forensic genetics mainly address how forensic geneticists redefine their self-conception and presentation of forensic genetics, this section explores how imaginaries of publics impact upon actual communication experiences with members of the criminal justice system. Most of the venues and material structures for communicating forensic genetics to publics-in-particular are pre-formatted by the criminal investigation and judicial settings. These routine practices entail, for instance, the production of written reports and the provision of expert testimony in courts at the request of judges or lawyers. Nevertheless, some forensic geneticists also use alternative spaces and formats to respond to what they perceive as being the needs of publics, for instance the need to clearly understand the potential and limitations of DNA evidence.

Based on the premise that members of the criminal justice system are not properly informed about forensic genetics and DNA evidence, many of our interviewees claim that there is a need for training designed to fill knowledge gaps, as the following quotation illustrates:

> The investigators are often not the people who do the work in the laboratory and they may not have learned the same kind of knowledge. So, one of the problems is the collection of samples, for example, doing this properly. So there needs to be an educational program, which makes sure that everybody is aware of what they should be doing. [Q01]

By attempting to construct a shared knowledge base about DNA analysis, forensic geneticists take on the role of public educators. In doing so, they are therefore delineating hierarchies of knowledge, attempting to assure their epistemic authority (i.e., their role as experts), protecting the autonomy of forensic genetics, and creating new forms of scientific legitimation and consolidation of expertise claims (Gieryn 1983; Kruse 2016).

The narratives of most of the forensic geneticists we interviewed highlighted the belief that, by occasionally engaging with members of the criminal justice system through educational courses and direct interactions – at least in more exceptional criminal cases, they might reduce the overall risk of potential misinterpretation of certain DNA evidence. This is illustrated by the following quotation:

> I think it is important to educate the police officers about your own work. … We are doing it because we are offering educational workshops, trainings, where we invite police to give them an update about our work. … Normally [when] we are involved in a major case, like a capital crime, then we have direct contact with … police officers. They like this very much because they can come to our institute and then we can discuss the case, and we can demonstrate what we have found and what it means. [O01]

When addressing publics-in-particular, forensic geneticists thus occasionally attempt to actively engage them in training, education, and joint discussion. Such moments enrich forensic geneticists' imaginaries of their publics by giving them access to the needs of publics-in-particular, as articulated by those publics themselves. They further provide an opportunity to actively share forensic geneticists' understanding of DNA evidence, thereby somewhat (re)distributing responsibility for (correctly) interpreting DNA evidence.

However, the willingness of forensic geneticists to engage directly with their publics-in-particular remains limited. Entertainment media is generally understood as limiting their capacity to reach out to wider publics and to influence exaggerated views about the potential of DNA technologies. In this sense, although forensic geneticists acknowledge the need to provide education and information, some may in fact contribute to the power of the CSI effect by overlooking the influence of their own claims to shape public opinion. Feeling unable to compete with media impact on audiences, some forensic geneticists end up demonstrating a certain resignation about challenging dominant perceptions:

> And we need to make improvements, and all roads lead to education and information. I worry about living in a world where everything is part of the news, not a world where we value education, instead everything becomes breaking news, everything ends up on newspapers or television. It's all CSI. But where's the education? [C05]

Beyond communication experiences with members of the criminal justice system, publics-in-general are, at least to a certain extent, perceived as being 'out of reach': 'We are interested in public perception, but it is not as important to us as police perception' [C04]. Consequently, forensic geneticists tend to give priority to communication with their publics-in-particular, who are in principle the greater threat to the credibility of forensic genetics.

11.6 CONCLUSION

This chapter has addressed the particularities of communicating forensic genetics and shown how forensic geneticists respond to these particularities. It has also elaborated on forensic geneticists' imaginaries of public audiences, and how these imaginaries shape their experiences of communication.

Forensic geneticists feel that the conditions under which they communicate DNA evidence in the criminal justice system are shaped by widely shared media representations of the capacities of DNA technologies. These representations are understood as being beyond their control, producing considerable 'misconceptions' among both publics-in-particular and publics-in-general. Consequently, confronted with what they describe as overly 'enthusiastic publics', communication of forensic genetics is frequently framed by a deficit model approach. Forensic geneticists' imaginaries of their publics-in-particular – judges, the police, or jury members – not only highlight their lack of knowledge, but also construct them as a potential threat to forensic expertise. Public misunderstanding of the nature of DNA evidence is framed as potentially putting into jeopardy both the credibility of forensic genetics and, ultimately, the ability of the criminal justice system to deliver justice.

As we have described, forensic geneticists develop coping strategies to manage these challenges. They emphasise the need to communicate the limitations of forensic genetics, and particularly the potential risks and uncertainties in the interpretation of quantitative probabilistic frameworks for forensic DNA analysis. They also point to the fact that interpretation frameworks can differ substantially: binary conventions of interpretation inherent in the criminal justice system are very different from the interpretation principles prevalent among forensic geneticists. Importantly, forensic geneticists work to (re)align the distribution of responsibility for the interpretation of DNA evidence. While they suggest that it is the responsibility of (good) forensic geneticists to highlight the contingencies of DNA evidence, and that of other parts of the criminal justice system to make final judgements concerning justice, they also propose educational initiatives for their publics-in-particular. Again, work is done here to outline the boundaries between the practices of forensic geneticists and members of the criminal justice system in the interpretation of DNA evidence and judicial decision making.

This case thus offers us an unusual approach to science communication: that of stressing science's limitations. This invites us to apply the deficit model in a new way. Studying the communication of forensic genetics means investigating a case in which the deficit not only applies to publics, but is applied by scientists to science itself (and other scientists). This emphasis on deficiencies becomes constitutive of a communication strategy for responding to what is perceived by the science community as 'too enthusiastic publics'. As such, this case study might reveal insights relevant to other situations where publics may be too 'enthusiastic', for instance in the context of 'breakthrough' medical knowledge, or space science imagined as realising utopian dreams of life beyond the Earth.

While the deficit model of publics is instrumental in the sense that it serves as a justification to argue for increasing scientific literacy or for excluding lay publics from some types of decision making, the deficit model, as it is here applied to science, serves as a gateway to renegotiate responsibilities for the non-trustworthy and illegitimate use of scientific findings. In the case of forensic genetics, the misuse of scientific findings may turn into miscarriages of justice. Therefore, when forensic geneticists emphasise the need to take the process of appropriately interpreting scientific results for criminal investigation purposes or judicial decisions seriously, at the same time they underline the fact that the responsibility to interpret all evidence so as to reach decisions – about investigative strategies, or about guilt or innocence – lies beyond the boundaries of the responsibility of forensic geneticists.

Forensic geneticists thus aim to renegotiate the meanings of forensic genetics that circulate in the courtroom and beyond. They seek to deconstruct the notions about DNA technologies conveyed by the media and to clarify the contingencies of DNA evidence. Forensic geneticists reaffirm what has been called the 'CSI effect' in relation to publics-in-particular present in the courtroom. Yet interestingly, the reference to 'the CSI effect' barely even refers to the television programme anymore. Instead, it has become a sense-making category for forensic geneticists to delineate any understanding of DNA evidence that is different from their own – and thereby a tool to create a unified identity for forensic geneticists.

ACKNOWLEDGEMENTS

This work received funding from the European Research Council (ERC) under the European Union's Horizon 2020 research and innovation programme (grant agreement No. 648608), within the project 'EXCHANGE – Forensic geneticists and the transnational exchange of DNA data in the EU: Engaging science with social control, citizenship and democracy', led by Helena Machado and currently hosted at the Communication and Society Research Centre (CECS), Institute for Social Sciences of the University of Minho, Portugal. The authors are extremely grateful for comments received from Ulrike Felt and Sarah Davies and an additional anonymous reviewer.

REFERENCES

Amorim, António. 2012. 'Opening the DNA Black Box: Demythologizing Forensic Genetics'. *New Genetics and Society* 31 (3): 259–270. doi:10.1080/14636778.2012.6 87083.

Amorim, António, Manuel Crespillo, Juan Luque, Lourdes Prieto, Oscar Garcia, Leonor Gusmão, Mercedes Aler, Pedro Barrio, Victor Saragoni, and Nadia Pinto. 2016. 'Formulation and Communication of Evaluative Forensic Science Expert Opinion—A GHEP-ISFG Contribution to the Establishment of Standards'. *Forensic Science International: Genetics* 25: 210–213. doi:10.1016/j.fsigen.2016.09.003.

Aronson, Jay. 2007. *Genetic Witness: Science, Law, and Controversy in the Making of DNA Profiling*. Piscataway, NJ: Rutgers University Press.

Biedermann, Alex, Christophe Champod, and Sheila Willis. 2017. 'Development of European Standards for Evaluative Reporting in Forensic Science: The Gap between Intentions and Perceptions'. *The International Journal of Evidence & Proof* 21 (1–2): 14–29. doi:10.1177/1365712716674796.

Bliss, Catherine. 2012. *Race Decoded: The Genomic Fight for Social Justice*. Stanford, CA: Stanford University Press.

Carracedo, Ángel, and Lourdes Prieto. 2018. 'Beyond the CSI Effect: Keys for Good Forensic Genetics Communication'. *Mètode Revista de Difusió de La Investigació* 9 (June). doi:10.7203/metode.9.10628.

Charmaz, Kathy. 2006. *Constructing Grounded Theory: A Practical Guide through Qualitative Analysis*. Thousand Oaks, CA: Sage.

Cole, Simon. 2013. 'Forensic Culture as Epistemic Culture: The Sociology of Forensic Science'. *Studies in History and Philosophy of Biological and Biomedical Sciences* 44 (1): 36–46. doi:10.1016/j.shpsc.2012.09.003.

Cole, Simon, and Rachel Dioso-Villa. 2009. 'Investigating the "CSI Effect" Effect: Media and Litigation Crisis in Criminal Law'. *Stanford Law Review* 61 (6): 1335–13374.

Davies, Sarah R., and Maja Horst. 2016. *Science Communication: Culture, Identity and Citizenship*. London: Palgrave Macmillan. doi:10.1177/1075547009339048.

Derksen, Linda. 2003. 'Agency and Structure in the History of DNA Profiling: The Stabilization and Standardization of a New Technology'. University of California, San Diego. www.academia.edu/1407355/Agency_and_structure_in_the_history_of_DNA_profiling_The_stabilization_and_standardization_of_a_new_technology.

Edmond, Gary. 2001. 'The Law-Set: The Legal-Scientific Production of Medical Propriety'. *Science, Technology, & Human Values* 26 (2): 191–226. doi:10.1177/016224390102600204.

Felt, Ulrike, and Maximilian Fochler. 2010. 'Machineries for Making Publics: Inscribing and De-Scribing Publics in Public Engagement'. *Minerva* 48 (3): 219–238. doi:10.1007/s11024-010-9155-x.

Gieryn, Thomas F. 1983. 'Boundary-Work and the Demarcation of Science from Non-Science: Strains and Interests in Professional Ideologies of Scientists'. *American Sociological Review* 48 (6): 781–795.

Gill, Peter, James Curran, Cedric Neumann, Amanda Kirkham, Tim Clayton, Jonathan Whitaker, and Jim Lambert. 2008. 'Interpretation of Complex DNA Profiles Using Empirical Models and a Method to Measure Their Robustness'. *Forensic Science International: Genetics* 2 (2): 91–103. doi:10.1016/j.fsigen.2007.10.160.

Hansen, Anders. 2016. 'The Changing Uses of Accuracy in Science Communication'. *Public Understanding of Science* 25 (7): 760–774. doi:10.1177/0963662516636303.

Howes, Loene M., Roberta Julian, Sally F. Kelty, Nenagh Kemp, and K. Paul Kirkbride. 2014. 'The Readability of Expert Reports for Non-Scientist Report-Users: Reports of DNA Analysis'. *Forensic Science International* 237 (April): 7–18. doi:10.1016/j.forsciint.2014.01.007.

Irwin, Alan. 2014. 'From Deficit to Democracy (Re-Visited)'. *Public Understanding of Science* 23 (1): 71–76. doi:10.1177/0963662513510646.

Irwin, Alan, and B. Wynne. 1996. *Misunderstanding Science: Public Reconstructions of Science and Technology*. New York: Cambridge University Press.

Jasanoff, Sheila. 1993. 'What Judges Should Know about the Sociology of Science'. *Jurimetrics Journal* 77 (2): 77–82. http://heinonline.org/HOL/Page?handle=hein.journals/juraba32&id=357&div=&collection=journals%5Cnhttp://www.heinonline.org/HOL/Page?handle=hein.journals/juraba32&id=357&collection=journals&index=journals/juraba.

Jasanoff, Sheila. 1995. *Science at the Bar: Law, Science, and Technology in America*. Cambridge, MA, and London: Harvard University Press.

Jasanoff, Sheila. 2004. *States of Knowledge: The Co-Production of Science and Social Order*. Abingdon and New York: Routledge. doi:10.4324/9780203413845.

Jasanoff, Sheila. 2006. 'Just Evidence: The Limits of Science in the Legal Process'. *Journal of Law, Medicine & Ethics* 34 (2): 328–341. doi:10.1111/j.1748-720X.2006.00038.x.

Kruse, Corinna. 2010. 'Producing Absolute Truth: CSI Science as Wishful Thinking'. *American Anthropologist* 112 (1): 79–91. doi:10.1111/j.1548-1433.2009.01198.x.

Kruse, Corinna. 2016. *The Social Life of Forensic Evidence*. Oakland, CA: University of California Press.

Lazer, David (ed.). 2004. *DNA and the Criminal Justice System: The Technology of Justice*. Cambridge, MA: The MIT Press.

Ley, Barbara L., Natalie Jankowski, and Paul R. Brewer. 2010. 'Investigating CSI: Portrayals of DNA Testing on a Forensic Crime Show and Their Potential Effects'. *Public Understanding of Science* 21 (1): 51–67. doi:10.1177/0963662510367571.

Lezaun, J., and L. Soneryd. 2007. 'Consulting Citizens: Technologies of Elicitation and the Mobility of Publics'. *Public Understanding of Science* 16 (3): 279.

Lynch, Michael. 2002. 'Protocols, Practices, and the Reproduction of Technique in Molecular Biology'. *British Journal of Sociology* 53 (2): 203–220. doi:10.1080/00071310220133304.

Lynch, Michael. 2003. 'God's Signature: DNA Profiling, the New Gold Standard in Forensic Science'. *Endeavour* 27 (2): 93–97.

Lynch, Michael, Simon A. Cole, Ruth McNally, and Kathleen Jordan. 2008. *Truth Machine: The Contentious History of DNA Fingerprinting*. Chicago, IL: University of Chicago Press.

Lynch, Michael, and Sheila Jasanoff. 1998. 'Contested Identities: Science, Law and Forensic Practice'. *Social Studies of Science* 28 (5–6): 675–686. doi:10.1177/030631298028005001.

Machado, Helena, and Rafaela Granja. 2018. 'Ethics in Transnational Forensic DNA Data Exchange in the EU: Constructing Boundaries and Managing Controversies'. *Science as Culture* 27 (2): 242–264.

Machado, Helena, and Filipe Santos. 2011. 'Popular Press and Forensic Genetics in Portugal: Expectations and Disappointments Regarding Two Cases of Missing Children'. *Public Understanding of Science* 20 (3): 303–318. doi:10.1177/0963662509336710.

Marris, Claire. 2015. 'The Construction of Imaginaries of the Public as a Threat to Synthetic Biology'. *Science as Culture* 24 (1): 83–98. doi:10.1080/09505431.2014.98 6320.

Mayring, Philipp. 2004. 'Qualitative Content Analysis'. In Uwe Flick, Ernst von Kardorff, and Ines Steinke (eds.), *A Companion to Qualitative Research*, pp. 266–269. London: Sage.

McNeil, Maureen. 2013. 'Between a Rock and a Hard Place: The Deficit Model, the Diffusion Model and Publics in STS'. *Science as Culture* 22 (4): 589–608. doi:10.1080 /14636778.2013.764068.

Michael, Mike. 2009. 'Publics Performing Publics: Of PiGs, PiPs and Politics'. *Public Understanding of Science* 18 (5): 617–631. doi:10.1177/0963662508098581.

Podlas, Kimberlianne. 2009. 'The "CSI Effect" and Other Forensic Fictions'. *Loyola of Los Angeles Entertainment Law Review* 27: 87–125.

PART III

CONCLUDING THOUGHTS

12

CONNECTIONS, ASSEMBLAGES, AND OPEN ENDS

This conclusion will do two things. It will draw together the key observations that have emerged across the book as a whole, from Chapters 2 and 3, which outlined what STS approaches and sensibilities could contribute to the study and practice of science communication, but also from the empirical chapters that followed. But it will also highlight some important things the book has not done, and which remain lacunae. We ask what is missing, and why.

Before we do this, though, it is worth stating again upfront what we wanted this volume to do. The book invites readers to ask new kinds of questions as we look at science communication. There is, as we discussed in Chapter 1, an interdisciplinary community of people studying science communication. Some of these existing approaches overlap with what is captured in this book, while others are quite different from it. Our discussion should not be read as a critique, but rather as a fruitful perspectival widening by taking STS sensitivities as a starting point. Our aim was to capture what an STS approach can contribute to the study of science communication, allowing us to reflect on it from a fresh perspective. A central aspect of this is to lay out science communication as a fluid concept, a space that allows for theorising and analysis across disciplinary boundaries by taking in less considered or sometimes even neglected dimensions of the ways in which science and technology are encountered in a broad range of communication events. Nothing we have said should be taken as prescriptive (even the encouragement to draw on STS thinking!): rather, the volume should act as a provocation, conversation-starter, or inspiration.

12.1 SOME TAKE-AWAYS

We started with a definition of STS: 'Science and technology studies … is an interdisciplinary field that investigates the institutions, practices, meanings, and outcomes of science and technology and their multiple entanglements with the worlds people inhabit, their lives, and their values' (Felt et al. 2017: 1). 'Entanglements' is perhaps the key word here. This book, and discussion of public communication of science more generally, is premised on the idea that science and technology have, over the last decades, evolved into highly significant activities that reimagine and reshape our societies continuously and in multiple ways. Science and technology 'permeate the social and material fabric of everyday life' and shape how we (can) 'experience, imagine, assemble, and order the worlds [we] live in' (ibid.: 1), while at the same time our ways of being in the world, our values, and the choices guided by them shape ways of knowing and of technologically making the world. STS, with its focus on studying these entanglements, orderings, and assemblies, is central to understanding science communication and its impacts on the world.

Chapter 2 outlined the key premises of an STS approach to science communication. Here the fundamental commitment of STS to a co-productionist perspective was particularly central. Such a perspective takes for granted that knowledge (and with it technological) orders and social orders are always mutually constitutive. How we know about and how we live in the world are inextricably intertwined. Science communication activities, in all their diverse forms, are therefore sites where we can see co-production in action. Based on this starting point of co-production, the rest of Chapter 2 described how we can look at science communication as a knowing space, as always being relational and formed through practices, and as a site where values are attributed and negotiated.

Chapter 3 then invited readers to zoom in further and engage with some more specific questions that emerge from the concerns of STS. How do ideas about readers, visitors, or audiences – 'the public' in all its many forms – shape and get shaped by public communication? How does public fact-making happen? How do expertise and evidence emerge out of and how are they used within different contexts of communication? How does materiality matter in science communication, even at moments when only discourse seems significant? What about space, time, emotions, and atmospheres within communicative engagements?

These are the main questions we opened up, always inviting the reader to ask specific questions when engaging with the many facets of science communication. These themes and sensitivities were then picked up by the empirical analyses of Chapters 4–11. Reading across the cases in the light of Chapters 2 and 3, one finds a number of recurrent emphases that add up to a suggestion of how to understand science communication in scientifically and technologically engaged societies. Here we want to draw these together in a series of cross-cutting observations.

12.1.1 SCIENCE COMMUNICATION AS NARRATIVE AND IMAGINATIVE INFRASTRUCTURES

Studying science communication ultimately entails investigating the narrative and imaginative infrastructures of contemporary knowledge- and innovation-centred societies. The narratives that are constructed and materialised by acts of communication, and the envisioning that happens within them, should not simply be considered a collection of stories sitting next to each other, with no overall connection or coherence. Rather they should be seen as 'contributing to and simultaneously being nourished and stabilised by a wider narrative infrastructure' (Felt 2017: 56) addressing how science and technology (should) relate to contemporary societies. To look at such science-related narratives is thus to investigate a specific kind of knowledge- and sense-making in one and the same move, particularly when it comes to complex and messy issues (Czarniawska 2004). Ways of telling science stories, in whatever form of space, at whatever point in time, and in whatever place, are therefore always linked to attributing meaning and agency and to communicating values. This is achieved through both discursive work and material instantiations.

The notion of infrastructure points to a network of at least temporally stabilised forms of public talk about science and technology and their relation to society. This narrative infrastructure allows the articulation of meanings and visions, but also their negotiation and contestation. While in any one of the case studies presented in Chapters 4–11 only specific kinds of narratives become visible, across the cases it becomes possible to understand how it might make sense to speak of them as an infrastructure that scaffolds contemporary technoscientific societies. Such narratives can take very different forms: they might be tales about good governance through science-based knowledge (as in Israel's nation-building nutritional guidance; Chapter 10); comprise future-oriented accounts that relate to environmental developments (as in representations of climate change in popular science magazines; Chapter 6); involve stories about threats and morality (for instance, with regard to health; Chapter 7); or point to the materialities involved in these narrative practices (for instance, on ecology through the construction of parks; Chapter 5). Despite this diversity, all of these stories ultimately relate to how social and technical orders are imagined together within (particular) societies. They define how public discourse about science can take place, but also encode hopes and expectations; these narrative infrastructures thus become 'the vehicles whereby [these hopes and expectations] are transmitted and made emotionally real' (Larkin 2013: 333).

It is thus important to understand that prevailing narrative infrastructures always enable or constrain possible ways of telling a story about science in public. This is visible across many of the cases discussed in this volume, which investigate a particular narrative that is situated and tied to a specific issue (obesity, climate change, synthetic yeast...): behind the immediate issue at stake, there are larger stories at play. However, even though these infrastructures might be robust, they are not fixed but evolve over time, and are reconfigured in different settings. Gradually, new constellations can emerge. Narrative infrastructures thus undergird any major subsystem of modern societies to form the ambient discursive environment (Felt 2017; Larkin 2013). The stories we (can) tell, and which are successful in attracting attention and circulating, thus contribute, in tacit ways, to how we can understand science, technology, and the society in which we live.

12.1.2 SCIENCE COMMUNICATION AS ASSEMBLAGE WORK

The book as a whole has emphatically moved us away from the idea that science communication is primarily about translating knowledge produced in scientific realms into terms that fit a new, public environment. This is of course implied by our central framework of co-production, but the analyses of Chapters 4–11 have also repeatedly demonstrated that science communication does substantive work in (re)assembling and constructing knowledge. Public communication of science makes public facts (Chapter 3), but as it does so it also connects those facts to everyday objects and events, encodes moralities, and tacitly frames ignorance and non-knowledge. We have seen, for example, how 'synthetic yeast' is assembled in public as an object that is not new or alien but that is essentially the same as familiar entities such as 'brewer's yeast' (Chapter 8). Similarly, Chapter 7 demonstrates the work that anecdotes do in assembling and arranging the obesity-related world in specific social and material patterns and in expressing specific moralities and values. Science communication is therefore a (co-)productive process, making knowledge rather than transmitting or translating it.

In doing so it ties to specific emotional registers and contributes to the creation of collective imaginaries about futures that can be realised through science and technology. But this is not a straightforward or unitary process. In embracing the notion of assemblage – the idea that any moment of science communication is assembled from diverse constituents and takes shape through specific connections between them, and that this assembly can always be done differently – we thus have to be attentive to multiplicity. This leads us away from making normative statements: there are not necessarily right and wrong ways of assembling a scientific object or fact in public. Different versions of a phenomenon 'may line up, contradict, include one another, never meet up – or combine some mix of these' (Law 2017: 43). Chapter 4, for example, tells of how a particular scientific object – a gene gun – is assembled in different ways in different spaces, and of how its nature (and the correct way of communicating about it) shifted slightly from space to space. In identifying how science is assembled within science communication, we should always be aware that those constructions could be done differently in other contexts or at other moments.

12.1.3 MATERIALITY IS KEY

Many of our case studies have pointed, in different ways, to the importance of the material aspects of science communication. This might be through communication being organised around a specific object, like the gene gun (Chapter 4); the material aspects of narratives around obese bodies (Chapter 7); the power of the visual to convey particular scientific facts (Chapter 6); or the affordances of the environments – whether digital or physical – in which communication takes place (Chapters 5 and 9). Materiality matters, and studies of communication need to take this into account.

One important implication of this is the need to pay attention to new spaces and places where knowledge orders are communicated, beyond those that are classically understood as science communication (newspapers, magazines, or museums, for instance). We have sought to open up an engagement with how objects travel across different spaces to trigger specific kinds of communication. Chapter 11 focused on the criminal and legal systems as spaces where the authority of scientific knowledge was negotiated, despite these systems rarely being framed as instances of 'science communication'. Chapter 5 (with its discussion of how ecological knowledge is embodied in public parks, more usually seen as places for playing frisbee and sunbathing than encountering science) and Chapter 10 (in exploring the work done by dietary advice and recipe columns) both similarly queried how science is made in public beyond the bounds of what is labelled public science communication.

12.1.4 SCIENCE COMMUNICATION AS TACIT GOVERNANCE

An instance of science communication is rarely, if ever, 'just' about science: it is also about social norms, morality, practices of attributing value, visions of the future, politics, or identity (for example). In short, science communication is always engaged in tacitly governing the ways in which we can (imagine how to) live in a world that is deeply entangled with science and technology. The lessons to be drawn are broad. Chapter 10 demonstrated how communication of knowledge – in this case knowledge about food – was essential to state-making and identity building, making women central actors in both. Chapter 7 took us to morality and to the ways in which anecdotal evidence functions to support a dominant health paradigm and to distribute responsibility and blame in specific ways. Similarly, Chapter 9 teaches us about how personal identities – whether one is a 'science lover' or not – are made and contested in online spaces dedicated to science. Chapter 6 demonstrates how even apparently neutral and objective visual communication about climate change is fundamentally engaged in doing politics by other means.

We might therefore see science communication as a kind of lens that can point us to wider social dynamics. Instances of communication will always take a specific view on the issue they focus on (however much that view is rendered implicit), and they will always imply a preferred way of relating science to society. Understanding science communication as working on society means that we will also come to interrogate the beliefs that lie behind science communication activities. At times, at least, the agenda is to bring about a world that falls in line with scientific and technological developments, and that supports a specific vision of technoscientific progress. Understanding the entanglement between science communication and society encourages us not just to look at science communication as making science public, but as making society, and ultimately to come to the question: what kind of societies do we want?

12.2 SOME (SEEMINGLY) MISSING MATTERS

We have said that we want this volume to offer a fresh perspective, and to open up questions and lines of thought for those who study, evaluate, and carry out science communication. But we are also very aware that, while we have sought to trace (in Chapters 2 and 3) and demonstrate (in Chapters 4–11) key STS ideas that might be put to work in science communication, the volume as a whole by no means offers a comprehensive or even complete introduction to doing so. In closing we want to briefly note some areas that remain lacunae, are less explicitly present in the book, or that are important to explore further in future research.

12.2.1 WHAT ABOUT METHODS?

Unusually for a book dedicated to inspiring those who carry out research, we have offered very little explicit guidance concerning methods (beyond the methodological descriptions outlined in the case study chapters). There are two reasons for this. First, as John Law (2017) has aptly formulated, we see STS as a method. In that sense, Chapters 2 and 3 should be read as theoretical and methodological framings of what is at stake when studying science communication: although they offer little advice concerning, for instance, sample sizes or how to carry out participant observation, they do suggest, rather concretely, a way of imagining and going about research. Based on these chapters, taking STS as a method means attending to practices and their performativity, being attentive to the situatedness of knowledge and its communication, being critical towards what is assumed to be unquestionable, and documenting the multiplicities of issues and objects that emerge through science communication. It also means working with case studies – in this book, we presented eight of them – as they 'evoke, illustrate, disrupt, instruct, and help STS to craft and recraft its theory' (Law 2017: 32).

The second reason is tied to the fact that STS, in common with many other qualitative and reflexive social science traditions, pays special attention to the way in which methods (just like science communication) are themselves performative: they 'do' the things that they seek to capture and describe. Law and Ruppert (2013: 233) invite us to '[reflect] on the devices of professional social science: on our interviews, our surveys and our focus groups; on the devices that we use as we seek to understand and represent the social', reminding us that they 'are shaped by the social and in turn they act as social operators to do the social'. As a consequence, an STS approach does not treat 'social research methods as techniques alone' (ibid.), but views them as actors within the knowledge-making process. This does not mean that we should not know about the considerations that have gone into defining particular methods, or that it is not necessary to carefully reflect on how to perform research – indeed, one can find excellent resources that engage with qualitative methods in social research. But it does mean that this is not enough. We should simultaneously be asking: 'what is it that our methods are doing? What do they imply? What kinds of worlds are they opening up to us? And what kinds of worlds are they closing off?' (ibid.).

In this context, it is important to highlight that the volume is already an interdisciplinary enterprise. The essays in this collection serve as case studies that illustrate how science communication can take different shapes in different sociocultural contexts, how it involves and addresses different publics, and how it relates to different sites and spatio-temporal configurations. These studies thus exemplify an STS approach to science communication across diverse situations – but many of the authors would not describe themselves as belonging to the field of STS. They are, among other things, historians, sociologists, or scholars of architecture, public health, or museums. All, however, engage with STS as a way of elaborating their case. While the exact methods used may vary, and may come from diverse research traditions, STS approaches thus have something to offer scholarship of science communication, whether that is in the shape of a general analytical focus, orientation, or set of research sensitivities.

12.2.2 WHAT ABOUT ENGAGEMENT AND PARTICIPATION?

This book has neither a specific section speaking to public engagement with and participation in science in Chapters 2 and 3, nor an empirical chapter that addresses a 'classical' case study of participation. This is perhaps surprising at a time in which science communication practice tends to frame itself around notions of dialogue, engagement, and interactivity (Kaiser et al. 2014; Trench 2008), especially given that STS has been instrumental in promoting these developments (Chilvers & Kearnes 2016; Delgado et al. 2011).

In part, this lacuna emerged for practical reasons, because of a lack of the right case study of engagement as we were compiling this volume. But we also think it is important to move away from a sharp distinction between engagement, generally understood as more participatory and oriented to public policy, and science communication, understood as oriented to informing, education, and/or leisure (Bucchi & Trench 2014; Davies & Horst 2016). As discussed in Chapter 1, we have deliberately used a generous definition of science communication, and are interested in all kinds of public spaces where science is talked about, represented, drawn upon, contested, or negotiated. It is actually the relation between these different ways of encountering science and how citizens engage with scientific knowledge which might in the end be the key question. In our view, science communication thus includes consultation processes, citizen juries, dialogue events, consensus conferences, and the many other formats for 'engagement' (Rowe & Frewer 2005) as well as diverse media outlets, science exhibitions, and webpages – and, indeed, courtrooms and parks.

Having said this, it is important to note that there has been a flowering of activities and formats that promote the involvement of diverse (public and stakeholder) voices in science communication and policy over recent decades, from consensus conferences to citizen science (Horst & Irwin 2010; Irwin 1995; Lewenstein 2016). We have gestured towards some of this work, for instance by discussing (in Chapter 2) Chilvers and Kearnes' (2016) arguments about the 'ecologies of participation' that exist around particular issues and topics. Participation, this line of thought suggests, should rightly take many different forms, some of which will involve traditional 'communication' formats, others of which might involve public deliberation or participation in policy, as well as forms of material participation such as engagement with particular technological devices (Lezaun et al. 2017; Marres 2012). Rather than placing labels on science communication practice – 'engagement', 'one-way', 'dialogue', and so forth – our view is that it is more productive to examine all the diverse moments and places in which communication about science takes place, and to investigate the practices (relating to citizenship or otherwise) they involve, the orders they try to impose, and the visions and versions of science–society relations they promote or support, regardless of their naming and framing.

12.2.3 WHAT ABOUT SCIENCE COMMUNICATION TO POLICY AND POLITICS?

Even though we have taken the reader to different, sometimes unusual, places and spaces where science gets communicated, we have not touched on one broad but important realm: the explicitly political. This might include expert scientific and technical advice, the ways in which scientists and scientific knowledge are drawn into political decision making, or major technopolitical public controversies such as those over genetically modified food or climate change (Doubleday & Wilsdon 2013; Fealing 2011; Hilgartner 2000; Jasanoff

2012; Maasen & Weingart 2005). It would be a significant endeavour in its own right to look into the broad repertoire of encounters between science and politics and to study how science is being communicated within these.

Such an endeavour would embrace looking into the concrete practices of scientific advice that involve being an intermediary or broker (Pielke 2007), as well as the way in which certain actors aggregate and synthesise knowledge to develop a specific situated expertise (Collins & Evans 2002). We could look into the many expert bodies, such as ethics committees[1] or bodies like the European Commission's Group of Chief Scientific Advisors,[2] who develop policy briefs on issues as diverse as ageing, microplastics, or food security. The documents produced by such bodies are certainly one way of communicating and engaging with diverse kinds of scientific knowledge. Scientific advisors in all of these forms champion the role of science in governing contemporary societies, support decision making, and provide expertise and evidence.

This form of science communication incorporates a new set of complexities: scientific advisors frequently have to point to unknowns and to complexity, while at the same time offering concrete guidance and direction. Given this deeply practical role in the functioning of contemporary democracies, as such expert bodies and science advisors gain increasing importance it is essential to investigate what vision of science gets communicated by their work. Following Jasanoff (2013), this would mean looking for the kinds of values that are expressed in the context of this kind of political communication of science. This means asking, for example, 'which facts and disciplines are relevant; when is new knowledge reliable enough for use; which dissenting viewpoints deserve to be heard?' (ibid.: 64). At a moment when our future is more than ever imagined as dependent on and driven by innovations, careful consideration is needed as to how the very idea of 'societal progress' and its relation to science is imagined and practised.

12.2.4 WHAT ABOUT THE DIGITAL?

While Chapter 9 does address online communication, and we discuss aspects of digital communication in Chapters 2 and 3, this topic deserves much

---

[1]The European Group on Ethics (EGE) would be a good example for such a body providing the European Commission with advice on ethical aspects of science and new technologies in relation to EU legislation or policies. Through publishing their 'opinions', they are an important source of science communication – even if they would not frame their activity as such. https://ec.europa.eu/info/research-and-innovation/strategy/support-policy-making/scientific-support-eu-policies/european-group-ethics-science-and-new-technologies-ege_en#what-is-the-ege

[2]https://ec.europa.eu/research/sam/index.cfm?pg=hlg

broader engagement (in this volume, in studies of science communication, and in STS generally). This is a growing area of scholarship. There are many studies that look at social media in the context of science communication (Brossard & Scheufele 2013; Hargittai et al. 2018); there has been research on search engines, including how they rank the knowledge that is to be presented and thus open up or close down access (e.g., Gerhards & Schafer 2010); and, as in Chapter 9 of this volume, there have been studies looking at the online lives of social groups discussing issues of science and technology (Riesch & Mendel 2013; Ritson 2016). In STS, issue mapping, in which one seeks to trace out the ecology of a controversy by observing its digital traces, is one approach that has sought to combine STS sensibilities with the affordances of big data (Marres 2015; Venturini 2012).

However, there is still much more to do. It is worth pointing out that it is not straightforward to investigate digital life. Too many studies that use (big) data from diverse social media environments flatten out the complexity of online social worlds or take an overly instrumental approach, while it is difficult to empirically investigate the complex, diversely mediated ways in which individuals consume and engage with online content in specific material contexts (Davies & Hara 2017; Marsh 2018). Key challenges for science communication scholarship of the digital include some of the themes of this book. How does materiality come to matter in how scientific content is performed and encountered online? How are diverse publics formed and re-formed – and how are they forming and re-forming themselves – within online spaces? What digital and data practices are brought into being and are being contested around science communication? Looking into these questions also means considering a whole new infrastructure, as well as the practices relating to this, which is rarely attended to when studying discourses. These practices and infrastructures, as we have argued, are essential to making sense of digital media and what they (can) do. This also invites us to move beyond studying new forms of representation or other ways of creating identities, and to explore the possible agencies emerging out of and being shaped by the very design of these new platforms (Plantin et al. 2018; Van Dijck 2013).

In considering these questions, it is, in our view, important not to see the digital as a separate domain with clear-cut boundaries. Rather, it opens a space of practices that overlap and engage with those of the 'real world', though clear distinctions between real and virtual worlds themselves seem increasingly problematic. Relatedly, Jennifer Gabrys and co-authors (2016) have explored 'data practices' in the context of citizen science, outlining how community needs, technical knowledge, homemade sensors and measurement devices, and the datasets produced through these give rise to 'alternative ways of creating, valuing and interpreting datasets' (ibid.: 2) and thereby offer new ways of doing data. Such new forms of (access to) data shape the way people relate to the scientific knowledge available, and reflect both emergent practices of data gathering and of making knowledge claims on the basis of such data. We encounter similar developments in the aftermath of Fukushima, when concerned citizens started to develop their own radiation mapping platform in order to assess 'the nuclear situation of the country, creating alternative sources of information that competed with official reports' (Plantin 2015: 906). Even more pertinent to the themes of this book, such forms of online participation are always tied to a specific place (the digital location of the platform) as well as to a specific temporality (tied to citizens' interest in updating the platform once the urgency of the problem has become less evident).

The key point is that we should not see digital science communication as necessarily different from other forms of public communication, while at the same time maintaining interest in its specific affordances and materialities, the spaces and temporalities it opens up, and how different kinds of practices and knowledges are articulated within it. There is need for further research, for instance, in how the digital world shapes specific communication practices and vice versa; how the flurry of audiovisual presentations of science and technology shape viewers in new ways and need new practices of selecting and connecting; how all this changes our practices of writing and documenting; and much more. Much remains to be done.

12.2.5 WHAT ABOUT THE SITUATEDNESS OF SCIENCE COMMUNICATION?

Finally, it is important to reflect on our discussion, the cases that have been featured, and the degree to which they speak to science communication in a global context. Our cases have largely drawn on science communication in Europe and the US. How can they speak to the vibrant science communication scenes in South America, or Australasia, or China, for instance?

We believe that the approaches we have outlined and the kinds of questions we asked are valuable entry points to understanding diverse cultural contexts, and are not necessarily tailored to a specific empirical context. What we have described, from co-production to the importance of materiality and from the relationality of communication to the importance of values and care, offers a repertoire of approaches and sensibilities for the investigation of science communication in different kinds of places, carried out in different kinds of ways. In a sense, what is central are the ways in which the concepts we have described are mobilised within empirical study.

However, this does not free us from looking for exactly how differences matter in science communication. Indeed, as science communication activities have become so central and are so frequently performed, there is a certain danger that they could 'become highly "ritualised", i.e., performed "by the book" and thus not sufficiently reflecting the differences across ... contexts' (Felt et al. 2013: 4). Furthermore, it seems essential to acknowledge the existence of a 'tacit geography' (Felt & Stöckelová 2009), which casts certain countries as role models in how to engage with science through science communication, 'while others are set up or set themselves up as the followers/as in need of catching up' (Felt et al. 2013: 22). This carries the danger of creating 'a centre–periphery model when it comes to science–society activities and reflections, imposing a dominant reading of what is the "gold standard" to do these reflections' (ibid.). Thus, we need to remind ourselves that what is represented makes a difference (as we argued in Chapter 2), and so does where we speak from, as well as the wider scientific and political context in which communication happens.

Describing our approach as one that is fundamentally sensitive to difference, specificity, and contingency (Law 2017) therefore obliges us to ask questions such as: How do particular formats travel (Horst & Irwin 2010)? How are scientific objects assembled differently in different cultural contexts? What differences are there in the narrative infrastructures that shape and enable science communication in particular sites? What are the politics of science communication in Turkey, Brazil, India, or New Zealand (for instance)? Similarly, gender, race, disability, and other ways of doing difference have only been mentioned in passing. These dynamics will also be central to how the specificities of how instances of science communication are articulated, and to the particular work that they (can) do. (We have seen, for example, how nation building through good nutrition became a task for women, in a process that constructed gendered identities alongside those of the Israeli state; Chapter 10.) Future research, and researchers, should thus be attentive not only to their own positionality, but also to the ways in which science communication operates along, and contributes to, particular ways of valuing diverse ways of being in the world (Fahy 2015).

These questions – and many more besides – are outside the scope of this volume. But we hope that scholars take up the STS approach we have described, and take it to many places and moments of science communication beyond those with which we are personally and professionally most familiar.

12.3 CONCLUSION

This book frames science communication as important. This might not be for the reasons we started by describing, in the very first pages: it is not because science needs to be sold in order to get support, or to create an innovation-friendly climate, or even (perhaps) because it is about taxpayers' money and scientists should therefore be open and accountable. Instead, we have demonstrated its importance by showing just how much work science communication does in articulating science and society. It plays a powerful role in defining the nature of contemporary democratic societies.

To give some examples: following the gene gun (in Chapter 4) showed how issues could be opened up or closed down for public discussion based on the space in which communication was taking place. We have witnessed how media anecdotes about 'living with obesity' made factual and moral statements simultaneously, while not being questionable on empirical grounds (Chapter 7). Chapter 8 showed us how synthetic yeast has been rendered recognisable and familiar by bringing it close enough to everyday life to turn it in something we need not further consider. And we have seen how an environmental issue such as climate change can be made political, or not political, by different framings within popular science accounts (Chapter 6).

These are just a few examples of the way in which science communication always relates to questions of responsibility. It is never simply about communicating science in order to inform the public: it is always normative and performative. Work is always being done on the world by it. We therefore want to close by reiterating the importance of thinking about science communication in the context of (our) responsibilities and values. Science communication demands responsibility from those who produce it, those who study it, and also, in the end, from all of us who engage with or consume it.

Taking responsibility for science communication seriously asks a number of things of us as researchers or practitioners. We should be sensitive to the concerns and needs of potential audiences, critically reflective about the choices made when science is communicated, and constantly concerned with the work that is being done by science communication practices. If science communication is such a powerful actor in the shaping and imagination of contemporary societies, ultimately it should, we believe, contribute to imagining, critically scrutinising, and finally realising those technoscientific worlds that seem worth inhabiting.

REFERENCES

Brossard, Dominique, and Dietram A. Scheufele. 2013. 'Science, New Media, and the Public'. *Science* 339 (6115): 40–41.

Bucchi, Massimiano, and Brian Trench. 2014. 'Science Communication Research: Themes and Challenges'. In Massimiano Bucchi and Brian Trench (eds.), *Handbook of Public Communication of Science and Technology* (Vol. 2), pp. 1–14. Abingdon: Routledge.

Chilvers, Jason, and Matthew Kearnes. 2016. *Remaking Participation: Science, Environment and Emergent Publics*. Abingdon: Routledge.

Collins, Harry M., and Robert Evans. 2002. 'The Third Wave of Science Studies: Studies of Expertise and Experience'. *Social Studies of Science* 32 (2): 235–296.

Czarniawska, Barbara. 2004. *Narratives in Social Science Research*. London: Sage.

Davies, Sarah R., and Noriko Hara. 2017. 'Public Science in a Wired World: How Online Media are Shaping Science Communication'. *Science Communication* 39 (5): 563–568.

Davies, Sarah R., and Maja Horst. 2016. *Science Communication: Culture, Identity and Citizenship*. New York: Palgrave Macmillan.

Delgado, A., K. Lein Kjolberg, and F. Wickson. 2011. 'Public Engagement Coming of Age: From Theory to Practice in STS Encounters with Nanotechnology'. *Public Understanding of Science* 20 (6): 826–845.

Doubleday, Robert, and James Wilsdon (eds.). 2013. *Future Directions for Scientific Advice in Whitehall*. www.csap.cam.ac.uk/media/uploads/files/1/fdsaw.pdf

Fahy, Declan. 2015. *The New Celebrity Scientists: Out of the Lab and into the Limelight*. New York: Rowman & Littlefield.

Fealing, Kaye Husbands (ed.). 2011. *The Science of Science Policy: A Handbook*. Stanford, CA: Stanford Business Books.

Felt, Ulrike. 2017. '"Response-able Practices" or "New Bureaucracies of Virtue": The Challenges of Making RRI Work in Academic Environments'. In Lotte Asveld, Rietje van Dam-Mieras, Tsjalling Swierstra, Saskia Lavrijssen, Kees Linse and Jeroen van den Hoven (eds.), *Responsible Innovation 3: A European Agenda?*, pp. 49–68. Cham: Springer International.

Felt, Ulrike, Daniel Barben, Alan Irwin, Pierre-Benoît Joly, Arie Rip, Andy Stirling, and Tereza Stöckelová. 2013. *Science in Society: Caring for Our Futures in Turbulent Times*, Policy Briefing 50. Strasbourg: European Science Foundation (ESF).

Felt, Ulrike, Rayvon Fouché, Clark A. Miller, and Laurel Smith-Doerr (eds.). 2017. *Handbook of Science and Technology Studies* (4th edition). Cambridge, MA: The MIT Press.

Felt, Ulrike, and Tereza Stöckelová. 2009. 'Modes of Ordering and Boundaries That Matter in Academic Knowledge Production'. In Ulrike Felt (ed.), *Knowing and Living in Academic Research: Convergence and Heterogeneity in Research Cultures in the European Context*, pp. 41–124. Prague: Academy of Sciences of the Czech Republic.

Gabrys, Jennifer, Helen Pritchard, and Benjamin Barratt. 2016. 'Just Good Enough Data: Figuring Data Citizenships through Air Pollution Sensing and Data Stories'. *Big Data & Society* 3 (2). doi: 10.1177/2053951716679677.

Gerhards, Jürgen and Mike S. Schafer. 2010. 'Is the Internet a Better Public Sphere? Comparing Old and New Media in the USA and Germany'. *New Media & Society*, 12 (1): 143–160. doi: 10.1177/1461444809341444.

Hargittai, Eszter, Tobias Füchslin, and Mike S. Schäfer. 2018. 'How Do Young Adults Engage with Science and Research on Social Media? Some Preliminary Findings and an Agenda for Future Research'. *Social Media + Society* 4 (3).

Hilgartner, Stephen. 2000. *Science on Stage: Expert Advice as Public Drama*. Stanford, CA: Stanford University Press.

Horst, Maja, and Alan Irwin. 2010. 'Nations at Ease with Radical Knowledge: On Consensus, Consensusing and False Consensusness'. *Social Studies of Science* 40 (1): 105–126.

Irwin, Alan. 1995. *Citizen Science: A Study of People, Expertise and Sustainable Development*. Abingdon: Routledge.

Jasanoff, Sheila. 2012. *Science and Public Reason*. Abingdon: Routledge.

Jasanoff, Sheila. 2013. 'The Science of Science Advice'. In Robert Doubleday and James Wilsdon (eds.), *Future Directions for Scientific Advice in Whitehall*, pp. 62–68. www.csap.cam.ac.uk/media/uploads/files/1/fdsaw.pdf

Kaiser, David, John Durant, Thomas Levenson, Ben Wiehe, and Peter Linett. 2014. 'Report of Findings: September 2013 Workshop'. MIT and Culture Kettle. www.cultureofscienceengagement.net.

Larkin, Brian. 2013. 'The Politics and Poetics of Infrastructure.' *Annual Review of Anthropology* 42 (1): 327–343. doi: 10.1146/annurev-anthro-092412-155522.

Law, John. 2017. 'STS as Method'. In Ulrike Felt, Rayvon Fouché, Clark A. Miller and Laurel Smith-Doerr (eds.), *Handbook of Science and Technology Studies* (4th edition), pp. 31–57. Cambridge, MA: The MIT Press.

Law, John, and Evelyn Ruppert. 2013. 'The Social Life of Methods: Devices'. *Journal of Cultural Economy* 6 (3): 229–240.

Lewenstein, Bruce. 2016. 'Can We Understand Citizen Science?' *Journal of Science Communication* 15 (1): 1–5.

Lezaun, Javier, Noortje Marres, and Manuel Tironi. 2017. 'Experiments in Participation'. In Ulrike Felt, Rayvon Fouché, Clark A. Miller and Laurel Smith-Doerr (eds.), *Handbook of Science and Technology Studies* (4th edition), pp. 195–221. Cambridge, MA: The MIT Press.

Maasen, Sabine, and Peter Weingart. 2005. *Democratization of Expertise? Exploring Novel Forms of Scientific Advice in Political Decision-Making* (Sociology of the Sciences Yearbook). Dordrecht: Springer.

Marres, Noortje. 2012. *Material Participation: Technology, the Environment and Everyday Publics*. Basingstoke: Palgrave Macmillan.

Marres, Noortje. 2015. 'Why Map Issues? On Controversy Analysis as a Digital Method'. *Science, Technology, & Human Values* 40 (5): 655–686.

Marsh, Oliver Martin. 2018. '"Nah, musing is fine. You don't have to be 'doing science'": Emotional and Descriptive Meaning-Making in Online Non-Professional Discussions about Science', Doctoral thesis, University College London.

Pielke, Roger A. Jr. 2007. *The Honest Broker: Making Sense of Science in Policy and Politics*. Cambridge: Cambridge University Press.

Plantin, Jean-Christophe 2015. 'The Politics of Mapping Platforms: Participatory Radiation Mapping after the Fukushima Daiichi Disaster'. *Media, Culture and Society* 37 (6): 904–921.

Plantin, Jean-Christophe, Carl Lagoze, Paul N. Edwards, and Christian Sandvig. 2018. 'Infrastructure Studies Meet Platform Studies in the Age of Google and Facebook'. *New Media & Society* 20 (1): 293–310.

Riesch, Hauke, and Jonathan Mendel. 2013. 'Science Blogging: Networks, Boundaries and Limitations'. *Science as Culture* 23 (1): 51–72.

Ritson, Sophie. 2016. '"Crackpots" and "Active Researchers": The Controversy over Links between ArXiv and the Scientific Blogosphere'. *Social Studies of Science*, June, doi: 10.1177/0306312716647508.

Rowe, Gene, and Lynn J. Frewer. 2005. 'A Typology of Public Engagement Mechanisms'. *Science, Technology & Human Values* 30 (2): 251–290.

Trench, Brian 2008. 'Towards an Analytical Framework of Science Communication Models'. In Donghong Cheng, Michel Claessens, Toss Gascoigne, Jenni Metcalfe, Bernard Schiele, and Shunke Shi, *Communicating Science in Social Contexts*, pp. 119–135. Dordrecht: Springer.

Van Dijck, José. 2013. *The Culture of Connectivity: A Critical History of Social Media*. Oxford: Oxford University Press.

Venturini, Tommaso. 2012. 'Building on Faults: How to Represent Controversies with Digital Methods'. *Public Understanding of Science* 21 (7): 796–812.

INDEX